Gilles Deleuze, Postcolonial Theory, and the Philosophy of Limit

Suspensions: Contemporary Middle Eastern and Islamicate Thought

Series editors: Jason Bahbak Mohaghegh and Lucian Stone

This series interrupts standardized discourses involving the Middle East and the Islamicate world by introducing creative and emerging ideas. The incisive works included in this series provide a counterpoint to the reigning canons of theory, theology, philosophy, literature, and criticism through investigations of vast experiential typologies—such as violence, mourning, vulnerability, tension, and humor—in light of contemporary Middle Eastern and Islamicate thought.

Other titles in this series include:
The Qur'an and Modern Arabic Literary Criticism: From Taha to Nasr, Mohammad Salama
Hostage Space of the Contemporary Islamicate World, Dejan Lukic
On the Arab Revolts and the Iranian Revolution, Arshin Adib-Moghaddam
The Politics of Writing Islam, Mahmut Mutman
The Writing of Violence in the Middle East, Jason Bahbak Mohaghegh
Iranian Identity and Cosmopolitanism, edited by Lucian Stone
Continental Philosophy and the Palestinian Question, Zahi Zalloua

Gilles Deleuze, Postcolonial Theory, and the Philosophy of Limit

Réda Bensmaïa

BLOOMSBURY ACADEMIC
LONDON • NEW YORK • OXFORD • NEW DELHI • SYDNEY

BLOOMSBURY ACADEMIC
Bloomsbury Publishing Plc
50 Bedford Square, London, WC1B 3DP, UK
1385 Broadway, New York, NY 10018, USA
29 Earlsfort Terrace, Dublin 2, Ireland

BLOOMSBURY, BLOOMSBURY ACADEMIC and the Diana logo
are trademarks of Bloomsbury Publishing Plc

This collection first published 2017
Reprinted by Bloomsbury Academic

Copyright © Réda Bensmaïa, 2017
Réda Bensmaïa has asserted his right under the Copyright,
Designs and Patents Act, 1988, to be identified as Author of this work.

For legal purposes the Acknowledgements on p. vii-ix constitute
an extension of this copyright page.

All rights reserved. No part of this publication may be reproduced or
transmitted in any form or by any means, electronic or mechanical,
including photocopying, recording, or any information storage or retrieval
system, without prior permission in writing from the publishers.

Bloomsbury Publishing Plc does not have any control over, or responsibility for,
any third-party websites referred to or in this book. All internet addresses given
in this book were correct at the time of going to press. The author and publisher
regret any inconvenience caused if addresses have changed or sites have
ceased to exist, but can accept no responsibility for any such changes.

British Library Cataloguing-in-Publication Data
A catalogue record for this book is available from the British Library.

ISBN: HB: 978-1-3500-0438-2
PB: 978-1-3500-0439-9
ePDF: 978-1-3500-0437-5
ePub: 978-1-3500-0440-5

Library of Congress Cataloging-in-Publication Data
Names: Bensmaèia, Râeda, author.
Title: Gilles Deleuze, postcolonial theory, and the philosophy of limit / by Râeda Bensmaèia.
Description: New York: Bloomsbury Academic, 2017. |
Series: Suspensions: contemporary Middle Eastern and Islamicate thought |
Includes bibliographical references and index.
Identifiers: LCCN 2016036510 | ISBN 9781350004382 (hb) | ISBN 9781350004405 (epub)
Subjects: LCSH: Deleuze, Gilles, 1925-1995. | Postcolonialism.
Classification: LCC B2430.D454 B46 2017 | DDC 194–dc23
LC record available at https://lccn.loc.gov/2016036510

Series: Suspensions: Contemporary Middle Eastern and Islamicate Thought

Typeset by Fakenham Prepress Solutions, Fakenham, Norfolk NR21 8NN

To find out more about our authors and books visit
www.bloomsbury.com and sign up for our newsletters.

Contents

Series Foreword		vi
Acknowledgments		vii
Preface: Gilles Deleuze and How to Become a *Stalker* in Philosophy		x
1	Postcolonial Haecceities: On Deleuze's Names	1
2	The Subject of Art: Prolegomena to a Future Deleuzian Aesthetics	23
3	*Cinéplastique(s)*: Deleuze on Élie Faure and Film Theory	45
4	On the "Spiritual Automaton," or Space and Time in Modern Cinema according to Gilles Deleuze	55
5	The Singularity of the Event: Gilles Deleuze, Paul Virilio, François Jullien	69
6	The Kafka Effect: Considerations on the Limits of Interpretation in Deleuze and Guattari's Book on Kafka	83
7	On the Concept of "Minor Literature": From Kafka to Kateb Yacine	99
8	Becoming-Animal, Becoming-Political in Rachid Boudjedra's *L'escargot entêté*	113
Notes		129
Bibliography		169
Index		175

Series Foreword

Poets, artists, theologians, philosophers, and mystics in the Middle East and Islamicate world have been interrogating notions of desire, madness, sensuality, solitude, death, time, space, etc. for centuries, thus constituting an expansive and ever-mutating intellectual landscape. Like all theory and creative outpouring, then, theirs is its own vital constellation—a construction cobbled together from singular visceral experiences, intellectual ruins, novel aesthetic techniques, social-political-ideological detours, and premonitions of a future—built and torn down (partially or *in toto*), and rebuilt again with slight and severe variations. The horizons shift, and frequently leave those who dare traverse these lands bewildered and vulnerable.

Consequently, these thinkers and their visionary ideas largely remain unknown, or worse, mispronounced and misrepresented in the so-called Western world. In the hands of imperialistic frameworks, a select few are deemed worthy of notice and are spoken on behalf of, or rather *about*. Their ideas are simplified into mere social formulae and empirical scholarly categories. Whereas so-called Western philosophers and writers are given full leniency to contemplate the most incisive or abstract ideas, non-Western thinkers, especially those located in the imagined realms of the Middle East and Islamicate world, are reduced to speaking of purely political histories or monolithic cultural narratives. In other words, they are distorted and contorted to fit within hegemonic paradigms that steal away their more captivating potentials.

Contributors to this series provide a counterpoint to the reigning canons of theory, theology, philosophy, literature, and criticism through investigations of the vast experiential typologies of such regions. Each volume in the series acts as a "suspension" in the sense that the authors will position contemporary thought in an enigmatic new terrain of inquiry, where it will be compelled to confront unforeseen works of critical and creative imagination. These analyses will not only highlight the full range of current intellectual and artistic trends and their benefits for the citizens of these phantom spheres, but also argue that the ideas themselves are borderless, and thus of great relevance to all citizens of the world.

Jason Bahbak Mohaghegh and Lucian Stone

Acknowledgments

This book is composed of essays that cover more than ten years of work on issues related to Gilles Deleuze's work as it pertains to francophone literature and postcolonial theory. It would never have seen the light of day had it not been for Jason Mohaghegh and Lucian Stone's friendly offer to include aspects of my work in the series they edit for Bloomsbury. I owe them my awareness that these texts, which have been produced in very specific and punctual circumstances, together revealed an extension of the territories I had previously explored in my previous work on francophone literature of the Maghreb and philosophy. It also gave me the wonderful opportunity to render homage to Gilles Deleuze, a mentor and a friend, who taught me the art of thinking as a surveyor of the invisible and the inaudible in literary texts. I am also indebted to those who invited me to contribute to specialized journal issues on the work of Gilles Deleuze and to Liza Thompson, Senior Editor at Bloomsbury, for the help she provided in putting together the essays that compose this book, giving me extra time to have the texts translated and an extension for editing the book's final version. It is also my great pleasure to thank the friends and family members whose encouragements, critiques, and suggestions have certainly helped me to produce a better work than it would have been without their support and dedication to my efforts: Maurizia Natali, 'first reader' of everything I have ever written and whose encouragements and keen critique have helped me to go deeper into some important issues involved in my book, as well as Paul Patton, Simone Bignall, Ian Buchanan, Birgit Mara Kaiser, and Constantin V. Boundas for their confidence in me and their invitation to contribute to the beautiful books they have edited on the work of Gilles Deleuze. I want also to thank Hamza Bounoua for having allowed us to use one of his painting for the cover of the book.

My deepest thanks go also to the translators of these texts. Namely: Jennifer C. Gage for "On the Concept of Minor Literature: From Kafka to Kateb Yacine" and the Preface; Patricia Krus for "Becoming-Animal, Becoming-Political in Rachid Boudjedra's *L'Escargot Entêté*"; Denise Davis for "On the Spiritual Automaton"; Bryan Lueck for "*Cinéplastic(s)*," "The Subject of Art," and "Philosophy, Rhetoric and Cinema: The Time to Take Stock"; Terry Cochran for "The Kafka Effect"; Sarah-Louise Raillard for "The Singularity of the Event"; and Paul Gibbard for "Postcolonial Haecceities: The Names of Gilles Deleuze."

It would have been impossible to go forward on that journey had I not gotten inspiration from the following pioneers: Emily Apter, Dorothea Olkowski, Rosi Braidotti, Eric Clément, Dana Polan, Marie-Claire Ropars-Wuilleumier, Ronald Bogue, Jean-Clet Martin, Gregg Lambert, Charles Stivale, Tom Conley, Alain Ménil, David N. Rodowick, Timothy Murray, Rey Show, Timothy Bewes, Enric Bou, Nick Nesbitt, Anne Sauvagnargues, and Pierre Taminiaux.

Many academic institutions have played a crucial role in the conception and the production of the texts that constitute this book. I am thinking here of the journals and university presses where these texts were first published. My warmest thanks go to the editors of *CinéMas*, *Hors-Cadre*, *Iris* (Revue de Théorie de l'Image et du Son), Princeton University Press (*Translation/Transnation Series*), University of Minnesota Press (THL Series), University of Edinburgh (Connections Series), L'Harmattan (Champs Visuels Series), and the Routledge Interdisciplinary Perspectives on Literature Series.

Material for the chapters of this book was previously published and appears here in revised and (sometimes) expanded form:

"Cineplastic(s): Gilles Deleuze Reader of Élie Faure," reprinted by permission from Cinéma Art(s) plastiques(s), Pierre Taminiaux and Claude Murcia (eds), Champs Visuels Series, Cerisy, L'Harmattan, 2004.

"The Subject of Art: Prolegomena to a Future Deleuzian Aesthetics," reprinted by permission from CinéMas, Revue d'Études Cinématographiques, Journal of Film Studies, Vol. 16/Nos 2–3, Réda Bensmaïa (ed.), University of Montréal, 2007.

"The Singularity of the Event. Gilles Deleuze, Paul Virilio, François Jullien," reprinted by permission from *Singularity and Transnational Poetics*, Birgit Mara Kaiser (ed.), Routledge, Taylor & Francis, New York and London, 2015.

"On the Concept of Minor Literature: From Kafka to Kateb Yacine," reprinted by permission from *Gilles Deleuze and the Theater of Philosophy*, Constantin Boundas and Dorothea Olkowski, Routledge, New York and London, 1994.

"Becoming-Animal, Becoming-Political in Rachid Boudjedra's L'Escargot Entêté," reprinted by permission from *Postcolonial Literatures and Deleuze*, Lorna Burns and Birgit M. Kaiser (eds), Palgrave Macmillan, 2012.

"The Kafka Effect," reprinted by permission from *Kafka: Toward a Minor Literature*, translation by Dana Polan, foreword by Réda Bensmaïa, University of Minnesota Press, Theory and History of Literature, Volume 30, 1986.

"Postcolonial Haecceities (or the Names of Deleuze)," reprinted by permission from *Deleuze and the Postcolonial*, Simone Bignall and Paul Patton (eds), Edinburgh University Press, 2010.

"On the 'Spiritual automaton': Space and Time in Modern Cinema According to Gilles Deleuze," reprinted by permission from *Deleuze and Space*, Ian Buchanan and Gregg Lambert (eds), Edinburgh University Press, 2005.

Preface: Gilles Deleuze and How to Become a *Stalker* in Philosophy

If multiplicities are defined and transformed by the borderline that determines in each instance their number of dimensions, we can conceive of the possibility of laying them out on a plane, the borderlines succeeding one another, forming a broken line.

Gilles Deleuze, A Thousand Plateaus[1]

As soon as one thinks, one necessarily comes up against a line between life and death, reason and madness, and this line draws you along. It is only on this line of sorcery that one can think.

Gilles Deleuze[2]

"A great philosopher," writes François Regnault of Gilles Deleuze, "is one who convinces his readers and listeners to lead a philosophical life from that point on. Gilles Deleuze convinces them. It matters not whether all of them succeed; it is sufficient that all those who read or hear him perceive that such a life is now open to them."[3]

Deleuze's text on Spinoza—an "open letter" that Deleuze addressed to me in response to the special issue of *Lendemains* that I edited in 1989 on the subject of his work[4]—confirms this judgment. Whether or not they are "professional" philosophers, all those who have had the opportunity to read or to hear Deleuze will agree with Regnault's appraisal: Deleuze engenders the desire to enter into the philosophical *Ritournelle* or refrain[5] as it is elaborated in his work. For Deleuze, "doing philosophy" no longer means juggling with abstractions inherited from the history of philosophy, but rather learning to read, write, and think in three new "languages" at once: that of the "creation of concepts," that of "affects," and that of "percepts," as renewed in *meaning* and *practice* by philosophers and artists.

In composing the present collection of essays, I started out from the notion that thought had found through Deleuze's work a new means of "intercession" and of actualization, and in Deleuze himself a new type of philosopher: the philosopher as stalker,[6] tracking as a *practice* of philosophy that has definitively broken with the alternative that Deleuze never stopped denouncing in his work: the obsidional *Aut-Aut*, a malignant *either/or* that must always choose one or the other form: "*either* an undifferentiated ground ... *or* a supremely individuated Being and an intensely personalized Form."[7]

It is for this reason that in each of the texts I have chosen to include here, I have attempted to traverse one or another swath of Deleuzian text *like a surveyor* whose task is to circumscribe a singular "field": one that is vaster or more "open" than those we have been bequeathed by the history of philosophy, which Deleuze has transformed into a territory as enigmatic as the "zone" of Tarkovsky's film.

By gathering together the texts that make up this book, one of my objectives has been to invite the broadest possible readership to share in the pleasure of venturing forth along *unmarked paths* and eventually tracing maps of territories that are *still unexplored*. I hope to impart a taste for philosophical "stalking" as inaugurated by Deleuze, and above all a passion for conceiving of philosophical practice as surveying a "field" that has metamorphosed, in the manner of Tarkovsky, into a *zone*. This explains why, in one way or another, all of the texts included herein explore questions of edges, frontiers, thresholds, fringes, margins, borders, limits—between multiplicities, subjects, zones (zones of presence or absence, zones of power, zones of proximity or distance, or again zones of invisibility or imperceptibility): regarding the self, for example, didn't Deleuze and Guattari themselves say that in fact "the *self is only a threshold*, a door, a becoming *between two multiplicities*"? This accords with the principle that "*Each multiplicity is defined by a borderline functioning as Anomalous*, but there is *a string of borderlines, a continuous line of borderlines (fiber)* following which the multiplicity changes. And at each threshold or door, a new pact?"[8] This "abnormality" or "string of borderlines" is what Deleuze, in his role as surveyor of the history of philosophy, doggedly sought to identify, pursuing as an adroit *Stalker* all these "aberrant movements" or "forces" that run through matter, life, thought, nature, and the history of societies:[9] hence the title I have chosen for this collection of texts, all of which address what at first glance seems "off" or dissonant, what oscillates between (at least) two zones, two realms of power, two territories, two musical or pictorial tonalities. And if the question still persists—why the emphasis on *borderline(s) and limits?*—I would simply echo Deleuze and Guattari themselves:

> The reason is simple. *It is because no one, not even God, can say in advance whether two borderlines will string together or form a fiber, whether a given multiplicity will or will not cross over into another given multiplicity, or even if given heterogeneous elements will enter symbiosis, will form a consistent, or cofunctioning, multiplicity susceptible to transformation.* No one can say where the line of flight will pass: Will it let itself get bogged down and fall back to the Oedipal family animal, a mere poodle? Or will it succumb to another danger, for example, turning into a line of abolition, annihilation, self-destruction, Ahab, Ahab …?[10]

Lines, more lines, all these borderlines or divides (of the perceptible): against these lines Deleuze, like Jacques Rancière, continually takes his bearings in order to tease out, from the chaos of the real, certain forms that are still invisible or inaudible.

As will become evident, all the texts that appear in this book—whether they deal with the initially enigmatic notion of haecceity as it relates to postcolonial theory or "Deleuze's names" (Chapter 1), the subject of art (Chapter 2), plasticity (Chapter 3), the spiritual automaton (Chapter 4), the event (Chapter 5), Kafka and the desire of the law (Chapter 6), minor literature (Chapter 7), or becoming-animal (Chapter 8)—are overspread with the "wings" (to use Deleuze's evocative term) of this desire (to survey or measure) that constitutes philosophical "stalking", and with the aerial joys of tracking down and short-circuiting these "invisible fences" of thought implicit in "common sense" and "good sense."[11] Comprising texts born of a particular time and set of circumstances, this book makes no claim to offer a new "interpretation" of Deleuze's work: how could one undertake such a goal in the case of a philosopher who has devoted his every effort to combatting the dual "passions" of philosophy: the hunger for a closed system and for dogma?

In fact, as the reader will discover, despite the constant resonance among the questions tackled in these essays, each one is offered first and fundamentally as an attempt to follow through to its end the path or paths down which a specific concept of Deleuze's work might lead me. Once again, since these are *occasional* texts, so to speak, each was impelled by a personal urge to explore and by a desire to better understand his body of work as a process of "*apprenticeship*."[12] As a result each chapter is offered as an attempt to trace a new map, to chart some of the diagrammatic lines underlying the configuration of a hitherto unexplored territory. And in this sense, the book must be read as if it were a Turing machine made up of heterogeneous series[13] (in this case, book chapters) whose mutual resonance—thanks to the concepts mobilized in each chapter—aims to uncover the algorithm that accounts for a unique journey. My intention is not one more attempt at "introducing" Deleuze "*himself*" (see my discussion of "Deleuze's names" in the first chapter); after all, has he not consistently endeavored to remain "imperceptible," as well as refused the role of master in relation to "disciples"? Rather, I have sought to begin signaling the philosophical and political cartography that Deleuze has passed on to us, to make a preliminary inventory of the territories he discovered, with a view to taking our own particular bearings and pointing toward some new directions of thought. This explains the place I have given here to the exercise of bringing Deleuze's thought face to face with postcolonial theory—a theory that never appeared explicitly in his own books, but which has played a central role in my own work for at least two decades (see Chapters 7 and 8) and in the work of major postcolonial theorists. Clarifying this encounter, trying to explain what made it possible, finding the singular points where this junction could become legible: these are some of the preoccupations that will become apparent in the following essays.

In parallel with the undertaking I have just outlined, it has also been my intention to try to convey a sense of the deterritorialization that is at work in Deleuze's writings, which means that in every case, at my own risk, I have had to become in my own turn an *apprentice-Stalker*: first, a *Stalker* of the immense zone that Deleuze laid open to thought with the veritable *Magna Cartae* of his books; but also, because Deleuze's writing shuns facile distinctions between "artificial" and "natural," "content" and "expressions," "forms" and "substances," I have had to become a *Stalker* of the *Real* to which Deleuze's maps refer, to penetrate rhizome-like the worlds revealed by the maps I was unfolding. At the same time, always on the "wings of desire," I have tried to unleash new horizons of thought, of visions, and of affect: to unfurl a world by unfolding a map, or by superimposing the contours and lines of demarcation of multiple maps at once.

For obvious reasons, the pathways that can be traced with the texts collected in this book are partial and certainly provisional. Happily, they are still being pursued elsewhere with new maps, new stakes, new *Stalkers*, in new locales. If these paths whet the reader's appetite to blaze their own trails through Deleuze's work, if they provide new tools for drafting the reader's private map, I will consider my purpose fulfilled.

Translated by Jennifer Curtiss Gage

1

Postcolonial Haecceities: On Deleuze's Names

If philosophy of the future exists, it must be born outside of Europe or equally born in consequence of meetings and impacts between Europe and non-Europe.
Michel Foucault, A Stay in a Zen Temple[1]

It is impossible to understand how they have got as far as the capital: however, they are there, and every morning their numbers seem to grow.
Franz Kafka, The Great Wall of China[2]

Sorcerers have always held the anomalous position, at the edge of the fields or woods. They haunt the fringes. They are at the borderline of the village, or between villages. A thousand Plateaus.
Gilles Deleuze and Félix Guattari, A Thousand Plateaus[3]

Arnaud Bouaniche has recently drawn attention to the curious way in which Gilles Deleuze opens his *Spinoza: Practical Philosophy* (1988b) with a dialogue excerpted from Bernard Malamud's novel *The Fixer* (1966), a dialogue which Bouaniche describes as "a perfect *mise en abyme* of the change in perspective" that, in his opinion, occurred in Deleuze's work after May 1968, and which points to the position that Spinoza occupied in Deleuze's thought.[4] What Bouaniche emphasizes, and what is of particular interest for us as we try to understand the nature of the relations between Deleuze and his "mediators," is that when one character in the dialogue is ordered by the other, a judge, to explain what brought him to read Spinoza and what meaning he took from this encounter, the character in question "emphasises *not the speculative content or the theoretical propositions in Spinoza's thought, but the* PRACTICAL

EFFECTS *that they have had* not only on him as a reader and an individual ('After that I wasn't the same man'), but also on their author ('[Spinoza] was out to make a free man of himself'), having decided, in the words of the judge, to approach the problem 'through the man rather than the work.'"[5]

For those of us who wish to gain a better understanding of the popularity that Deleuze has attained among postcolonial writers, what is interesting about this story is that it gives a first hint of the direction we must take in order to approach the question correctly. Spinoza was, as we all know, an important point of reference for Deleuze in the area of philosophical theory, but also in the area of "encounters" between philosophers and non-philosophers, between professional theorists and the "general public." This "pedagogical" concern can be found in the major texts, but also in more "spontaneous" ones, letters, interviews, etc.: a concern that philosophy should be produced—enjoyed and understood—*by all* and not just by the "professionals." This point appears clearly in a reply that Deleuze sent to me when I was editing a collection of articles about his work for the German journal *Lendemains*. I asked him whether he thought his work was "accessible" to the general public, and what place he allotted to philosophical discourse. This is how Deleuze answered, again making reference to Spinoza:

> The paradox in Spinoza is that he's the most philosophical of philosophers, the purest in some sense, but also the one who more than any other addresses non-philosophers and calls forth the most intense non-philosophical understanding. That is why absolutely anyone can read Spinoza, and be very moved, or see things quite differently afterward, even if they can hardly understand Spinoza's concepts.[6]

Deleuze adopts the same position when discussing the status of philosophy in "How Philosophy is Useful to Mathematicians and Musicians: What directly orients the teaching of philosophy," wherein he tells us that it "is the question of how useful it is to mathematicians, or to musicians, etc., even and especially if this philosophy does not discuss mathematics or music. *This kind of teaching has nothing to do with general culture; it is practical and experimental*, always outside itself, precisely because the students are led to participate *in terms of their own needs and competences.*[7]

One inference we can draw from these two statements, made many years apart, is that postcolonial writers, activists, and intellectuals encounter Deleuze not so much through the *speculative* content of his thought but through the "practical effects" that his work has for each one of them. In what follows I shall try to bring out the critical and theoretical elements that have made the encounter between Deleuze and the postcolony possible. As we shall see, this assumes that we *start* by considering the multiple "avatars" of Deleuzean thought, and that we are able to determine *which* "Deleuze" we are dealing with when his "name" is linked to different strands of postcolonial theory.

Few exponents of postcolonial and subaltern theories now dispute the influence that Deleuze's work exerted on the intellectuals and theorists who developed those theories. Some cite his political stances (on Algeria, Palestine, and colonialism, as well as on prisons and societies of control) as the reason why he became one of the chief inspirations for postcolonial theory, while others point to particular concepts he forged with Félix Guattari. What is problematic about this sort of theoretical appropriation is its tendency to assume too lightly and uncritically what logically ought to be the object of preliminary analysis. The current postcolonial orthodoxy, particularly in the United States, holds that Deleuze's writings from the 1970s onward *unquestionably* form part of what is called "postcolonial theory." But what "theory" is being referred to here? Should such specialized and complex work as Deleuze's be assimilated, without any kind of qualification, into a theory of this sort which has its own particular framework as well as a strong tendency to resist any form of ideological annexation or appropriation? By taking as a given something that ought to be the object of initial enquiry, is there not a danger of blurring boundaries and losing sight of what is genuinely important in the "encounter" between the work of Deleuze and the movement of postcolonialist thought? We are obliged to make a careful assessment and show that it is indeed "Deleuze" that we are dealing with when we refer (only) to the texts he wrote with Guattari; and the same applies when we proceed *as though* what Deleuze wrote *before* his collaboration with Guattari "amounted to the same thing." Isn't it a misrepresentation of his thought simply to assume that the Deleuze we are dealing with in *A Thousand Plateaus* is "the same" Deleuze of *The Logic of Sense*?

There are other questions of this kind that must be raised. Have the promoters of a generalized Deleuzeanism taken care to check whether the borrowings they have made from such specialized work as his do him justice?

Have they considered the distortions that can occur when concepts arising in Deleuzean *philosophical practice* are applied or borrowed non-problematically to a different field of research and thinking? And lastly, where is the "crossroads" of their meeting? Where exactly does the encounter take place between a philosophy supposed to be "untimely" and which rejected the idea of the philosopher as a political leader or an ideological guru, and a theory which had as one of its chief goals direct action on current circumstances and the transformation of the social and political forms of a world inheriting decolonization?

One of my contentions in this essay is that postcolonial and subaltern theorists have engaged with Deleuzean thought in ways that have perhaps produced a long series of misunderstandings for which Deleuze himself is not responsible. Nevertheless, it is important for us to consider how Deleuze's work has come to play such a crucial role in the development of postcolonial theories and to understand, as François Cusset says in *French Theory*, "how such trenchant texts, often quite difficult to access, could come to be woven so deeply into the American cultural and intellectual fabric," as well as into the intricate weft of what would emerge as "a new global discourse on micropolitical resistance and subalternity."[8] The best critical strategy for approaching this, it seems to me, is not to review the obvious cases in which the Deleuzean "graft" has taken, but to reveal the "elements" which enable us to understand— if I may be allowed to employ a Derridean concept here—the "dissemination" of Deleuze's "names" across the broad field of postcolonial theory. What I hope to show in the following pages is that the encounter between Deleuze and the postcolonial movement can only be understood through the idea of a "field," we could even call it an "empirico-transcendental" field, in which Deleuze and his postcolonial followers find themselves "captured."

As numerous commentators have noted, in comparison with that of other philosophers, Deleuze's work was slow in gaining recognition for the important influence it had on the major intellectual debates of the 1970s and 1980s.[9] If the work he published on Hume, Kant, Bergson, Nietzsche, and Spinoza won him recognition among professional philosophers, it was only with the publication of *The Logic of Sense* and, especially, *Difference and Repetition* that the "name" of Deleuze began to emerge as a genuine intellectual "event" for those who had realized that his early books were something more than the straightforward work of a "historian of philosophy." And while these readers were beginning to suspect that he was doing more than simply accepting the torch from the great historians of philosophy (Guéroult, Hyppolite, Delbos, etc.), there was nothing yet to indicate that his work was on its way to becoming (along with that of Jacques Derrida, Jean-François Lyotard, and Michel Foucault) an essential point of reference in what would first be called "French Theory" and soon afterwards "postcolonial theory." Deleuze's innovative style and the difficulties in his texts created barriers to the quick adoption of his ideas and made it hard (notwithstanding his study of *Sacher Masoch*) for others to "adapt" them to the debates of the time, whether these were concerned with questions about the status of language, the subject, power, gender theory, the theory of sexuality, and perhaps, most problematically, postcolonial theory.[10] It would be necessary to wait until the 1990s before it was definitively recognized that any understanding, not just of essentially European philosophy, but of philosophy on a global stage, was impossible without taking into account the "Deleuzean project" (as Alain de Beaulieu very aptly calls it).[11]

Moreover, since Deleuze's death, the influence and impact of his work has continued to grow. In 2002 and 2003, in addition to the publication of *Desert Islands and Other Texts* and *Two Regimes of Madness*, the "Gilles Deleuze documentary archive" was established at Saulchoir in France, and the lectures that Deleuze gave at Vincennes were published online. What we should also add, concerning the reception of Deleuze's work, is how, as Arnaud Bouaniche puts it, "even before his influence became apparent in the conscious or deliberate use that was made of his themes and analyses, it could be seen in the enriching and stimulating effects it had on all those involved in intellectual and artistic matters."[12] It is through these effects that many figures who might at first be thought to have little in common are able to come together and unite around Deleuze's work: the historian of science Isabelle Stengers, the composer Pierre Boulez, the philosopher Dionys Mascolo, as well as the Portuguese film-director Manoël de Oliveira, who wrote to Deleuze saying how much he had been moved by a talk Deleuze gave on cinema at the French national film school FÉMIS, and that Deleuze's comments about the creative process had dazzled him. Oliveira's response is particularly interesting as it gets to the heart of what many artists will say about their "encounter" with

Deleuze's writings on film, music, painting, or literature, and does so in very clear terms. All speak of the "curious disquiet" they experience as they read one or another of Deleuze's texts, and of the "secret" affinities they uncover between what they have tried to do in their work and the way Deleuze describes his own experience of the creative process. Themes change and questions vary, but all whom Deleuze's work has touched share the feeling that he has revealed something of great importance to them. It is as though, they say, Deleuze's work makes them suddenly aware of a dimension of their own work which, until then, they had sensed but had not been able to define conceptually. Examples abound of artists and thinkers who have testified to the profound significance an "encounter" with Deleuze's work has held for them and the "joy" it engendered in them.

The poet Jean-Philippe Cazier, for example, recounts in an interview with Stéfan Leclerq: "As I read Deleuze more closely, my work took new directions, *related to developments in Deleuze's thought and his idea of minor literature.* My 'encounter' with a very bold style and very intense movements of thought all generated poetry in me."[13] For his part, the painter Ange-Henri Pieraggi is quick to attribute a broadening in the scope of his work and the discovery of new creative directions to a similar sort of "encounter": "Reading *The Movement-Image* was very important for me. The way it demonstrates that a face in close-up loses its connections in space and time, and so loses any capacity for individuation, socialisation and communication, raising itself to the level of another entity expressing the affect ... *gave me great intellectual pleasure.*"[14] What a great many other "encounters" with Deleuze show, as Bouaniche observes, is that the perception that Deleuze has something of the "oracle" or "seer" about him "stems not so much from the difficulty of identifying something like a monologic main thread in what he says or writes, and even less from the way he marshals his conceptual arsenal," but, more commonly, from a "listening" or "understanding through percepts and affects" which in some way resonates directly with a concept that "hits home" and connects with something important. In these types of "encounter" there is an experience of the same order as that described by Roland Barthes when he speaks of a relationship with a text "according to pleasure" rather than according to a "tactical aim," a "social usage," or even an "image-reservoir": "I cannot," writes Barthes, "apportion, imagine that the text is perfectible, ready to enter into a play of normative predicates: it is too much this, not enough that; the text (the same is true of the singing voice) can wring from me only this judgement, in no way adjectival: that's it! And further still: that's it for me!" And Barthes goes on to specify, in a Deleuzean vein: "This 'for me' is neither subjective nor existential, but Nietzschean."[15]

As we shall attempt to show, the writers and critics who will serve here as "mediators" testify to exactly this type of experience in relation to Deleuze's work: work which wrings from them a *That's it! That's exactly it for me!*—coming from an elsewhere which they are not always able to locate or even name, but which they experience neither as simply "subjective" nor uniformly "existential," but … Deleuzean! There are thinkers, and Deleuze is one, whose work provides the occasion for such "intuitive transition." This is why, as Jean-Hugues Barthélémy says of Gilbert Simondon, in words which could apply equally well to Deleuze, his work "enthrals" and is often "used" by many "without being deployed or even explained in detail and for itself absolutely."[16] From one text to another, from one concept to another, the same type of experience is intensely encountered and shot through with extremely strong affects: the individual undergoing the experience has just recognized a "scene of language" which delights her, and has just encountered a "conceptual persona" which cleaves her in two and causes her to enter in an unprecedented way into a "bloc of becoming," an "a-parallel evolution."[17]

Having said that, it is not the case that all "encounters" with Deleuze's work occur under the same auspices. While we have discussed the "pythic" or "psychopompal" Deleuze, the Deleuze who inspires creators and whom they consider to be the thinker who has best explored certain of their concerns, the situation becomes much more complex if we decide to look at all the texts whose relations to the work of Deleuze—and in particular to the texts he wrote with Guattari—appear without the same degree of transparency:[18] texts which show that the Deleuze of artists and creators is not always the same as the Deleuze of professional philosophers, for example, or postcolonial theorists. Foucault was perhaps referring to this Promethean quality when he declared that "one day, perhaps, the century will be Deleuzean"[19]—a quip which, in my view, did not imply that Deleuze's ideas would one day come to dominate the global intellectual scene, with Deleuze being acknowledged as its ruling figure and the century's greatest thinker, but rather alluded to something much more profound, which we shall call *Deleuze's "names"*. Wasn't it Deleuze "himself" who said that "individuals find a truly proper name for themselves ... only through the harshest exercise in depersonalisation, by opening themselves up to the multiplicities everywhere within them"?[20] What Foucault sensed and very quickly understood is that a thinker who "complicates" the idea of a radical univocity of being with a theory of multiplicities and pre-individual identities can never be "reduced" to a (single) name; the century would be "Deleuzean," above all, because of this *dispersion of names*, and consequently, of the *problematics* that it draws in its wake. The century would be Deleuzean because it would "perhaps" find in his work a resonance chamber for its own great tumult, for its waves of thought, for its movements of ideas and events—whose intense energies could only be seized by an individual who was prepared to *surf* on them.[21] The century would be Deleuzean due to the apparatuses [*dispositifs*] that he set up: he ended up transforming himself into a "mediator," and by doing so enabled "a new light, new enunciations, new forms of subjectivation" to emerge. But doubtless Foucault did not insert that "perhaps" inadvertently or as a manner of speaking: in the context in which it was uttered, Foucault's "quip" was perhaps alluding to a danger that Deleuzean thought—that true "nomadic war machine"—might be transformed into a "toolbox" (another of Deleuze's terms, of course), which would owe nothing to the initial radicality of the task that Deleuze undertook in his writings. Foucault understood that the "Deleuze effect," along with the apparatuses [*dispositifs*] that mediated it, could go just as easily towards bringing about a revolution in "images of thought" and "morals" as they could go in the opposite direction: molar "stasis," the hardening of identity, communitarianism, etc. This ought to be clear to us from the warning that Deleuze (and, in this case, Guattari) repeatedly issued to their readers: that a rhizome can always hide roots, and a line of flight can always hide strata, segmentarities, and even a repressive apparatus of the state: "Sometimes," write Deleuze and Guattari, "*one overdoes it*, puts too much in, works with a jumble of lines and sounds; then instead of producing a cosmic machine [for music and painting!] capable of 'rendering sonorous,' *one lapses back to a machine of reproduction* that ends up reproducing nothing but a scribble effacing all lines, a scramble effacing all sounds ... . All one has left is a resonance chamber well on the way to becoming a black hole."[22]

What these "examples" show is that many different "names" try concurrently to attach themselves to the avatars of a Deleuze who is a historian of philosophy, all arriving with the same (false) supporting evidence. In this way, a *poststructuralist Deleuze* belonging to "French theory" is hastily hitched to a multitude of different strands of thought (aesthetic theory, literary theory, queer studies, feminist theory, "artistic practices," etc.).[23] We come across, for example, a Deleuze who is a *pop philosopher*, who gathers artists around him (painters, musicians, poets, etc.); we also come across a *schizo-analyst Deleuze*—that is to say, a Deleuze who now writes his books "using four hands," with Guattari, and who has radically distanced himself from his work as a historian or as a poststructuralist "pure and simple" in order to embark on a more directly political program. And at this point, as will be seen, he is hitched to other strands of thought: altermondialism, anarchism, neo-fascism, postcolonialism, subalternism, identity politics, etc. Now, it is precisely this proliferation of names (Deleuze's names) which led us to delay the moment at which Deleuze became enlisted without further ado in the postcolonial movement.

While it is always possible to adduce (Deleuze's) texts to justify or defend any of these interpretations of Deleuze's œuvre—doesn't Spinoza say that "no heresy has difficulty or is in trouble finding a text [that justifies it]"?—it remains the case that: (1) the names to which these texts refer are not always consistent at a theoretical level[24]—the pop philosopher Deleuze can exist alongside the schizo-analyst Deleuze, but nobody can claim that the two display the same outlook on things, or that she is dealing with the "true" or the "real" Deleuze because she has managed to reconcile the two "currents" of thought; (2) as such, no one and/or other of these "hypotheses" is able to *define* what conditioned the setting up of the "Deleuze-postcolony" apparatus [*dispositif*] and to specify the name under which Gilles Deleuze makes his theoretical "entry" into it. This question seems all the more legitimate to us because for so long Deleuze was viewed as a difficult writer, and seemed incapable of being linked with any particular current of thought.[25] As one very acute commentator, Alain Badiou, has perceived, Deleuze remained "at a slant to all blocks of philosophical opinion" and was neither "a phenomenologist, nor a structuralist, nor a Heideggerian, nor an importer of Anglo-Saxon analytical 'philosophy,' nor a neo-humanist liberal,"[26] and we could add, no more was he a subaltern or postcolonial theorist in the works he wrote *in his own name*. His favorite (or even "fetish") authors were not Kateb Yacine, Edouard Glissant, Aimé Césaire, Albert Memmi, or Frantz Fanon, but rather Kafka, Melville, Beckett, and Proust, and it is in this sense that it can indeed be said that "in perfect harmony with the aristocratism of his thought ... Deleuze [created] *a polarity all his own*."[27] How can we, from this point of view, account for the fact that he is considered, along with Derrida, Foucault, and Lyotard, to be one of the inspirations for postcolonial or subaltern theory? How do we explain the fact that so many theorists and critics of these two currents of thought do not hesitate to insert him into the movement of their work when he in fact superbly ignored all of their *fetish authors*? What apparatus [*dispositif*] do we look to in trying to understand the way in which Deleuze has been adopted as a "mediator" of postcolonial thinkers? We can also think about this question by reflecting on the *name* and the conditions under which Deleuze enters the "postcolonial theory" apparatus [*dispositif*], and by asking what, then, are its characteristics?

What seems to us to have conditioned the actualization of this singular apparatus [*dispositif*] is an insistence on the "appeal" that can be found in practically all the texts that *Deleuze wrote with Guattari*, to the production of subjectivities capable of resisting the different forms of control that colonization imposed on the colonized. Deleuze was not perhaps *directly* interested in the leading figures of postcolonial theory (Frantz Fanon, Albert Memmi, Antonio Gramsci, or even Edward Said, Homi K. Bhabha, Gayatri C. Spivak, Ranajit Guha, Gyan Prakash, Dipesh Chakrabarty, Valentin Mudimbe, and Achille Mbembe), but he always took careful account of the *political* consequences of the ideas he advanced in his work. In any case this is one of the reasons that led him to engage in the genuine "conversion" that he carried out in the work he did with Guattari, but also with Carmelo Bene, Dyonis Mascolo, and many others. This, anyway, is how I understand the place he gave to the idea of the "encounter" in his work, and the "pathos" he attached to it: "When you work," he argues, in a book written with Claire Parnet, "you are necessarily in absolute solitude. *You cannot have disciples, or be part of a school. The only work is moonlighting and is clandestine. But it is an extremely populous solitude. Populated not with dreams, phantasms or plans, but with encounters. An encounter is perhaps the same thing as a becoming, or *nuptials*. It is from the depth of this solitude that you can make any encounters whatsoever. You encounter people (*and sometimes without knowing them or ever having seen them*) but also movements, ideas, events, entities."[28]

Deleuze was also fond of saying that "philosophers aren't reflective, they are creative,"[29] by which he meant he was not interested in "thinking on"[30] (cinema, politics, etc.) or "speaking for" (the public, minorities, etc.), but rather he was interested in "setting things in motion," in creating concepts which do not remain simply at the level of words or sentences—or "phrase-making"—but rise to the level of utterances: "thought as archive!"[31] And, from this, we arrive at the hypothesis that postcolonial theories were developing *at the same time* (that is, in the same *epistemic frame*) as Deleuze's thought was taking shape, in an a-parallel evolution: once again, the wasp and the orchid!

We recall that in his short text about "mediators" Deleuze discusses the factors that condition the relations between radically different practices: "How is it possible—*in their completely different lines of development*, with quite different rhythms and movements of production—*how is it possible for a concept, an aggregate, and a function to interact?*"[32] In this text we also come across the "elements"—in the Kantian sense of *Elementarelhere*—which enable us to understand how the most demanding philosophical practice can resonate with practices that seem completely alien to it. "Creating concepts," writes Deleuze, "is no less difficult than creating new visual or aural combinations, or creating scientific functions. What we *have* to recognise is that the *interplay between the different lines* isn't a matter of one monitoring or reflecting another. A discipline that set out to follow a creative movement *coming from outside* would itself relinquish any creative role. You'll get nowhere by latching onto some parallel movement, you have to make a move yourself. If nobody makes a move, nobody gets anywhere. Nor is interplay an exchange: it all turns on giving or taking."[33] All the same, it is not entirely by chance that many of the "examples" which Deleuze offers in this text by way of "illustrating" the manner in which "mediations" function relate to questions linked to colonization and the necessity of escaping the discourse of the "master": "Perrault thinks," writes Deleuze, "that if he speaks on his own, even in a fictional framework, *he's bound to come out with an intellectual's discourse, he won't get away from a 'master's or colonialist's discourse*,' an established discourse … . So, to the established fictions that are *always rooted in a colonialist's discourse*, we oppose a minority discourse, with mediators."[34]

At this point in our analysis, we might be tempted to "close the circle" and defend the argument that it is precisely as a *mediator and intercessor* that Deleuze comes into play in the postcolonial debate—or *ritornello*. To achieve this, all we would have to do, as many commentators have done, is allude to the multitude of works, familiar to both scholars and the general public, which profess a direct "debt" to the work of Deleuze, or which boldly declare their allegiance to Deleuze.[35] We could support this argument by, for example, citing the concepts that nowadays define what might be called the *Deleuzean postcolonial orthodoxy*. And indeed can any text claiming to belong to the postcolonial or subaltern movement ignore the concepts of "minor literature," "multitude," "nomadic war machine," "becoming" (-minor, -animal, -woman, -intense), "rhizome," "*ritornello*," or "faciality"? Can any critic ignore the adaptation (to postcolonial problematics) of concepts that Deleuze and Guattari introduced in *Anti-Oedipus*, *A Thousand Plateaus*, and *What is Philosophy*? Can anyone neglect the schizo-analytic concepts of "desiring-machine," "body-without-organs," "anomal," "aberrant movements," and many other "Deleuzo-Guattarian" concepts without feeling she has missed a "plateau" or an important "encounter"? But we might ask: what's left of Deleuze in all this? Which Deleuze is being spoken of when we observe that most of the concepts that have "passed" into postcolonial theory are drawn from works that Deleuze wrote *with* Guattari? Which of Deleuze's *names* is being referred to in this case? Which Deleuze is being referred to when postcolonial theory engages with one or other of the concepts listed above without concerning itself with the ruptures (in style or theme) which have marked the development of Deleuzean thought over the years? Doesn't one run the risk of *instrumentalizing* his thought by ignoring the transformations that have marked the evolution of his thought and the progression from the work he did alone to that done with Guattari? Is it not a great oversimplification to integrate the *pre*-Guattarian Deleuze with the *post*-Guattarian Deleuze without any qualification whatsoever?[36] These, in any case, are the types of questions which have led us from the outset to enquire into Deleuze's "names"—an enquiry which, it should now be clearer, is less concerned with casting doubt on Deleuze's theoretical involvement in the postcolonial movement than with mapping certain *critical* aspects of the question.

These types of questions also lead us on to another problem, one which is concerned, paradoxically, with the idea of "mediation" itself. We have seen that the concepts and the theoretical and political problematics which Deleuze and Guattari engaged with in the books they wrote together enabled a "connection" to be made between their work and the "spin-offs" that their work produced for postcolonial theory. Deleuze and Guattari perhaps never engaged in direct "dialogue" with their postcolonial colleagues, but all the texts they published in tandem or individually reveal that they were perfectly aware of the implications that their ideas might have for the global theoretical field. We have only to reread that "concept accelerator," *A Thousand Plateaus*, from this point of view to realize it could never have been written without its authors' possessing the sharpest sensitivity to the great global questions of the moment. Isn't it from chapters such as "November 20, 1923: Postulates of Linguistics," "1933: Micropolitics and Segmentarity," "1227: Treatise on Nomadology:—the War Machine," and "7000 BC: Apparatus of Capture" that the leading theorists of postcolonialism draw certain of their key concepts on the status of language "*en pays dominé*" ("in a dominated country" or "under a colonial dominion")[37] on questions of space, territory, and borders, but also on questions relating to the "formation of subjectivity" and identity, of socius and state, and finally to the relations between Power and Knowledge? When, in September 1999, Didier Eribon asked Deleuze, in relation to *What is Philosophy?*, that is, a text which does not at first sight appear to make any trenchant political attacks, whether this book of "geophilosophy," co-authored with Guattari, did not amount to a "political manifesto," Deleuze gave an unexpected response: "The current political situation is very muddled. People tend to confuse the quest for freedom with the embrace of capitalism. *It seems doubtful that the joys of capitalism are enough to liberate a people.* The bloody failure of socialism is on everybody's lips, but no one sees capitalist globalisation as a failure, *in spite of the bloody inequalities that condition the market, and the populations who are excluded from it.*"[38] As other texts reveal, everything concerned with globalization held great importance for Deleuze and Guattari—particularly France's postcolonial situation, and the neo-colonialist aspirations of the United States. All the "ingredients" of encounter and mediation are there, and yet the original paradox remains: at no time did our authors, and in particular Deleuze, engage in direct dialogue with the representatives of postcolonial militants[39] or join in the political debate (or "conversation," as some commentators call it) which raged elsewhere: across India, Latin America, and Algeria, as well as across Italy, Spain, and before long the whole world.[40] And how consequently do we overcome this problem and escape from this apparent impasse? How do we interpret the *gap* that exists between the "influence" of Deleuze and Guattari's work on theorists of the postcolony and the absence we have already referred to of any direct relation between them? It is through the notion of the *mediator* that we can find a "way out." What exactly, we must then ask, does Deleuze mean by *mediator*? What characterizes a *mediator* for him?

"Mediators are fundamental," writes Deleuze. "*Creation's all about mediators. Without them nothing happens.* They can be people—for a philosopher, artists or scientists; for a scientist, philosophers or artists—but things too, even plants or animals, as in Castaneda." So much for the generic definition. But Deleuze immediately goes on to specify: "Whether they're real or imaginary, animate or inanimate, you have to *form* your mediators. *It's a series. If you're not in some series, even a completely imaginary one, you're lost.* I need my mediators to express myself, *and they'd never express themselves without me*: you're always working in a group, even when you seem to be on your own. And still more when it's apparent: Félix Guattari and I are one another's mediators."[41]

It is impossible to read this passage without recalling what Deleuze said when pursuing a different line of thought in *The Logic of Sense*, one relating to the idea of "structure." It is interesting to note the parallels that can be established between the two definitions, along with the importance allotted to the idea of "series" for both mediator and structure. Deleuze describes the minimal conditions for a "structure in general" as follows:

> 1) There must be *at least two* heterogeneous series, one of which shall be determined as "signifying" and the other as "signified" (a single series never suffices to form a structure). 2) Each of these series is constituted by *terms which exist only through the relations they maintain with one another* .... 3) The two heterogeneous series converge toward a *paradoxical element*, which is their "differentiator." This is the principle of the emission of singularities.[42]

What is striking in both cases is of course the reference to heterogeneous series. But, for those of us trying to arrive at a better understanding of the composition of this structure and the place that the *series* occupies in its functioning, a new element makes its appearance—one which was not present in the text concerning mediators, but which will acquire here an extremely important status and play a fundamental role: we are referring to the "paradoxical element" that Deleuze mentions, the "differentiator," which, as we know, can assume a *multitude of names*, but which can never be "pinned down," never reduced to a single name. It is of this atopic element, this element always in movement, that Deleuze will say: "it *does not belong to any series*, or rather [it] belongs to both at once, and never ceases moving through them."[43] Our attention is inevitably drawn to other characteristics attributed to this element, which is gradually endowed with greater and greater powers, and with a capacity for metamorphosis all the more extraordinary: always "displaced in relation to itself," always "lacking its own place," "its own identity," "its own resemblance and its own equilibrium," it is constantly "becoming" and "in the middle."

I do not believe that I am giving way to interpretive delirium in saying that Deleuze defines his philosophical practice on the model of this "element": the philosopher as "differentiator" who never ceases moving between series, between discourses; the philosopher-*Stalker* always displaced in relation to himself, lacking his own place and his own identity, and who, by this fact, can never be bound to ideologies or doctrines that are "fixed" and closed upon themselves. It is this characteristic, in our view, that has conditioned the different types of relations that can be entered into with regard to Deleuze's work and which enables us to understand the multiplicity of "names" that he has been able to "embody" for a "public" more and more numerous and heterogeneous. It is from this position (of "differentiator") that Deleuze will tackle all the questions that characterize his philosophical practice: a position which dispenses with the centered and unified "subject," as it appears in transcendental philosophy and metaphysics, in favor of a "free, anonymous, and nomadic singularity which traverses men as well as plants and animals independently of the matter of their individuation and the forms of their personality."[44] Just like Nietzsche (of whom Deleuze was a remarkable interpreter, and who was the "mediator" *par excellence* of all Deleuze's work), in his discovery of impersonal and pre-individual singularities, Deleuze also saw a "new way of exploring the depth, of bringing a distinct eye to bear upon it, *of discerning in it a thousand voices, of making all of these voices speak*—being prepared to be snapped up by this depth which he interpreted and populated as it had never been before."[45] Moreover, it is all these "actualizations," along with this "atopicality" and the constantly changing nature of a "subject" that is always other than what it "founds,"[46] that ensure that (the name of) Deleuze is capable of being associated with the diversity of "encounters" to which his work gives rise. It will always be necessary, in this sense, to recognize that there is a *virtual and/or undifferentiated* (name of) Deleuze which remains always to be discovered *despite all its actualizations*, and that his readers reinvent him, just as "himself" but always "other," each time that an affect or a percept drawn from one of the concepts of his work speaks to them.

It is, in our view, just such an apparatus [*dispositif*] that conditions the *different natures* of the "encounters" that Deleuze's work gives rise to in its readers. And so, for example, it is with full awareness of the obstacles he must overcome and the theoretical precautions he must take that a philosopher like Žižek writes his book "on" Deleuze. He immediately warns us that "a Lacanian book on Deleuze cannot ignore *all these facts* [*that is, the debate between Lacan and Badiou on the relationship between psychoanalysis and philosophy*]. Consequently, *Organs without Bodies* is not a 'dialogue' between these two theories [those of Badiou and Lacan via Deleuze?] but something quite different: an attempt to trace the contours of *an encounter between two incompatible fields.*" And Žižek then adds an observation which is close in nature to the questions we raised about Deleuze's concept of "encounter": "An encounter cannot be reduced to symbolic exchange: what resonates in it, over and above the symbolic exchange, is *the echo of a traumatic impact.* While dialogues are commonplace, encounters are rare."[47] *Dont acte!* as the French saying goes! Let's take this for granted for the time being! But what is remarkable in this case is the sensitivity Žižek displays regarding the nature of the type of "encounter" that one can have when one is dealing with philosophical work of the calibre of Deleuze's. Žižek "understands" that the encounter cannot be reduced or related to a simple "symbolic exchange" and doesn't hesitate to evoke the idea of "a traumatic impact" because he realizes that in writing a book "on" Deleuze, *arising out of his own disagreement with Badiou and Lacan,* he must marshal "all the facts," that is, get to the bottom of things and settle his account with Badiou and Lacan through the mediation of Deleuze. And, this being the case, it is perhaps not entirely by chance that the concept of "Bodies without Organs" ("BwO") is used as the catalyst between series and the release mechanism for the "encounter": "the limit of deterritorialisation of the schizo body and created in concert with the fragmented body and bad partial objects,"[48] converted into *OwB* ("Organs without Body") in the title of the book, it is transformed into the "dark precursor" of the critical ambitions that Žižek will develop in his book and functions as a connector between the questions that will be treated in it. But by saying that he must marshal "all the facts," Žižek is also indicating that one of the aims of his book is to "track down" the Deleuze who threads his way between the ideas expressed in his own books or those written with Guattari. For Žižek, it is less a question of *providing a better explanation* of Deleuze's thought than of testing out his own hypotheses and concepts through a systematic reading of Deleuze's work. To undertake such a venture, it is first of all necessary to know *who* you are dealing with. You may *know*, but what is the nature of your knowledge? Taking Deleuze as a "mediator," Žižek seeks to test his thought and the problematics it is based on at the same time that he once more works through the reading he has done *via Deleuze* of Lacan, Foucault, Derrida, Badiou, and Butler, using this reading to serve his own system. The "encounter" has a "traumatic" dimension because *in this particular case* it runs the risk at every moment of giving up what it has for an uncertain alternative, taking *for Deleuze* (or *Deleuze's thought*) what may yet reveal itself to be only one of his avatars. This is why, in our view, having set out in search of the "true"(?) Deleuze, Žižek finds himself having to peel away and discard what he sees as certain of Deleuze's names (or *false* names): "So, why Deleuze?" he asks at the very start of his book. "In the past decade, Deleuze emerged as *the central reference of contemporary philosophy*: notions like 'resisting multitude,' 'nomadic subjectivity,' the 'anti-Oedipal' critique of psychoanalysis, and so on are the common currency of today's academia—not to mention the fact that *Deleuze more and more serves as the theoretical foundation of today's anti-globalist Left and its resistance to capitalism.*"[49] In less than two sentences, Žižek has already confronted two of Deleuze's "names" that have "emerged" over the years, but in which he does not recognize his "own" Deleuze or, to put it another way, the most "authentic" Deleuze (who has been "hidden" behind his other incarnations). Several lines later, an apparently even more "traumatic" encounter takes place with another of Deleuze's "ghosts," the Deleuze who is "much closer" to psychoanalysis and Hegel: "*Organs without Bodies* here goes 'against the current': its starting premise is that, *beneath this Deleuze* (the popular image of Deleuze based on the reading of the books he co-authored with Félix Guattari), *there is another Deleuze*, much closer to psychoanalysis and Hegel, a Deleuze whose consequences are much more shattering."[50]

Other philosophers, including some of the subtlest interpreters of Deleuze's thought, have had to confront the same problem, which relates to "capturing" Deleuze, enclosing him within a system and *giving him a name*. Alain Badiou is a case in point: his book is intended as a homage to Deleuze but is unable to resist the temptation of reducing Deleuze's thought to a single dominant strand, or to a particular "taste" even, all in the name of the so-called Deleuzian "Univocity of Being."[51] The idea of mediation takes on its full meaning in this work, and Badiou presents to us a Deleuze with whom he feels great affinity and with whom—in what makes him the perfect "mediator"—he has the most profound philosophical and theoretical disagreements. Deleuze's names inundate the text: he is described as the "philosophical inspiration for the *anarcho-désirants*" during the Vincennes years; at the same time, no less, he is presented as "an enemy [who was] all the more dangerous because he was inside the [leftist] movement." Later in the same text, Badiou recounts how once he didn't hesitate to "label as 'fascist' the defence [which Deleuze made] of spontaneous movement, his theory of 'spaces of freedom,' his hatred of dialectics, [and] in summary: his philosophy of life and of natural all-One."[52] Elsewhere, in the same text, Badiou dismisses Deleuze's thought as being nothing more (or less) than "reworked Platonism." Badiou concludes that Deleuze and he ended up forming a "paradoxical duo," based on "active divergence." And, having criticized the "dubious role of the disciples" who tended to rally round their master for "the wrong reasons" and ended up betraying him, Badiou himself arrives at the same conclusion: *there is an equivocity between the different names of the Master, an equivocity which bears the name* "Deleuzeanism." Badiou explains: "There exists in fact a *cynical Deleuzeanism* which is the diametric opposite of the sobriety and asceticism of the Master."[53] And what if the notion of the "Master" itself is flawed? What if it is simply the "spin-off," both fortuitous and necessary, of the "logic" which underlies the proliferation of Deleuze's names within the field of philosophy *as well as outside it*? And what if, to put it another way, "Deleuzeanism" (as philosophers call it) were only a "machine" (a *"machine-desirante"* even!) with multiple fissures and "spin-offs"? And what if finally the "Deleuze" that philosophers have tried so hard to pigeonhole was only ever the "dark precursor" of the "differentiator" that Deleuze discusses in *Difference and Repetition*, and of which he says: "it has no place other than that from which it is 'missing,' no identity other than that which it lacks: it is precisely the object = *x*, the one which is 'lacking in its place' as it lacks its own identity?"[54] In this particular case, it is not "Deleuze" who should be asked to explain certain (conceptual, affective, or perceptive) "spin-offs" produced by the dark precursor's "coupling" of divergent series—rather it is his readers. To criticize Deleuze for "deviating" from certain norms or transcendental principles, and to attribute to him, without any qualification, an identity at the end of one or other of the series that he has caused to resonate—Bergson-duration-cinema, Nietzsche-Spinoza, Virtual-Actual, time-truth, chance-eternal return, fold-outside, etc.—is to ignore the multiple warnings that Deleuze gives about the nature of the relationship that the differentiator maintains with what it conditions in any intensive system. Deleuze specified very clearly:

> If difference is related *to its differentiator, and if we refrain from attributing to the differentiator an identity that it cannot and does not have*, then the difference will be small or large according to its possibilities of fractionation—that is, *according to the displacements and disguise* of the differentiator. In no case will it be possible to claim that a small difference testifies to a strict condition of resemblance, any more than a large difference testifies to the persistence of a resemblance which is simply relaxed. Resemblance is in any case an effect, a functional product, an external result—an illusion which appears *once the agent arrogates to itself an identity that it lacked*.[55]

If in *Difference and Repetition* and *The Logic of Sense* the theory of the subject and the event is explained within the (post)structural(ist) framework of the "differentiator" which causes heterogeneous series to resonate, in *Dialogues* Deleuze approaches the question in a completely different way and opens it out into a radically new dimension.[56] We remember that in Chapter 3 of his *Dialogues II* with Claire Parnet, Deleuze indicates that one must distinguish between "two types of planes": a plane which is "as much as one wishes, structural and genetic," which he calls "one of *organisation*," and which essentially concerns "the development of forms and the formation of subjects"[57] and a "completely different plane" which he calls the "*plane of consistency*," whose distinctive characteristic is that it "knows only relations of movement and rest, of speed and slowness, between unformed, or relatively unformed, elements, molecules or particles borne away by fluxes," and which, moreover, "knows nothing of subjects, but rather what are called 'haecceities.'" We learn indeed, in the same text, that on the one hand "no individuation takes place in the manner of a subject or even of a thing. An hour, a day, a season, a climate, one or several years—a degree of heat, an intensity, very different intensities which combine—have a perfect individuality which should not be confused with that of a thing or of a formed subject"; and, on the other hand, that "it is not the *moment*, and it is not *brevity*, which distinguishes this type of individuation," and that "a haecceity *can last as long as, and even longer than, the time required for the development of a form and the evolution of a subject*." When we appreciate that haecceities are not concerned with *the same type of time* but with "floating times"[58] as distinct from *Chronos*, we are perhaps beginning to assemble the elements which will enable us to understand better how this mysterious entity, the haecceity, is linked with the problematics of the multiplicity of Deleuze's names, which we have discussed above. Because it serves to "determine an impersonal and pre-individual transcendental field, … which nevertheless is not confused with an undifferentiated depth [and] cannot be determined as that of a consciousness," and refers to "what is neither individual nor personal,"[59] the concept of haecceity is revealed to be what, from now on, *presides over* the genesis of individuals and people as emitters of singularities:

> It is haecceities that are being expressed in *indefinite, but not indeterminate*, articles and pronouns; in proper names which do not designate people *but mark events*, in verbs in the infinitive which are not undifferentiated but constitute becomings or processes.[60]

The one explains the other: haecceities allow the naming of the singularities which characterize "forces, events, movements and moving objects, winds and typhoons," but equally the naming of a period of time, even of a century: What a terrible five o'clock in the afternoon! What a terrible twenty-first century![61]

What do Deleuze (and Guattari) undertake in *Anti-Oedipus* if not to locate and give a name to all the waves of force which formed the century, as well as to those which silently approach—still "indefinite, but not indeterminate"? Deleuze knew that we belonged to the apparatuses [*dispositifs*] corresponding, between other becomings or processes in formation, to the haecceities which we shall call *postcolonial*[62] and which have the names: "movements of national liberation," "decolonization," "emigration," "crisis in the struggle of the working class," "crisis in the republican model," "post-history," "diasporization of knowledge," "postmodernism," "conflicts between civilizations," "racialization of social conflicts," "whiteness," "witnessness,"[63] "death of the grand narrative," "third world," "fourth world," "AIDS"...

Deleuze and Guattari did not *invent* these haecceities but, by reviving the concept of haecceity, they allowed new light to be thrown on the way the present could be tackled, while being quite aware, as Deleuze aptly observed, that "the present [*actuel*] is not what we are but rather what we become, what *we are in the process of becoming, in other words the Other, our becoming-other*."[64] In our view, it is this "process of becoming ... Other," and the haecceities to which it relates, that Deleuze (and Guattari) were pursuing when they created the concepts they have left to posterity, concepts which they hoped would allow us to map out better new modes of subjectivation and socialization: "What new modes of subjectivation do we see appearing *today* that are certainly *not Greek or Christian*?" Deleuze asked, in a text devoted to Foucault,[65] so many questions which, understandably, in light of the way they "overflowed" a strictly European frame, appealed to and even enthralled postcolonial writers, thinkers, and researchers. *Appealing* because, even if they were not always addressed directly to them, they touched on what was unfolding in the world and shared in this according to the principle which, in this case, holds that: HAECCEITIES = WHAT CENTURY ARE WE IN? WHAT WAVE IS SWEEPING US ALONG? WHAT HISTORY? WHAT NEW VISIBILITIES ARE POSSIBLE AFTER THE POSTCOLONY? etc. *Enthralling* because, even if the encounter did not always take place on a speculative level, there was always a concept that could come and *cleave* in two: postcolonial poets, musicians, and film-makers who went to encounter Deleuze's work and who discovered themselves to be "Deleuzean" not "without realizing it" but through "something that seems to have been brought about by him alone."[66]

We nowadays know that this "something = x" which carries the philosopher and the non-philosopher onwards comes from the multiplicity of Deleuze's "names" and the rich concepts he created in order to give an account of the haecceities that fascinated him so much and which turned out to be the very haecceities which writers such as (confining ourselves just to postcolonial writers of the Maghreb) Kateb Yacine, Abdelwahab Meddeb, Assia Djebar, Abdelkébir Khatibi, Hélé Béji, Rachid Boudjedra, and Nabile Farès explore in their work.

Translated by Paul Gibbard

2

The Subject of Art: Prolegomena to a Future Deleuzian Aesthetics

If there is a "constant" in Deleuze's thought *about art* [*au sujet de l'art*], and at the same time ON the subject (of art) [*SUR le sujet (de l'art)*], it is the reference to Kant.[1] What an attentive reading of his texts makes clear is also the insistence with which Gilles Deleuze returns to, and appears to rely on, Kant when he engages with the question of aesthetics, and more specifically with the question of the status of (the subject of) art within the economy of philosophical thought. Viewed from a certain angle, Deleuze appears to have wanted to make a return to Kant in the way that others have attempted a return to Freud, Nietzsche, or Hegel. There is obviously the short book that he devoted to Kant, which can be seen as a book of self-initiation and of the general repetition of properly Deleuzian theses to come.[2] But there is above all the multiplicity of articles devoted to Kant's work as well as the sections of analysis that can be found scattered throughout practically all of Deleuze's books. This is very much the case in *The Logic of Sense* and *Difference and Repetition*, but also for example in *What is Philosophy?*

Kant as reference, Kant omnipresent to be sure, but not just any Kant. What is striking, especially when we are interested in the question of the subject (of art)—and we will understand this expression henceforth with all the ambiguity contained in the nominal form—is the importance assumed by the detour that Deleuze takes through the *Critique of the Power of Judgment*, and primarily through the critique of the Transcendental Aesthetic.

But what can Kant's Transcendental Aesthetic represent for Deleuze? Why a critique of Kant rather than of Hegel, for example, since it is the aesthetic theory of the latter that will serve as Deleuze's foil? The response is found first in Kant himself, a Kant whose theses the early Deleuze—the Deleuze who still presented himself as a "historian" of philosophy—merely "repeated." What does the Transcendental Aesthetic represent, indeed, for the still Kantian Deleuze of the first critical texts? One could take almost word for word what Jean-Luc Nancy and Philippe Lacoue-Labarthe told us about the "romantic" renewal of Kantianism: as with the German "romantics," what interests Deleuze in Kant's Transcendental Aesthetic is that it no longer refers to the traditional division between the sensible and the intelligible, but more profoundly to the division between "two forms (*a priori*) within the 'sensible' or intuitive itself":[3]

> Aesthetics suffers from a wrenching duality. On the one hand, it designates the theory of sensibility as the form of possible experience; on the other hand, it designates the theory of art as the reflection of real experience.[4]

The first consequence of such a "division," for Deleuze, and it is without doubt the most important aspect of our analysis at this stage, is indeed "that there is no *intuitus originarius*":[5] the instance that gave its support to philosophical discourse as *Arche* or *Telos* will be absent from Deleuze's discourse. Inquiring into "the conditions of the true genesis" of thought in the series on Singularities in *The Logic of Sense*, Deleuze will be led to wonder how "the transcendental field is to be *determined*."[6] Now the question of the status of the subject presents itself to him completely naturally:

> It seems impossible to endow it [the subject], in the Kantian sense, with the personal form of an I, or the synthetic unity of apperception, even if this unity were to be given universal extension … But it is no more possible to preserve for it the form of consciousness, even if we define this impersonal consciousness by means of pure intentionalities and retentions, which still presuppose centers of individuation.[7]

Nothing remains as *subject*, then, except the "I" as "empty form" accompanying my representations (pure logical necessity, Kant says, or grammatical requirement according to Nietzsche, whom Deleuze does not hesitate to summon in his return to Kant—a "Kant with-Nietzsche" as it were). If we add to this that the subject is only an empty form because the form of time is, as we know, "the form of internal sense," which does not permit any substantial representation, or because the cogito is "empty," then we already understand what could be of interest to Deleuze in Kant's work. In fact, what Deleuze appreciates in the Kant of the three *Critiques*, and particularly in the Kant of the third, is at bottom the *displacement* that Kant effects between the categories inherited from classical philosophy and the hitherto unseen—and "unforeseeable"—relation that he will be able to establish between aesthetics and philosophy: a "knotting" that, far from being a simple dialectical "setting into relation," will provoke a "crisis" that no later philosophy will successfully resolve.

What, in fact, was the object of the third *Critique* or *Critique of the Power of Judgment*? What was it that could make it a necessary detour in Deleuze's eyes, or a kind of "prolegomenon to any future aesthetics?" Why, finally, must the question of the subject (of art) be posed starting from the problematic of an "aesthetic common sense" that underlies the *Critique*?

As Éric Clemens has shown so well in the pages devoted to Kantian aesthetics in *La fiction et l'apparaître*, it was a matter for Kant of bridging "the immeasurable abyss" between *theoretical* philosophy, that is, the concepts of nature produced by the understanding, and *practical* philosophy, which concerns the concept of freedom and of (moral) reason.[8] Consequently, the "abyss" in question would come from the fact that the "objects" of nature are *represented* in intuition, but (only) as *phenomena*, whereas if the object of freedom (morality of action, moral principle) represents a "thing in itself," then it is impossible to associate it with any sensible intuition. This "abyss" thus seems to separate irremediably the world of nature from the world of freedom.

> Yet the latter [the world of freedom] *should* have an influence on the former, namely the concept of freedom should make the end that is imposed by its laws real in the sensible world; and nature must consequently also be able to be conceived in such a way that the lawfulness of its form is at least in agreement with the possibility of ends that are to be realized in it in accordance with the laws of freedom.[9]

It is this type of "knotting"—one that traverses Kant's doctrine of the faculties as a whole and whose goal is to define the *a priori* conditions of the legitimation of the higher *interests* of reason and of the higher *objects* of culture (and thus of art)—that holds Deleuze's attention in Kantianism.

In Kant, the faculty that would permit in principle the bridging of "the abyss"—and this will be the great discovery of the third *Critique*—is "judgment," which is situated between the understanding and reason. For Kant, "to judge" is (paradoxically, at first sight) before all else to *sense*, to *experience* a feeling of pleasure or pain. No doubt the act of judging consists first of all in a "thinking of the particular as contained under the universal."[10] But it is necessary very quickly to *distinguish*, as Kant explains, between *determining* and *reflecting* judgment. In the former, the law, rule, or principle, i.e., the universal, is given and determines the particular, or if you prefer, the object. In the latter, on the contrary, only the *particular* is given and the universal must be found without deriving it from elsewhere, *by a pure act of reflection*. Of course a "principle" of judgment is necessary—for example of the beauty of an object of art—but this principle can only be found through the subject's returning to itself. This is borne out, for example, in the case of the judgment called "teleological," which attributes a purposiveness to nature—a judgment that will be called "reflecting" in that its principle is purely subjective. It is at this stage that things become complicated (even by Kantian standards), since the understanding cannot legitimately attribute this principle to particular empirical laws, even though these are essential to its activity. It will thus have to proceed *as if* these laws fell under a universal order, a necessary purposiveness: it will then be the role and function of judgment to posit *analogically*, or "transcendentally" if you prefer, this universal principle:

> Now this transcendental concept of the purposiveness of nature is neither a concept of nature nor a concept of freedom, since it attributes nothing at all to the object (of nature), but rather only represents the unique way in which we must proceed *in reflection on the objects of nature* with the aim of a thoroughly interconnected experience, consequently it is a subjective principle (maxim) of the power of judgment.[11]

Thus, as Éric Clemens has noted, the final agreement of nature with knowledge is *contingent*, but it will nonetheless be necessary to "imagine," to feel this agreement as necessary, which is what judgment is supposed to provide. An *endless* heterogeneity of empirical laws of nature and a permanent disagreement or "discord" between the faculties would leave us in the greatest confusion. It will be *thanks to the idea of end*, which has its origin in reason, that judgment will be able to assure the link with the laws of the understanding.

One might already suspect what will awaken Deleuze's (meta-"critical"?) attention in this leap into the "subjective" and what will make him want to distance himself from Kant. But it is not this gesture alone that will cause Deleuze to distance himself from Kantian transcendentalism. Even if he had already located certain slippages that had ended up reducing the "critique" to the tandem of "common sense" (as *concordia facultatum*) and "good sense" (as "the distribution which guarantees this concord"), that is, to a deceptive and reductive "image" of thought, it is not this that will pose the most serious problem.[12] While it is still only a matter of teleological judgment, Deleuze only notes and critiques a certain incapacity correctly to pose the problems (as regards the nature of the relations between the faculties):

> Because the Kantian critique remains dominated by common sense or the dogmatic image, Kant still defines the truth of a problem in terms of the possibility of its finding a solution ... We always find the two aspects of the illusion: the *natural illusion* which involves tracing problems from supposedly pre-existent propositions, logical opinions, geometrical theorems, algebraic equations, physical hypotheses, or transcendental judgments; and the *philosophical illusion* which involves evaluating problems according to their "solvability"—in other words according to the extrinsic and variable form of their finding a solution.[13]

However it is only when we have recourse to the idea of a *reflecting aesthetic judgment* that things will become complicated and will end up taking the turn that will give Deleuze's thought its own characteristics. Indeed, why is it this "sensibility" at this level of reflection and not starting from the entrance onto the scene of teleological judgment? To respond to this question, we will need to take a new detour through that *other reflecting judgment* which is *aesthetic judgment*. For Kant, what determines the specificity, or perhaps better, the *singularity* of reflecting aesthetic judgment, is the fact that its "subjective" character is much more marked. No *empirical law*, no *concept of the understanding*, nor any brute sensation can confirm it or transcendentally establish its theoretical validity.

It is at present, facing the object (of art), and not through the intermediary of reason or the understanding, that a "form" emerges from the whole (for the subject). But what must be noted immediately in this regard is that in speaking of "forms," and in particular of what is "beautiful" in things, Kant has in mind neither the stiff regularity of geometric shapes nor the functional symmetry of organic forms. Kant tends rather to think of such forms as *uninteresting* and even "boring":

> Now geometrically regular shapes—a circle, a square, a cube, etc.—are commonly adduced by *critics of taste* as the simplest and most indubitable examples of beauty; and yet they are called regular precisely because they cannot be represented except by being regarded as mere presentations of a determinate concept, which prescribes the rule for that shape (in accordance with which it is alone possible). Thus one of the two must be wrong: *either the judgment of the critics* that attributes beauty to such shapes, *or ours*, which finds purposiveness without a concept to be necessary for beauty.[14]

And Kant adds to this that,

> No one is likely to think it is necessary for a person to have taste in order to find more satisfaction in the shape of a circle than in a scribbled outline, or more in an equilateral and equiangular quadrilateral than in one that is lopsided and irregular, as it were deformed; for this takes *only common understanding and no taste at all* … All stiff regularity (whatever approaches mathematical regularity) *is of itself contrary to taste*: the consideration of it affords no lasting entertainment, but rather, insofar as it does not expressly have cognition or a determinate practical end as its aim, it induces boredom.[15]

Thus there is "form" and there is "form," and it is certain that the classical notion of form as grid or outline, or simple Gestalt, is not what is at issue in aesthetic judgment; its reflexivity is not situated there. What an attentive reading of these texts shows is that, for Kant, "beautiful form"—which means that a form is beautiful or that beauty is prior to all form—is not some prominent structure or other that I recognize in the object or that I "extract" from it (in an empiricist manner of the old style?), but rather *the dynamic, unstable play between figures without conceptual resolution*.[16] To consider the idea of form and to associate it with an unstoppable play between figures is to treat it as what is at stake in a *perpetual instability*. And it is at this *intersection* where the *encounter* takes place between Kantian and Deleuzian aesthetics concerning "beautiful form" as internal differentiation or, if you prefer, as difference that self-differentiates and affirms (imposes) its difference without negation. The faculty of judgment thus poses at once the question of "the form of things (of nature as well as art)" and that of "the intersubjective communication of felt pleasure and the taste for the beautiful and of the feeling of the sublime."[17] The singularity of the beautiful (as well as of the sublime, even if it has a different function and status) would result from an *internal coherence with which we cannot associate any transcendental concept*.[18] For example we cannot isolate an element in a work of art that would be inessential or superfluous in applying external criteria because in the appreciation of beauty (which Kant will call "free" in opposition to "adherent," so called "impure beauty") the judgment of taste must be pure:

> No concept of any end for which the manifold should serve the given object and thus which the latter should represent is presupposed, *by which the imagination, which is as it were at play in the observation of the shape, would merely be restricted*.[19]

Kant will never have been so close to what Deleuze would propose in his analyses of literature, music, cinema, and of art in general. In any case we can see Deleuze making use of this idea since the beginning of the 1960s, beginning with the fine text devoted to what he called already "the method of dramatization." As we will recall, it is a matter in that text of bringing out the elements of a theory of the "Idea," aiming primarily to wrest it away from the Platonic "Intelligible" and to inscribe it within a dialectic of "vice-diction" that would enable us to think of it as intensive multiplicity.[20] But when it is a matter of defining the nature of this "Idea" and of the "drama" that will come to dynamize the concepts, it is naturally Kant to whom Deleuze refers us once again:

> What I am calling a drama particularly resembles a Kantian schema. The schema, according to Kant, is indeed an *a priori* determination of space and time corresponding to a concept: *the shortest* schema is the drama (dream or nightmare) of the straight line.
>
> And he explains just after this passage that in a certain way, all the post-Kantians have tried to elucidate the mystery of this hidden art, according to which dynamic spatio-temporal determinations genuinely have the power to dramatize a concept, although they have a nature totally different from the concept.
>
> The answer perhaps lies in a direction that certain post-Kantians have indicated: pure spatio-temporal dynamisms have the power to dramatize *concepts*, because first they actualize *incarnate Ideas*.... So, we have to ask ourselves about the nature of the Idea, about its difference of nature from the concept.[21]

Pierre Zaoui has spoken of "the great Nietzsche-Spinoza identity" in Deleuze's work; but what we can see taking shape here would be the great "Nietzsche-Deleuze-Kant" identity, or if you prefer, a re-reading of Kant through Nietzsche.[22] Indeed it is not a matter for Deleuze of proceeding to a "deconstruction" of Kantianism, but rather of forcing certain of Kant's axes (and axioms), of *dramatizing* them, in order to "lift up" some of the virtualities, some of the possibilities, or some of the Ideas that Kant would not have been able to "actualize" or bring to light. So there is rather a desire on Deleuze's part to meet Kant and to establish a connection with what "vice-diction" as procedure of dramatization will have enabled him to discover:

> The problem of thought is tied not to essences but to the evaluation of what is important and what is not, to the distribution of singular and regular, distinctive and ordinary points, which takes place entirely within the inessential or within the description of a multiplicity, in relation to the ideal events which constitute the conditions of a "problem." To have an Idea means no more than this ... It is vice-diction which engenders cases, on the basis of auxiliaries and adjunctions.[23]

The meticulous critical inventory that Deleuze will make of the three *Critiques* in his book on Kant will bring to light the "knot" on the basis of which his thought will begin to be distinguished from what he will *owe* to Kant. Once we know how much the later works will owe to transcendental philosophy, we will not be surprised to see Kant's aesthetic theory, and in particular his theory of *sensibility*, occupying such a prominent place in Deleuze's thought. This could be seen very clearly in the introduction to the article that Deleuze had devoted to "the genesis of the faculties" in Kant, published before the book on Kant:

> The difficulties of Kantian aesthetics in the first part of the *Critique of Judgment* have to do with the diversity of points of view. On the one hand, Kant proposes an esthetics of the spectator, as in the theory of the judgment of taste; on the other hand, Kant proposes an esthetics or meta-esthetics of the creator, as in the theory of genius. Then again, he proposes an esthetics of the beautiful in nature, but also an esthetics of the beautiful in art. Sometimes it's a "classically" inspired esthetics of form, and sometimes a meta-aesthetics of form and Idea, which is closer to romanticism. The systematic unity of the *Critique of Judgment* can be established only by encompassing these various points of view and understanding the necessary transitions between them. Such a comprehension must

explain the apparent organizational difficulties, in other words, both the place of the Analytic of the Sublime (sandwiched between the Analytic of the Beautiful and the deduction of the judgments of taste) and the place of the theory of art and genius (at the end of the deduction).[24]

In fact, in the "Transcendental Aesthetic" of the *Critique of Pure Reason*, "aesthetic" referred to a "theory" that gave a very particular status to sensibility and perception, namely to the possibility of knowing and experiencing sensible objects through the *a priori* categories of space and time. From this point of view, Kantianism presents itself as a "monism of the phenomenon" where the human capacity to experience sensations would be defined as purely "receptive," indeed "passive." In these conditions, what characterized our relation to the world above all was *conformity to the conditions of all possible experience*.

On the contrary, in the *Critique of the Power of Judgment*, "aesthetic" will refer to judgment, and in particular to *reflecting* judgment which, as we know, has as its "domain" the feelings of pleasure and pain no longer as *a priori* conditions of possible experience, but rather as the subject's reflection on itself and on the operation of the mind based on an "indirect" relation to the object or on a relation implying a mediation (by form and, before long, the symbol).[25]

Forced to ascend from the particular given in experience (of nature) to the universal, aesthetic reflecting judgment will require a principle that it cannot derive from experience. Judgment

> can only give itself such a transcendental principle as law, and cannot derive it from anywhere else (for then it would be the determining power of judgment) nor can it prescribe it to nature: for reflection on the laws of nature is directed by nature, and nature is not directed by the conditions in terms of which we attempt to develop a concept of it that is in this regard entirely contingent.[26]

To summarize this last point, we might say that aesthetic judgment—"this is beautiful"—is "subjective" in that it bears witness to an immediate feeling (of pleasure) caused by the representation of a given object. But what characterizes it as a (reflecting) "judgment" is that it "claims" to be valid for all subjects who would be in accordance with *objectivity*, if it could be justified.[27]

What such a perspective leads to is that in every judgment of taste there is a "claim," or if you prefer, a "need" in virtue of which one is required to pre-judge *what the taste of the other ought to be.* This is to say that for Kant—and without doubt it is at this stage that Deleuze distances himself—the judgment of taste poses a problem of *right*: how to justify the universalizing claims of this type of judgment? It is in approaching this kind of question that Kant offers the famous "deduction" of aesthetic judgment, that is, a procedure in which there is no question of *proving* the correctness of this or that aesthetic judgment considered by itself (which Kant thinks is impossible), but which is concerned instead with showing how the *function* of aesthetic judgment in general, such as it is present to consciousness, is possible. Now for Kant, taste is present to consciousness in such a way as to constitute, strictly speaking, a "common sense," a name, Kant hastens to explain, that is given improperly to the uncultured understanding, but which suits better and more legitimately the faculty of aesthetic judgment:[28]

> If judgments of taste (like cognitive judgments) had a determinate objective principle, then someone who made them in accordance with the latter would lay claim to the unconditioned necessity of his judgment. If they had no principle at all, like those of mere sensory taste, then one would never even have a thought of their necessity. They must thus have a subjective principle, which determines what pleases or displeases *only through feeling and not through concepts*, but yet with universal validity. Such a principle, however, could only be regarded as *common sense*, which is essentially different from the common understanding that is sometimes also called common sense (*sensus communis*), since the latter judges not by feeling but always by concepts, although commonly only in the form of obscurely represented principles.
>
> Thus only under the presupposition that there is a common sense (by which, however, we do not mean any external sense but rather the effect of the free play of our cognitive powers), only under the presupposition of such a common sense, I say, can the judgment of taste be made.[29]

One will notice that the *sublime*, for its part, is absent from this problematic, for its deduction takes place almost immediately and raises no "juridical" problem.[30] The transcendental analysis demonstrates, from its first descriptions, that two faculties are in play which, by their very opposition, reveal the destination of man:

> because there is in our imagination a *striving to advance to the infinite*, while in our reason there lies a *claim to absolute totality*, as a real idea, the very inadequacy of our faculty for estimating the magnitude of the things of the sensible

> world awakens the feeling of a supersensible faculty in us; and the use that the power of judgment naturally makes in behalf of the latter (feeling), *though not the object of the senses*, is absolutely great, while in contrast to it any other use is small. Hence it is the disposition of the mind resulting from a certain representation occupying the reflective judgment, but not the object, which is to be called *sublime*.
>
> Thus we can also add this to the foregoing formulation of the explanation of the sublime: *that is sublime which even to be able to think of demonstrates a faculty of the mind that surpasses every measure of the senses.*[31]

Thus for Kant the faculties are found in every human being, and the object called "sublime" would only be an occasion to perceive the link that unites them. To be less clear at first, the deduction that allows us to include judgments pertaining to the beautiful is not very different at bottom. The beautiful object is not the one that presents some sensible quality or other ("agreement") nor the one that sets some of the fundamental faculties of man harmoniously in motion, here the imagination (again) and the understanding. The subjective universality of the judgment stems before all else from the fact that these faculties are found in all men and, in this case, the deduction of the judgments of taste enables us to bring out the main idea that traverses the three *Critiques*, which is precisely that of the "harmonious play" of the faculties.[32]

It is in relation to this, no doubt, that Deleuze breaks with what he had hailed at different points in his work as the Kantian *coup de force*. For Deleuze, the problem in Kant is that the genesis of thought is a genesis that betrayed its own principles and that failed to keep its promises. What is problematic for Deleuze in Kant's doctrine of the faculties is the "equivocity" that undermines the process of deduction. Since its goal was to define the *a priori* conditions that legitimate the higher interests of reason and the higher objects of culture, the doctrine of the faculties had to conform, as it were, to transcendental principles at each stage of the deduction. Now on the one hand, according to Deleuze, Kant claimed that he wanted to ground these conditions objectively, in a determinate agreement of the faculties. On the other hand, he is led to envision a "subjective foundation" that refers to an "aesthetic common sense" which is supposed to be "more profound than any other."[33] For Deleuze, this "double foundation," this kind of "epistemological dissonance," has catastrophic consequences for the whole system. The first is that, as empty cogito, the transcendental subject seems at present to presuppose a shareable universality, a community and a culture of which the "aesthetic common sense" becomes the only evident "guarantor." The other problem that arises at the same time is to know how if it is the aesthetic common sense—"our common sense of the beautiful" as Kant says—that would ground the "free agreement of the faculties" of which Kant speaks, or if it is instead the free transcendental agreement that justifies the universality of aesthetic judgment. This brings us back, among other things, to the question whether, in the name of such a "higher" interest of reason—the desire for "absolute totality" for example—Kant had not had recourse surreptitiously to the old-fashioned subject of (the history of) metaphysics: "the 'solitary' subject," as Alberto Gualandi has well noted, "seems to make an appeal here to a *community of subjects* who communicate with each other and who constitute a higher type of transcendental, an *a priori* intersubjective form."[34]

The other difficulty that Gualandi has very aptly noted in analyzing Deleuze's theses is that, since it is now the aesthetic common sense that provides the subjective ground of "logical common sense" and of the agreement of the faculties from the point of view of the higher interest of knowledge *and of morality*, one will conclude that if the "beautiful" is what satisfies our common sense of the beautiful, then the "true" will be nothing other than what will satisfy our common sense of the true. As one might guess, one of the first consequences that Deleuze will draw from this return to the psychological (subject) through the beautiful and the sublime is that the universal subject evoked by the aesthetic common sense will be revealed at the end of the account as merely an "abstract singular." Where he claimed to fix forever the *a priori* structures of a universal subject, Kant had simply fixed the necessary conditions for any *possible* experience. For Deleuze, because of this sliding, the Kantian transcendental is shown to be no more than a "false transcendental" and the "universal" to be nothing more than the image abstracted from the (dominant?) culture of its time. Deleuze demonstrates this point well in a passage from *Difference and Repetition*:

> Kant seemed … equipped to overturn the Image of thought. For the concept of error, he substituted that of illusion … For the substantial self, he substituted a self profoundly fractured by a line of time; while in the same movement God and the self encountered a kind of speculative death. However, in spite of

everything, and at the risk of compromising the conceptual apparatus of the three Critiques, Kant did not want to renounce the implicit presuppositions. Thought had to continue to enjoy an upright nature, and philosophy could go no further than—nor in directions other than those taken by—common sense or "common popular reason."³⁵

This is to say that what causes the problem in the "genesis" of thought proposed by Kant—and this is *decisive for questions pertaining to the genesis of the status of art and of the subject (of art)*—is that it is only a genesis *in fact* and *not by right*, despite its juridical pretentions. For Deleuze, the "true" right that should be accorded to thought is the right to "disagreement" that Kant himself noted at certain points in his deduction. It is only in the *discordant* exercise of the faculties that thought has a chance to reach the genuine "higher objects" and that a *truth* (of art, for example) can be affirmed or established.

In his *Manifesto for Philosophy*, Alain Badiou speaks of a "blockage" that most philosophical systems encounter whenever they "delegate" their functions to some external "condition" or generic procedure:

> The most frequent cause of such blockage is that instead of constructing a space of compossibility through which the thinking of time is practiced, philosophy *delegates* its functions to one or other of its *conditions*, handing over the whole of thought to *one* generic procedure. Philosophy is then carried out in the element of its own suppression to the great benefit of that procedure.
> I shall call this type of situation a *suture*.³⁶

The thesis I would like to advance concerning the relation of Deleuze to the question of art (*contra* Badiou, who places him among the philosophers for whom philosophy is "sutured" by—or "under the condition of"—literature) is the following: it is rather *under the condition of a "desuturation of the play" of the faculties* that a Deleuzian conception of art (and of the subject) can be established.

"Desuturing" Kantianism for Deleuze involves returning to an intuition of the possibility of a "disagreement" of the faculties that Kant himself had had. In fact, one of Deleuze's most constant affirmations in all the texts where the question of art is raised (but we will see that it affects the question of philosophical or scientific thought as well) involves the recognition of the ontological necessity, so to speak, of a *disagreement of the faculties* in order to discover what is truly at stake in the genesis of thought.

Indeed, as Alberto Gualandi has shown, if the analytic of the sublime holds a privileged place in Deleuze's reading of Kant, it is precisely because it is the "place" where the relation between the faculties is still not under the control of any other faculty (objective, determinant, or subjective). From this point of view, the imagination finds itself in a "discordant relation," in a "differend" with reason, according to Gualandi, and is pushed toward its finite limits while discovering the infinite character of reason. Now for Deleuze, if we abstract from the moral foundation on which this "accordant discord" rests, the unharmonious oppositions that can arise from the conflict of the faculties could constitute a radically *new model for the transcendental relations between the faculties*; but *also for* the definition of the transcendental conditions which will no longer be the conditions of a "justification of the empirical," as Deleuze says, but of *the transcendental conditions of invention*: conditions of the authentic event of thought in scientific production, artistic creation, and philosophical invention. Starting from the "disagreement" of the faculties, Deleuze will commit himself resolutely to a new genesis of thought which will itself be grounded in the need for a deduction of new (unheard of) faculties.[37] The chance of encounters will have to become a necessity that gives birth to thought. "Every act of thought," Gualandi writes, "will always be both the effect of a *contingent* encounter and the product of a methodical construction that transforms chance into necessity."[38]

I cannot analyze within the space of this essay all of the consequences that Deleuze will draw from this reading of the *analytic of the sublime*.[39] However I will note the importance of the status that he will be led to give to sensibility, which is transformed from a passive, non-creative faculty in Kant into one of the elements—in the sense of an *Elementarlehre*—of what we could rightly call a Deleuzian *aesthetics*: an aesthetics founded on the surpassing of the arbitrary rift that Kant had established, according to Deleuze, between aesthetics as a theory of sensible intuition and aesthetics as a theory of art and of the beautiful. It is in radically opposing this division that Deleuze was able to develop an "aesthetics" in which art would no longer be a simple activity of representation and in which the subject (of art) would not be limited to the subjectivity of the artist.

Art will be presented henceforth as a true practice of experimentation and of problematization of the real. This can be seen in the text devoted to the idea of "genesis" in Kant's aesthetics: "But if the *Critique of Judgment* opens up a *passage*," he writes in a movement where he proceeds to a veritable reversal of Kantianism, "it is first and foremost because it unveils a *ground* that had remained hidden in the other two Critiques."[40] It is to this "ground"—which will be assimilated to a primordial chaos—that Deleuze will push, as it were, in order to proceed to a new genesis of thought and to formulate an "aesthetics" that will be founded on a new economy of the relation between the faculties: that is, "a primeval free imagination that cannot be satisfied with schematizing under the constraints of the understanding; a primeval, unlimited understanding that does not yet bend under the speculative weight of its determinate concepts, no more so than it is not already subjected to the ends of practical reason; a primeval reason ... which frees itself when it frees up the other faculties."[41] It is the same "deduction" that will condition the two "objects" relating to the questions raised in this work, which I have called art and its subject.

Once the play of the faculties is *de*-sutured, we must no longer speak of a subject unified around a self, but rather of "subjectivities" (in the plural). Kant's error, or rather his "illusion," was to fold the dynamisms aroused by the violence of the conflict of the faculties back to a unique instance of subjectivity, to the unicity of a molar subject. What the new "deduction" brings to light in order to surpass this unicity is the folding back or the reduction of the "subject" to transcendent and constituted significations, monopolizing and annihilating the rich proliferation of scattered subjectivities, of the marginalities of life that the unleashing or "desuturation" of the faculties enable us to experience, and in particular, the opening of the vast field of experimentation that is sensibility "freed" from the transcendental limits assigned to it by Kant:

> We paint, sculpt, compose, and write with sensations. We paint, sculpt, compose, and write sensations. As percepts, sensations are not perceptions referring to an object (reference): if they resemble something it is with a resemblance produced with their own methods; and the smile on the canvas is made solely with colors, lines, shadow, and light.[42]

Against transcendental significations, the new transcendentalism made possible by the "empirical" deduction is to affirm the "a-signifying." "Where there was folding back," or even the withdrawal into consciousness, it will be a matter of "bringing about the deployment" or the unfolding of singularities.[43] It will be in the difference between the faculties, in their essential "disparation," indeed in the distance that separates the act of thought from all acts of simple recognition of the object, that sensibility, imagination, and reason will be able to reach their proper transcendental dimension. The faculties are arranged, then, "like the parts of the body imagined by Empedocles' cosmology, scattered across the surface of the earth, errant multiplicities at the birth of the world,"[44] to set in motion the series of subjectivities and errant singularities that the originally synthetic apperception of a "transcendental over-*conscioused* I"—*[un JE sur-conscientisé]*—tends to neutralize:

> Singularities are the true transcendental events, and Ferlinghetti calls them "the fourth person singular." Far from being individual or personal, singularities preside over the genesis of individuals and persons; they are distributed in a "potential" which admits neither Self nor I, but which produces them by actualizing or realizing itself, although the figures of this actualization do not at all resemble the realized potential.[45]

The play of faculties now forms "knots"—"chaoids"—which can be undone in order to come together elsewhere in new organizations, giving rise to new configurations of thought, of desire, or of ever new blocks of sensation. It is, as Deleuze rightly says, by a connection that resembles a "fuse" that each faculty transmits to the other a *violence* that pushes it to its own limits. This violence, as I mentioned above in describing the process of desuturation, is the result, each time, of an encounter with an "insensible," an "unimaginable," an "unthinkable," or an "incommunicable," according to the "object" of the experience: in all these cases, *it is a matter for (the subject of) art*, as for science and philosophy, of "throwing a plane over chaos."[46] But where the philosopher must signal an infinite variation of concepts through relinkings, the artist will bring back from the chaos "*varieties* that no longer constitute a reproduction of the sensory in the organ but set up a *being of the sensory*, a being of sensation, on an anorganic plane of composition that is able to restore the infinite."[47] In each case, there is no need for a "subject" *per se*. According to Deleuze, "we cannot accept the alternative which thoroughly compromises psychology, cosmology, and theology: either singularities already comprised in individuals and persons, or the undifferentiated abyss." He adds that "only when the world, teeming with anonymous and nomadic, impersonal and pre-individual singularities, opens up, do we tread at last on the field of the transcendental."[48] We could in our turn reverse this proposition and say that "when the transcendental field is desutured, the world teeming with anonymous singularities opens up." Nonetheless we must note that, as regards the "object" of thought, given that we are dealing henceforth with a higher sensualism founded on a transcendental-experimental principle that counter-actualizes—between science, art, and philosophy—the Kantian revolution in undermining its epistemological base, the question will no longer be that of "the *methodological* dependence of the object in relation to the subject," as Éric Alliez has seen, "but of the *ontological* auto-constitution of a new subject on the basis of its objects."[49]

If "faculty" designates the relation that the subject maintains with the object, or if you prefer, the transcendental relation that thought maintains with its higher objects, then one must no longer consider the doctrine of the faculties as a "physio-psychology" of transcendental subjectivity, but as a transcendental doctrine of culture, and at the same time as a doctrine of artistic, scientific, and philosophical creation. In this sense, Badiou "distorts" things when he places Deleuze in the group of thinkers and writers tempted by the *poetic* "saturation"—or "suture"—of philosophy, or of a practice of philosophy, as he likes to say, "under the condition of literature."[50]

Here, for example, is what Badiou says in another chapter after having reviewed the different types or forms of "sutures" (positivist, Marxist, Lacanian, Levinasian, and Heideggerian):

> For philosophers sutured to the poem, or more broadly to literature, to art even, thought does without the object as well as the subject … Everyone concurs on a single point, which is so general an axiom of philosophic modernity that I can but rally to it: there is in any case no question of defining truth as a "likening" of the subject to the object. Everyone diverges when it comes to laying out the critique of likeness, since they do not agree on the status of the terms (subject and object) between which it operates.

And he adds:

> It should be noticed that this typology leaves a locus void: a locus of thinking which *would maintain the category of subject*, but would grant the poets the destitution of the object. The task of such thinking is to produce a *concept of the*

> subject such that it is supported by no mention of the object, a subject, if I might say, without a vis-à-vis.[51]

It is toward the "solution" of a "subject without object" that Badiou will orient his thought, for example in *Handbook of Inaesthetics*. But it is not in this direction at all, it seems to me, that Deleuze advances. In fact, as Antonio Gualandi and René Schérer have shown, each in his own way, what is different in Deleuze is that the "true" transcendental is neither in the subject nor in the object, but in the "Idea-structure," that is, in an "Idea" which, in Kant, was *undetermined* in its object, *determinable* only by analogy with the objects of experience, an embodiment of an ideal of "infinite determination" in relation to concepts of the understanding. In Deleuze, the *Idea* will enter into relations of a completely different nature! Let us judge for ourselves: "Once it is a question of determining the problem or the Idea as such," Deleuze writes, "once it is a question of setting the dialectic in motion, the question 'What is x?' gives way to other questions, otherwise powerful and efficacious, otherwise imperative: 'how much, how, and in what cases?'"[52] This indicates that "the problem of thought"—and I would add, of the relation of subject and object—is never tied "to essences but to the evaluation of what is important and what is not, to the distribution of singular and regular, distinctive and ordinary points"[53] but, as we can verify in reading practically all of the texts in which Deleuze approaches this question, this distribution "takes place entirely within the inessential or within the description of a multiplicity, in relation to the ideal events which constitute the conditions of a 'problem.'"[54] The true opposition, therefore, will never be the one between "subject" and "object," but between "Idea" (as structure-event-sense) and "representation"—and it is this, to my mind, that is at the heart of the problematic that "ties together" the question of art and the subject (of art) in Deleuze:

> With representation, concepts are like possibilities, but the subject of representation still determines the object as really conforming to the concept, as an essence. This is why representation as a whole is the element of knowledge which is realized by the recollection of the thought object and its recognition by a thinking subject ... The virtuality of the Idea has nothing to do with possibility. Multiplicity tolerates no dependence on the identical in the subject or in the object. The events and singularities of the Idea do not allow any positing of an essence as "what the thing is."[55]

And Deleuze explains what follows from this, which is important for our subject:

> No doubt, if one insists, the word "essence" might be preserved, but only on condition of saying that the essence is precisely the accident, the event, the sense; not simply the contrary of what is ordinarily called the essence but the contrary of the contrary: multiplicity is no more appearance than essence, no more multiple than one ... Learning to swim or learning a foreign language means composing the singular points of one's own body or of one's own language with those of another shape or element, which tears us apart but also propels us into a hitherto unknown and unheard-of world of problems.[56]

Deleuze will try to show in the rest of the text (particularly in the chapter titled "Ideas and the Synthesis of Difference") that what is "lacking" in the Kantian Idea, as multiplicity, is not "reality" but "actuality." Between the transcendental Idea (which is given to the subject) and the "things" that it gives rise to (in the subject), there is a "correspondence without resemblance," which means that what is engendered (this crystal, this oak, even this Idea) is not a simple "copy" of the Idea but rather a "new individual." Ideal without being abstract, real without being actual, the Idea is the virtual and pre-individual totality that is actualized along "lines of differentiation" that are like "so many solutions to a problem where it is the totality of being that resonates in a new creative chance."[57] We will have to deal, then, with a multiplicity of singular multiplicities: social multiplicity, physical multiplicity (sensibility and sign), biological multiplicity (vitality and the "monster"), and obviously aesthetic multiplicities. The discord of the faculties, defined by singularity—"exclusivity," Deleuze says—of the transcendental object that each one apprehends nevertheless implies an "accord" according to which each one transmits its *violence* to the other in following a *fuse*, but always a discordant accord that *excludes the form of identity*, of convergence, and of the collaboration of common sense:[58]

> There is thus a point at which thinking, speaking, imagining, feeling, etc., are one and the same thing, but that *thing* affirms only the *divergence of the faculties in their transcendental exercise*. It is a question, therefore, not of common sense but, on the contrary, of a "para-sense" (in the sense that a paradox is also contrary to good sense). The elements of this para-sense are Ideas, precisely because Ideas are pure multiplicities which do not presuppose any form of

identity in a common sense but, on the contrary, animate and describe the disjoint exercise of the faculties from a transcendental point of view.[59]

It is in this sense as well that the Ideas will be able to be called "differentials" of thought, "unconscious" of pure thought, at the very moment where the opposition of thought to every form of common sense remains more present and livelier than ever. We will understand all the better why Ideas "are related not to a Cogito which functions as ground or as a proposition of consciousness, but to the fractured I of a dissolved Cogito; in other words, to the universal *ungrounding* which characterizes thought as a faculty in its transcendental exercise."[60]

The "illusion" of classical philosophy was to believe that one could in a sense "confine" subjectivity and its processes within the subject and its substance—the subject that is also the celebrated *ego*, the "hypostasis of a thinking self" as René Schérer put it. This is also the umbrella of which Deleuze and Guattari speak in referring to D. H. Lawrence:

> People are constantly putting up an umbrella that shelters them and on the underside of which they draw a firmament and write their conventions and opinions. But poets, artists, make a slit in the umbrella, they tear open the firmament itself, to let in a bit of free and windy chaos and to frame in a sudden light a vision that appears through the rent ...[61]

In the texts prior to *What is Philosophy?*, what was new was the rupture with the idea of the subject as fixed self, of a self-center or pole. What was new, if we refer to psychoanalytic theory, was the refusal of a problematic which was once again that of the subject, even (and especially) when it is understood as empty place or "gap." The keyword was "becoming," which referred to processes that rush like waves, that come, go, peak, and disappear; to conceive of becomings and not the stable, of multiplicity and not unicity, of consciousnesses as transitivities and not as an origin: not a subject that is unique, even and including existentially, but *subjectivations without transcendence*, pure folds in the field of immanence where they come to manifest themselves and of which the subjectivized designation is "expression" or "vice-diction."[62]

In *What is Philosophy?* the "turning point" is no longer in the *ungrounding* of the subject but in the brain as new "differential" and particle accelerator: the novelty is present. "It is the brain that thinks and not man—the latter being only a cerebral crystallization."[63] But one will have understood, when it is a question of the domain of art, of "the plane that art throws over the chaos" (of the artistic chaoid?), it is no longer a matter of the brain as "superject"[64]—that is, as faculty of the creation of concepts—and even less as "eject"—that is, as faculty of "distinction" and of "discernment"—but as "inject," as instance where it is no longer a matter of contemplating Ideas "through concepts" but of transforming "the *elements of the matter that we contemplate through sensation.*"[65] The "inject" as accelerator and transformer of sensations! In this sense, the brain that says "I" is no longer the same as the brain of connections and secondary integrations of representation: "And this *I* is not only the 'I conceive' of the brain as philosophy, it is also the 'I feel' of the brain as art," according to Deleuze and Guattari, for whom, henceforth, "sensation is no less brain than the concept."[66] This is to say that the "desuturation," as we can now see, represents a true "turning point" for thought, which places it constantly before a chaos rendered consistent: *become* "thought." As Éric Alliez has nicely stated, "nature and art alike partake in a melodic vitalism which attains an expressionism but with the sudden appearance of the territory and the house"; expressivity, diffused in life, "becomes constructive and erects ritual monuments of an animal mass that celebrates qualities."[67] This is what will permit Deleuze to affirm that "there is no other aesthetic problem than that of the insertion of art into everyday life," and to explain the same context that

> the more our daily life appears standardised, stereotyped and subject to an accelerated reproduction of objects of consumption, the more art must be injected into it … in order to make its two extremes resonate—namely the habitual series of consumption and the instinctual series of destruction and death. Art thereby connects the tableau of cruelty with that of stupidity … It aesthetically reproduces the illusions and mystifications which make up the real essence of this civilisation, in order that Difference may at last be expressed …[68]

"Desuturation" of the faculties as theater of cruelty!

This is because, as René Schérer saw, the philosophy that Deleuze worked so hard to formulate is a "philosophy of expression," that is to say a philosophy in which, for the relation of cause and effect is substituted a relation "between equals," a reversibility between expresser and expressed which "rejects the subject just as much as it rejects causality and substance."[69] Henceforth only "intensities" or "dispersions" or "concentrations" will be "admitted" within a continuous space, that is, a continuum that runs from the soul to the body and vice versa. Deleuze's Spinozism.

It will be understood from this point on that as "philosophy of expression," Deleuzian philosophy will pass through a "semiotic reform" that will have to constantly take into account the "non-signifying" or the "a-signifying" within the always reductive system of signs. It is this kind of counter-actualization that will favor the liberation of multiplicities full of all the subjective virtualities that traverse works of art, virtualities not at all "subjective" but rather "pre-individual and anonymous" and to this extent "collective even though always singular." Thus, to the subject constructed around a centralizing self, Gilles Deleuze will oppose subjectivities dispersed in accordance with impersonal flows of desire.

We must be careful, though, and not be too quick to "pacify," in a sense, the concepts that Deleuze and Guattari so generously provided us to give an account of the "specificity" of art. Art, we will be told, has no other purpose than to bring into the world unknown and unheard-of percepts and affects. These celebrate the unprecedented coupling of forces in the joint *becoming sensitive* of the "sensing" and the "sensed," of the author and the aesthetic figures he creates. It is a matter in any case of making "perceptible the imperceptible forces that populate the world, affect us, and make us become":[70] becoming-other, or again as Éric Alliez has rightly put it, "non-human becomings of man merging into the non-human landscapes of nature."[71]

This should not make us forget that, for Deleuze in any case, "art is (before all else?) the sign of a mortal passion and of a desire for the eternal," that only the artist is capable of counter-actualizing, in an active work on sensible matter and in a production of vital forms in which sensations and emotions take on an objective consistency that is independent of all subjective experience.[72] "The artist," Deleuze and Guattari write, "brings back from the chaos *varieties* that no longer constitute a reproduction of the sensory in the organ but set up a being of the sensory, a being of sensation, on an anorganic plane of composition that is able to restore the infinite."[73]

Translated by Bryan Lueck

3

Cinéplastique(s): Deleuze on Élie Faure and Film Theory

When Gilles Deleuze refers to the texts of Élie Faure, it seems that what interests him at first are the theses pertaining to cinema as "collective agency of enunciation," that is, as the art which is still capable of mobilizing the masses, of assembling them and uniting them in the same vision of the world: cinema as "Catholic" art. Indeed it is in the chapter titled "Cinema and Thought" from *Cinema 2: The Time-Image*, where Deleuze approaches for the nth time the problem of "belief" in cinema, that one of the explicit references to the work of Élie Faure appears: "It is clear from the outset," Deleuze writes, "that cinema had a special relationship with belief. There is a Catholic quality to cinema … Is there not in Catholicism a grand *mise-en-scène*, but also, in the cinema, a cult which takes over the circuit of the cathedrals, *as Élie Faure said*?"[1] And in fact it is in Élie Faure that we find one of the very first defenses and illustrations of cinema as "the nucleus of the common spectacle which everyone demands, as being perfectly susceptible of assuming a grave, splendid, moving character, a religious character even, in the universal, majestic sense of the word."[2]

What already captivates Faure in cinema is its "collective" character and its power of gathering, indeed of "communion." As we know, one of his "theses" is that theater, music, dance, fresco, architecture, and even painting have lost their power of attraction and of the communion of men and that it is cinema that has taken over: we read in *The Art of Cineplastics* that "the cinema has nothing in common with the theater, save this, *which is only a matter of appearances, and the most external and banal appearances at that*: it is, as the theater is, but also as are dance, the games of the stadium and the procession, *a collective spectacle* having as its intermediary an actor."[3] And moreover this will be the leitmotiv of most of the texts that Faure will devote to cinema and to its specificity in relation to the other plastic arts. The "thesis" that underlies these affirmations is that "as far back as we look, among all the peoples of the earth, and at all times, *a collective spectacle* has been able to unite all classes, all ages, and, as a rule, the two sexes, in a unanimous *communion* exalting the *rhythmic power* that defines, in each of them, the moral order."[4]

To be sure, Deleuze will not go so far in the direction of this ecumenical optimism, but he will retain Faure's "lesson," above all when he is concerned with developing the idea of a "belief" of which cinema would be in a sense the bearer: an "art" that would be destined, in a democratic society, "to become *the art of the mass, the centre of a powerful communion* in which *new symphonic forms* will be born in the tumult of passion and used *with aesthetic ends capable of lifting the heart*."[5]

We know, on the other hand, the place that Deleuze will give to belief and the role that cinema will be able to play for him in the transfiguration of the world. "The modern fact," he writes, "is that *we no longer believe in this world. We do not even believe in the events which happen to us, love, death, as if they only half concerned us.*" And after a detour through Jean-Luc Godard, who was a privileged "intercessor" for him in his books on the theory of cinema, Deleuze adds that "the cinema must film, *not the world, but belief in this world, our only link.*"[6] A strong assertion which, because it was not related to what it owed to Élie Faure, was never understood and remained quite "enigmatic": a "Catholic" Deleuze?

This is one of the most massive and direct encounters between Faure and Deleuze. But although it is one of the most explicit references in the text, it is not the most important or the most meaningful and it is not related directly to the subject at issue here, which is the *plastic "dimension"* of cinema. This is a dimension, as we know, that Élie Faure was among the first to identify in its radical *specificity*. We are reminded, no doubt, of the clarity and the force of affirmation of the formulation of his thesis concerning the "plastic" in cinema that opens *The Art of Cineplastics*:

> The cinema is plastic *first*: it represents a sort of *moving architecture* which is in constant accord, in a state of equilibrium dynamically pursued—with the surroundings and landscapes where it is erected and falls to the earth again. The feelings and the passions are *hardly more than a pretext*, serving to give a certain sequence, a certain probability to the action.[7]

The statement is thus clear: the cinema *innovates* and marks the aesthetic domain with its seal, not insofar as it takes over for theater or the novel or dance—in sum, for "drama"—but at the moment when "independent of the acting of the cinemimics," and thanks to the wealth of its sensible "resources," it enables the establishment of "multiple and incessantly modified relationships with the surroundings, the landscape, the calm, the fury and the caprice of the elements, from natural or artificial lighting, from the prodigiously complex and shaded play of values."[8] What must be affirmed in any case, and what we must no longer doubt, is that "the starting point of the art of the moving picture is in plastics."[9]

In addition, when Élie Faure attempts to describe what the term "plastic" refers to, it is once again to define it *starting from cinema* (that "unknown art," as he likes to say):[10]

> Let us not misunderstand the meaning of the word "plastic." Too often it evokes the motionless, colorless forms called sculptural—which lead all too quickly to the academic canon, to helmeted heroism, to allegories in sugar, zinc, papier mâché or lard. Plastics is the art of expressing form in repose or in movement by all the means that man commands: full-round, bas-relief, engraving on the wall or on copper, wood or stone, drawing in any medium, painting, fresco, the dance; and it seems to me in no wise overbold to affirm that the rhythmic movements of a group of gymnasts or of a processional or military column touch the spirit of plastic art far more nearly than do the pictures of the school of David.[11]

In these conditions, what appears clearly is that the "encounter" between Élie Faure and Gilles Deleuze becomes dialogical and productive mainly because both tend to think of cinema not as a "machine of representation(s)" but, rather and primarily, as a "machine" that produces "plastic effects." Indeed I believe that what interests Deleuze in Faure's "theses" on cinema is what I would call his "prescience" about what cinema would *become*, but also about certain of its possibilities, or as he will say, its "secret." Those brilliant intuitions he had had concerning cinema's ability radically to renew the relations between cinematographic images, but also the relations these images maintained with the other components of the filmic image: speech, of course, but also the sounds, noises, writing, the contrasts of colors and tones, and obviously the music! There were so many relations that, as I will attempt to show, were already intuited in the notions of *cineplastie*, *cineplast*, and *cinemimic*, but also from Faure's reflections on the concepts "proper" to cinema, on its "intellectual automatism" for example, and more generally on what he will call its "mystical" significance.

> Don't worry, we have time, the cinema has only just begun. The new faith will find its aesthetic framework there, just as Catholicism found its in the cold basilicas of Rome, which its passion has populated, animated, and lifted up in bursts of flames. The faith comes from an obscure accord between the intrinsic development of the art itself and the mystique that it is called to serve ... It is not from the outside, and through the "subject" in itself that we ask cinema to educate us, it is from its nature itself that we can expect this benefit. Cinema is before all else an inexhaustible revelation of new passages, new arabesques, and new harmonies among tones and values, lights and shadows, forms and movements, the will and its gestures, the spirit and its incarnations.[12]

It is, I believe, this affirmative and ontological optimism concerning the aesthetic problem linked to cinema, this attention to what is new in the cinematographic art and "pedagogy," that attracted Deleuze. But it is also, much more specifically, such intuitions on the nature of the "automatism" of cinema and the "transcendent monism" that conditions it, which lead me to believe that it is more than a matter of a chance encounter.[13] There is, finally, in Faure's texts the constantly reiterated attempt not to reduce cinema to a simple mechanical instrument for the reproduction of movement or for the production of psychological "dramas." In a passage we might think was written by Deleuze, Faure argues that

> in truth, it is its *material automatism* itself that brings to light from the interior of these images the new universe that it imposes little by little *on our intellectual automatism*. It is in this way that there appears, in a blinding light, the subordination of the human soul to the tools it creates and vice versa. Between technicity and affectivity, there proves to be a constant reversibility. We find ourselves in the presence of a *transcendent monism*, objectively demonstrated ...[14]

It is this that is echoed in the theses on "spiritual automatism" or on cinema as "spiritual automaton" that run through all of *Cinema 2: The Time-Image*.[15]

But what seems to me to bring the two thinkers closest together, outside (or in addition to) this "subordination of the soul to the tools it creates"—a "subordination" that reveals an extremely fine sensitivity with regard to the very special nature of cinematographic "mechanism"—is their relation to the "audiovisual," to the "audiovisual archive" as Deleuze says. For both Faure and Deleuze, there is a *disjunction* and not a "dialectical" synthesis between speaking and seeing, between the visible and the sayable, and as regards cinema, between image and sound (whether it be the moment when someone speaks or when it is a question of music, noise, and the different forms of sonorous framing and deframing). We know that for Deleuze, "what we see never lies in what we say" and conversely, "the archive, the audiovisual is disjunctive."[16]

Scholars have detected this dimension in Deleuze's thought—what I would call his Spinozism—but I do not believe they have related it to his "reading" of the works of Élie Faure. Nonetheless, there is an enormous number of passages in the texts of Faure that I have mentioned which enable us to establish this "filiation" very precisely. We can show quite easily that it is the conflict of the faculties, the split between filmic components and the parallelism of the sonorous, musical, and speaking dimensions, that led Faure to the "intuitions" of what he called the "cineplastic," or conversely, that the cineplastic is the "prescience" in Faure's work of what Deleuze will call the "heautonomy" of the new audiovisual image: "The heautonomy of the two images does not suppress but reinforces the audio-visual nature of the image, it strengthens the *victory* of the audio-visual."[17] Or again, "what constitutes the audio-visual image is a *disjunction*, a *dissociation* of the visual and the sound, each heautonomous, but at the same time an incommensurable or 'irrational' relation which connects them to each other, without forming a whole, without offering the least whole."[18] It is moreover Élie Faure's sensitivity to this dimension of cinema that conditions the link he clearly establishes—and in this he anticipates the *theoretical* developments that Deleuze will go on to make—between cinema, the production of a *direct* image of time, and thought. Indeed, in "Introduction à la mystique du cinéma," Faure writes:

> We discover immediately in cinema the concrete realization of *philosophical intuitions* toward which the end of the 19th century was converging. It projects duration onto the planar limits of space. Not only that, it makes duration into a dimension of space, which confers on space a new and immense signification as active, and no longer passive, collaborator of the mind. Cartesian space, since Cinema and thanks to Cinema, is nothing but a topographical value, if I may put it that way. Practically, two planes that philosophers have always believed to be mutually impenetrable fuse together.[19]

With this, then, another "link" with Deleuze's thought on cinema is established, and thus what we might call, pastiching Deleuze himself speaking of Spinoza and Nietzsche, the "great Faure-Deleuze identity."[20] But to limit ourselves to a simple term-by-term comparison of the constitutive elements of each thought would be to remain at a level that is much too empirical and descriptive.

What is certain is that, as close as they are to some of Deleuze's "findings," the reflections of Élie Faure remain at an intuitive, not to say impressionistic, level: if the relations that obtain between cinema and thought, movement-image and time-image, cinemimic and cineplast are well identified, they never give rise to a theoretical development *sui generis*.

Everything happens as if Faure had stopped at the *intuition* of a phenomenon—which he calls "plastic drama in action," "new plastic poem," "moving symphony," or "cineplastic tragedy"—without ever managing to produce a concept of it. We will recall that it was Faure who, in a short text titled "La prescience du Tintoret," did not hesitate to attribute to Tintoretto the "presentiment" of precisely what cinema would do at the level of the plastic and that it was the 800 figures of Tintoretto's *Paradise* which had inspired the comparison between this "permanent spatial [and plastic] drama" that is this immense fresco and the "cinematograph": "Tintoretto does not seek these combinations of lines and these equilibria of movement, which film reveals and inspires today, in order to draw from them, by a kind of spiritual game, a *melodic arabesque*. He FORESEES it, which is more spectacular, and *plays* it, already with all the combined elements that cinema imposes on us, as an innumerable visual orchestra … See these profound landscapes where light and shadow alternate, etc …"[21] In *The Art of Cineplastics*, Faure will be even more explicit: "Cineplastics, in fact, presents a curious characteristic which music alone, to a far less marked degree, has exhibited hitherto."[22]

Pastiching him, we could say that Élie Faure "foresaw" some of the "concepts" (of the future theory) of cinema. What is certain is that he was not content to make these "combinations" that, in a sense, "amalgamated" cinema and painting, cinema and theater, cinema and photography, cinema and fresco or painting—so many comparisons that, for him, could never lead to any concrete explanations and that would not make possible an understanding of the true "nature" (of the plastic dimension) of cinema: a "dimension" that, for him, was systematically missed every time the attempt was made to reduce cinema to some dimension or other of the "plastic" arts that came before. And in fact when Faure evokes, like other critics of his time, the encounters or other "fusions" between these different artistic "regimes" or "languages," it is to demonstrate straightaway the frailty or inadequacy of the mixture. When they are compared with each other, it is never to make them resemble each other, or even less to "add" or even "fuse" their particular "imaging" power, but in the best case, to subject them to an analogy of proportionality that safeguards their radical heterogeneity.[23] In other words, for Élie Faure, the arts do not *resemble* each other. Rather it is through their differences—the differential system of rhythms, forms, movements, etc.—that they communicate and perhaps enrich each other. And so he says, for example, "that there are, between cinema and the societies that take form without complicity, or despite our resistance, the same relations that existed during the Middle Ages … between architecture and the Christian society of Europe, between architecture and the Buddhist society of Asia."[24] And if he happens to summon certain of its "plastic" or "dramatic" parameters during an encounter he is staging, it remains the case for him that "the cinema has nothing in common with the theater,"[25] nothing in common with pantomime, fresco, music, or painting, and that *only* the reference to dance, at the limit and only in certain relations, remains![26]

Kant wrote in the *Critique of Pure Reason* that "intuitions without concepts are blind" and that "thoughts without content are empty."[27] It is the invention of the theory of the "transcendental schematism" that bridges the "gap" that separates sensible intuition from the concept that corresponds to it. My reading hypothesis is that for Deleuze, the hybrid and intuitive character of Faure's theses on cinema will play the role of transcendental "schemas" for the concepts *to be produced*, while the "categories" that he creates to characterize the singularity of the play of cinematic forms and language—"cineplast," "cinemimic," *plastic* "drama," or "essay," etc.—will play the role of "conceptual personae."[28] And this perhaps explains why it is in the chapter devoted to "Thought and Cinema" that Deleuze "spontaneously"(?) makes reference to the work of Élie Faure. This is explained by what I attempted to highlight above, but also by a series of other "encounters" which are really not at all "fortuitous": in Faure, Deleuze discovers "found objects," or more precisely, "ready-made intuitions" which will serve, as they almost always do for him, as shifters of analysis ["*embrayeurs d'analyses*"] and, finally as generators of concepts (of cinema). For Deleuze, the "intuitions" of a critic like Élie Faure will be, in another analogy of proportionality, what the Kantian "transcendental schema" is to the concept. Moreover, in *What is Philosophy?*, there is a passage that enables us to understand the role that Faure's plastic "intuitions" were able to play in Deleuze's aesthetics of cinema and it is there that Deleuze explains the link between what he calls *percepts* ("artistic" percepts, but this is a pleonasm!) and *concepts*. We should not be surprised that it is in focusing on "aesthetic figures" that he makes the following clarification:

> Aesthetic figures, and the style that creates them, *have nothing to do with rhetoric*. [In other words, aesthetic figures are above all *plastic*! Does he not, in referring to Artaud, speak of a "plastic specter" that haunts works of art?] They are sensations: percepts and affects, landscapes and faces, visions and becomings. But is not the philosophical concept defined by becoming, and almost in the same terms? Still, aesthetic figures *are not the same as* conceptual personae. It may be that they pass *into one another*, in either direction, like Igitur or Zarathustra, *but this is insofar as there are sensations of concepts and concepts of sensations*. It is not the same becoming.[29]

We can translate the results of this clarification for our own purposes: just like Deleuze's "conceptual personae,"[30] the notions that Élie Faure invents in order to try to account for the idiosyncrasy of cinema—cineplast, cinemimic, plastic essayist, etc.—will have the status of "sensations of concepts," in sum, of these small scenarios that anticipate and prepare the terrain for the creation of "true" concepts of cinema: they *mime* the concept to come without being able truly to formulate it.

An "example" among others to illustrate my point: in "Vocation du cinéma," Faure raises the question—so important for him!—of the sequencing of images, but he ventures only very rarely into a detailed and, to be honest, *theoretical* analysis of the specific status of montage, of cutting, or of the impact of the image/sound/speech/music "assemblage." It is still to the category of "man" that he refers when it is a matter, for example, of naming the organizing instance that is at work in cinema: we read in "Vocation du cinéma" that "cinema records images mechanically. But then who, if not *man*, chooses the images to be organized?"[31] And when he creates the conceptual personae of the cineplast or the cinemimic, it is with hesitation and without knowing exactly where to situate them or in which filiation: "We discuss in order to know whether the author of the cinematographic scenario—*I hesitate to create* the word *cineplast*—must be a writer or a painter, the cinemimic a mime or actor. Charlot resolves all of these questions: a new art implies a new artist."[32]

There you have it, and there we will remain! But the fact remains that these "personae" have been productive: they enabled Faure to highlight the specificity and the importance of the *plastic dimension* of cinema for example, and it is in this sense that they will have for Deleuze the status of true "conceptual personae," a true "arresting of thought in a freeze-frame"[33] or "preconceptual intuitions" that call for their concept but that do not "expose" it, do not truly "produce" it. Deleuze's passion will be to do precisely that: to produce these concepts. In any case that is how Deleuze will read them in order to integrate and transform them into his "conception" of cinema, whether as "sensations of concepts," or better as "*mises en scène*" or "dramatizations" of concepts (to come, to create, to "specify"). And this perhaps enables us better to understand what Deleuze writes in his conclusion to *Cinema 2: The Time-Image*:

> A theory of cinema is not "about" cinema, but about the concepts that cinema gives rise to and which are themselves related to other concepts *corresponding to other practices* ... It is at the level of the interference[34] of many practices that things happen, beings, images, concepts, all the kinds of events.[35]

This is to say that in reading Faure's texts as he did, Deleuze sought not so much to salvage or to critique this or that thesis but, as with the "conceptual personae" provided by the other "intercessors" that traverse his texts (Artaud, Godard, Robbe-Grillet, Duras, Blanchot, etc.), to draw out the perfectly singular "plane of immanence" that their path enabled him to map out for the benefit of his own philosophy.[36]

In concluding his book on cinema, Deleuze writes that "the great cinema authors are like the great painters or the great musicians: it is they who talk best about what they do. But, in talking, *they become philosophers or theoreticians*—even Hawks who wanted no theories, even Godard when he pretends to distrust them. Cinema's concepts are not given in cinema."[37]

The *concepts of cinema* are not *given* in cinema, but are products, created by philosophy. We can see how they could have been intuited through a critique that had no *declared* philosophical ambition when it set itself to reflecting on cinema. Is it a matter here of a purely accidental encounter? Fortuitous? As soon as we know that Faure was a student of Bergson, part of the "mystery" of such an encounter can begin to fade.[38]

Translated by Bryan Lueck

4

On the "Spiritual Automaton," or Space and Time in Modern Cinema according to Gilles Deleuze

The unifying thread of this chapter is the "spiritual automaton," a "concept" that appears relatively late in Gilles Deleuze's work, in *Cinema 1: The Movement-Image* (1986) and *Cinema 2: The Time-Image* (1989), but one that nonetheless plays a crucial role in the general economy of the Deleuzian conception of the way(s) space and time are produced and negotiated in cinema.

A certain familiarity with the work of Deleuze makes readily apparent both that the concepts he creates need not appear in the title of a book or a chapter to play an important role in his analysis, and that any examination of these concepts must be taken up in light of the theoretical problematic in which he reworks and re-evaluates them. Apart from the very rare exception, a Deleuzian concept cannot be read as such, or left to posterity by a given philosophical "tradition." The originality with which Deleuze practices the history of philosophy and the broad versatility with which he uses his "canonical" concepts have been noted by a number of critics, and in the two books on film he wrote one just after the other Deleuze does not break with this practice. By detaching concepts from their original theoretical contexts, he is able to reactivate them, to reevaluate their tenor and make them play new roles—in a couple of words, he is able to transform them into "conceptual personae."[1] In this way, philosophical concepts are never, for Deleuze, static entities fixed once and for all, but are, rather, matters to be further worked through and reconnected, ever called into crisis and reinvented. The "spiritual automaton" is, in this sense, one of the finest examples of a philosophico-conceptual "persona" that film theory has ever invented to account for its "object."

The thought process animating the creation of such personae is exemplified by the notion of the "Body without Organs." Introduced for the first time in *The Logic of Sense* (1990a), Deleuze, we recall, presented it as borrowed from Antonin Artaud (a poet) and from Gisela Pankow (a psychiatrist). Some years later while working with Félix Guattari, Deleuze would again take up this figure, this time giving it a crucial role to play, in *Anti-Oedipus* (2009). By means of this transfer, the nature and definition of the concept would completely change: no longer drawing its valence and effect solely from the work of the authors who had originally fostered it as an intuition, the *BwO* would draw from at least two new systems of thought, themselves referring to two new theoretical regimes. Indeed, as Andre Pierre Colombat has aptly shown in his excellent article on the concepts at work, like "tools" in *A Thousand Plateaus*,[2] the concept of the *BwO*, articulated around the idea of non-sense as developed by Artaud and Lewis Carroll, is presented *at once* "as an egg" (that is, as a biological metaphor) *and* as a "Spinozist substance" (this time, as a properly philosophical concept). Inevitably, the juxtaposition of these two apparently "incompatible" fields of explanation creates nonsense or, if you will, an "excess of meaning" that sets the reader's intellect and imagination in movement: "The concept of the 'Body without Organs' will therefore be *defined in between* two heterogeneous series, thanks to a never-ending *to-and-fro motion* between Deleuze's conception of the egg, borrowed from François Dalcq, and his conception of the Spinozist substance,"[3] which he derived this time from his own interpretation of Spinoza's *Ethics* (1992).[4] In *A Thousand Plateaus* (1987), the *BwO* re-emerges to play a still more complex role, or more exactly, it crisscrosses and is crisscrossed by new determinations: here, the *BwO* still remembers having been an egg and a Spinozist substance, but it also reveals itself to be an "intensive and unshaped matter,"[5] the "plane of consistency specific to desire" of Spinoza's *Ethics*, Heliogabalus, *Logos Spermaticos*, and so on.[6] As a "rigorous and inexact concept," the *BwO* is in constant metamorphosis, "occupying the in between space that allows intensities and desiring flows to circulate before actualizing themselves in different shapes of thought and in living organisms, on a physical or a metaphysical plane."[7]

With the concept of the "spiritual automaton," we observe the same kind of thought process with respect to film. Although initially taken from Spinoza's

Ethics: Treatise on the Emendation of the Intellect,[8] the "spiritual automaton" would soon be transformed into a concept of the Jabberwocky, Snark, or *BwO* type. That is to say, we have once more to grapple with one of the so-called "inexact and rigorous" concepts traversing Deleuze's work and making for the richness of the theoretical and practical effects he draws from them.

The "spiritual automaton" is first and foremost an "inexact" concept, because it is difficult if not impossible to assign to it a singular and stable origin. Indeed, Deleuze does not hesitate to bring its use and effectiveness to bear on writers, artists, historians, creators, and theorists as different as Élie Faure, Jean Epstein, and S. M. Eisenstein, to name but a few, whom he immediately associates and connects in a complex and contradictory way to an author like Artaud and filmmakers like Pier Paolo Pasolini and Jean-Luc Godard, only to arrive at (and thus to take up the question anew) a poet like Paul Valery or philosophers like Spinoza and Heidegger.

At the same time, the concept of the "spiritual automaton" can still be called "rigorous" in that, as suggested above, what are clearly the "transference" and "translation" undergone by the concept are neither gratuitous nor improvised; on the contrary, they obey the most consistent thought process. Yet, according to what criteria are we to judge this consistency? How can we say of a concept that it is at once "inexact" and "rigorous"? Why the re-creation and re-activation of a concept on the particular occasion of a reflection on cinema? And finally: in what way does this "concept" affect time in film?

Deleuze's interest in the Spinozist concept of the "spiritual automaton" is not so much in any "automatic" or "mechanical" aspect—Spinoza is in no way a "mechanistic" philosopher—but, rather, in what has since in Spinoza been referred to as a "method" that, although borrowing its starting point from geometry, nonetheless only finds its intrinsic form of action in the thought process that makes it exceed its own ordinary limits, raising it to an essence as the "genetic reason of all knowable properties."[9] For Deleuze, interest in the Spinozist "spiritual automaton" stems from at least two inseparable factors: the immanence of thought and the theory of parallelism. "Spiritual automaton," Deleuze writes, "means first of all that an idea, being a mode of thought, has its (efficient and formal) cause nowhere but in the attribute of Thought. Equally, any object whatever has its efficient and formal cause only in the attribute of which it is a mode and whose concept it involves."[10]

These definitions may seem rather "abstract" when thus formulated out of context, but they become much more effective and concrete once we understand that, for Spinoza, they implied none other than the *power* of parallelism: to say that an idea or an object finds its efficient and formal cause "only in the attribute of which it is the mode" is to affirm that "all efficient or formal (and even more, material and final) causality is *excluded between ideas and things, things and ideas*"[11] (my emphasis). What holds Deleuze's attention in Spinoza's "automatism," then, is the multiple consequences he infers from Spinoza's first axioms: the affirmation of the independence of two series, the series of things from the series of ideas; and immediately thereafter, the independence of the series of images from the series of objects, things, or bodies—series of words from images, and so on. Deleuze would focus especially on the "autonomy" and "automatism" of thought.[12]

Like Spinoza's, Deleuze's method in *Cinema 1* and *Cinema 2* includes (at least) three moments, each narrowly implicated in the others: a first moment in which the apprehension of movement and the "objects" it carries is granted to intuition or to the "immediate contents of consciousness," also the moment of film analysis as simple "image movement" or "image-representation";[13] a second "moment" occurs when it is no longer movement as such, but the dislocation of movement (called "*mouvements aberrants*" in this case[14]) that precedes analysis; and a third moment, one of synthesis, albeit disjunctive, when it is an "unthinkable" Outside that takes on the order of thought—the thought of the un-thinkable: "spiritual automaton."

Such is, schematically drawn, the "program" laid out by the reactivation of the concept of the "spiritual automaton." From this, everything else unfolds because, as suggested above, in bringing this concept to bear, it was never a question for Deleuze of "applying" it as such to cinema; on the contrary, it was a matter of using cinema to transform an "exact" concept—too "exact" in the work of Spinoza—into an *operator of analysis* or an *accelerator of concepts* that would allow it to "give rise" in us to a new way of thinking cinema. In other words, the "spiritual automaton" acts as a "transformer" of the regime of concepts and images in film. As Deleuze writes: "*Automatic movement* gives rise to a *spiritual automaton* in us, which reacts in turn on movement." Furthermore, from the moment of its confrontation with the disjunctive logic at work in cinema, the concept of the "[s]piritual automaton" no longer designates—as it does in classical philosophy—the [merely] logical or abstract possibility of formally deducing thoughts from each other, but "the circuit into which they enter with the movement-image, the shared power of what forces thinking and what thinks under the shock: a *nooshock*."[15]

Thus, the effect of displacing the "automaton" from one given theoretical field to another is two-fold: *at the same time* that it unyokes Spinozist philosophy—and perhaps all philosophy—from its latent "formalism," it tears cinema from its patent "mechanism" (the simple "shock") to reveal therein what forces us to think (beyond the opposition of movement-image and action-image). As soon as the nature of the spiritual automaton's intervention in film is understood, it "is as if cinema were telling us: with me, with the image-movement, you can't escape the shock *that arouses the thinker in you*. A subjective and collective automaton for an automatic movement: the art of the 'masses.'"[16]

As long as they had available to them only a formal conception of movement and of the production of ideas in cinema—ideas that still remained *representative*—filmmakers and film theorists inevitably missed its *noetic* dimension, for they confused the "shock" with the "*noochoc*" and thereby reduced the vibrations of the movement-image to the "figurative violence of the represented." Such a "reduction," intensified by a *confusion*, would quickly and unduly assimilate cinema as "spiritual automaton" with cinema as the "art of propaganda" or the reproduction of reality! According to Deleuze, even a filmmaker with the genius of S. M. Eisenstein, with all his theoretical vigilance, could let himself be taken in by an entirely mechanical conception of the noetic dimension of cinematographic "automatism."

If Eisenstein did indeed locate the "movement" in cinema that goes from the shock of two images to the thought or, as he himself said, to the "concept"—if he had indeed exposed the twisted dialectic that turns the first movement upside down so as to pass from the "concept" to the "affect" and from the "organic" to the "pathetic"—he never managed to produce an adequate idea of the nature of the "automatism" at work in cinema. As Deleuze aptly put it, with Eisenstein, "we no longer go from the movement-image to the clear thinking of the whole that it expresses; we go *from thinking of the whole which is presupposed and obscure to the agitated, mixed-up images which express it*."[17] In this sense, Eisenstein managed to intuit the complex nature of the cinematographic "shock" "in the form of opposition," as well as the thought that it engaged "in the form of opposition overcome, or of the transformation of opposites."[18] But in order to be "dialectical," this transformation could not renounce the idea of a totality as a harmonic "synthesis" of parts ("shots") that pre-existed them in a "Subject" or a "World." If he clearly signals the (dialectical) passage of a *Logos* that "unifies the parts" to a *Pathos* that "bathes them and spreads out in them," that is, the shock rebounding from the unconscious concept (of a whole) to the matter-image—"fountains of cream, fountains of luminous water, spurting fires, zigzags forming numbers, as in the famous sequence in *The General Line*, for example—Eisenstein could still believe in cinema as a "device" that allowed him to go back to images and string them together according to the demands of an "interior monologue" that he could reduce "to the course of thought of a man."

To rid himself of a conception of cinema tending to close off the rhetorical dimension that determined it in logical and grammatical dimensions, Eisenstein would have had to appreciate the more purely *noetic*[19] range of cinema. For although cinema was awakened, with him, to the power of the "figure-image," that is, to the formal play, "that [in cinema] gives the image an affective charge that will intensify the sensory shock," he did not take account of what, again in cinema, can refer to an "outside" that is neither reducible to an "interiority" as subjectivity nor to an "exteriority" as *res extensa* or "exterior" world. We must therefore envision a third "moment" that no longer consists in going from image to thought (percept to concept) or from concept to affect (thought to image), but which surpasses this dialectic to create a movement *in which concept and image are one*: "The concept is in itself in the image, and the image is for itself in the concept. This is no longer organic and pathetic *but dramatic, pragmatic, praxis, or action-thought.*"[20] In this sense, for Deleuze, Eisenstein would have been the theorist filmmaker to detach "Narrative-Representative" cinema from its imperatives and who, following this, would have embarked on the course of a *cinematographic noetic*—except that everything happens as if he had reduced it too quickly to an "automatism," an instrument in the service of the historical revolution or of dialectical reason. With Eisenstein, the "spiritual automaton" became "revolutionary Man," as for Leni Riefenstahl it would become (the instrument of) "fascist Man." In both cases, the "audio-visual battle" ended in a belief that led them to abandon their prey to go chasing after shadows: in spite of everything, the audio-visual battle became a powerful instrument for capturing the exterior world—"our world"!—without knowing that it drew from the original forces of an "un-formable and unformed Outside."[21]

At this level, what we willingly call the "Spiritual Automaton Transformer" reveals its full effect because instead of leading to an impasse, this last acknowledgment participates in a revival of the *problems*. Indeed, thanks to the veritable "transformer"[22] of concepts that is the "spiritual automaton," Deleuze is able to point out that the failure of the movement-image and the action-image in cinema, as well as the gross mediocrity that lies in wait for its most commercial productions, can be attributed neither to the poverty of ideologies nor to the "fascism of production"[23]—after all, Riefenstahl made "beautiful" films—but more pointedly to a thought that did not always know how to raise itself to the height of the cinematographic automatism's intrinsic power. Everything happens for Deleuze as if cinema had failed to take account of and to play out fully its potentialities, not because of an *excess* of "automatism" but because of a lack of radicalism. It is at this level that the work of a writer like Artaud plays such an important role.

With Artaud, the S-A-T would be invested with new valence, allowing the renewed thinking of the economy of such key concepts as *montage* and *a whole* in cinema. Indeed, no longer conceived of as "the [simple] logical possibility of a thought which would formally deduce its ideas from each other" (for example, Eisenstein's "montage-king"), and even less as "the physical power of a thought that would be placed in a circuit with the automatic image"[24] (for example, the Expressionist shock-image), the S-A-T would instead be conceived of as a "Mummy" that would no longer serve as a caution to endeavors,[25] like those still played out in the Eisenstein aesthetic that undertake to re-center the Subject (as "People," "History," "Reason," and so on). Henceforth, cinema could finally be thought of not as a dialectical or logical instrument of referral to a "world" and a "subject" always already given, but as the indicator of a virtual world and subject (to come). With Eisenstein, the "automaton" allowed going from the image to the thought, having provoked the shock or the vibration that was supposed to give rise to "thought in thought";[26] but from thought to image, there was still the self-incarnating figure in the interior monologue "capable of giving us the shock again": "dialectical" automaton!

With Artaud, we witness an altogether different regime of thought, as well as the actuation of an otherwise more complex dialectic:

> What cinema [henceforth] advances is not the power of thought but its "unpower," which will no longer be conceived of in terms of a "simple inhibition that the cinema would bring to us from the outside, but of this central inhibition, of this internal collapse and fossilization, of this "theft of thoughts" of which thought is a constant agent and victim.[27]

Once raised to the height of "spiritual automatism," cinema would no longer be conceived of as an instrument serving to reproduce thought or represent the real, but would instead be understood as a machine of a superior order, one that sets thought in relation to an Outside that cannot be reduced to a world said to be "exterior." Cinema as spiritual automaton is this "machine" that puts thought into contact with an Outside that itself comes to subvert the nature of the relations of representation existing in cinema between image and reality. We might say that for Deleuze, cinema becomes the producer of an original composition of space-time that metamorphoses the real. Faced with such an Outside, given to us by cinema like an "offering," the represented reality appears as a fallout effect of cinematographic virtualities.

By way of illustration, I will take a specific example analyzed by Deleuze: that of the *Whole*, the idea of the whole in cinema. The Whole, Deleuze tells us, is a poetic notion that can be traced back to Rilke but is also a philosophical notion elaborated by Bergson. It is, therefore, also a "rigorous and inexact" concept. As Deleuze points out, however, it is important not to confuse the Whole—the idea of a whole in cinema—with the idea of a set. In fact, for all that a set unites very diverse elements, its structure must remain no less closed or sealed off. It may refer to or be included in a larger set, but this latter will in its turn wish for closure, and so on to infinity. But the Whole, Deleuze tells us, is of another nature entirely; it cannot be assimilated to a set because it "is of the order of Time."[28] To quote Deleuze: "[The Whole] traverses all sets and is precisely what prevents them from fully realizing their proper tendency, which is to say, from completely closing themselves off."[29]

Following Bergson, Deleuze says in his turn: "Time is the open, it is what changes and keeps changing its nature in each instant."[30] We can translate this thesis by saying that Time is the Open, it is what changes all things, not ceasing to change the nature of things in each instant. Time in cinema is this Whole, which is precisely not a set but is, rather, the perpetual passage from one set to another, the transformation of one set into another. My working hypothesis therefore becomes the following: Deleuze created the notion of the spiritual automaton in an attempt to think about the relation *time-whole-open*. He does not say that only cinema thinks of this relation; he merely says that "it is cinema that makes it easier for us to think it." In this sense, there is, for Deleuze, something like a "pedagogical" dimension proper to cinema. And in fact, its demonstration is relatively simple once cinema is used as an operator of analysis for intuiting such a singular phenomenon. To "illustrate" his point of view, Deleuze takes as a "model" the following three levels of organizing and articulating the image: framing, cutting, and movement. He argues that: "Framing is the determination of an artificially closed provisional set" that to all appearances does not exhaust what is at stake in a cinematographic image; yet it is constantly traversed by cutting, which is "the determination of movement or movements distributed in the elements of the set; but movement in its turn also expresses a change or variation in the whole, which is the job of montage."[31] In this sense, the Whole is the "power," the *Dunamis* that cuts across all sets and specifically prevents them from being "totally" closed off. To illustrate his "case," Deleuze takes the example of the notion of "off-camera" that refers, according to him, to two distinct realities. On one hand, he indicates that any given set is part of a greater set of two or three dimensions (there are objects found on this side of the door and objects that are "out-of-field," on the other side. *The secret beyond the door!* On the other hand, he indicates that all sets, "plunge into a whole of another nature, that *of a fourth and fifth dimension*, that keeps changing through the sets it traverses, no matter how vast they are. In the one case, it is a spatial and material extension, while in the other, it is spiritual determination."[32] Among the numerous "examples" Deleuze specifically analyzes are, of course, the works of Dreyer and Bresson, whose films show just how difficult it is to separate the two types of "dimensions": the material and the spiritual, the spatial and the temporal. Each filmmaker must recreate from the ground up the relation or relations to the Whole that will traverse the sets. For, as Deleuze says, in a great film as in all works of art, "there is always something open."[33] And anyone seeking to know what it is will discover it is time, it is the Whole, produced as they are by the "automaton"; because the automaton is none other than the "machine" that allows the adding of *n* dimensions to the first and the second dimensions of the image: "shot-reverse shot."

Here, then, is the idea of the Whole severed from any idea of organic or dialectic totality. But this is not the complete story, for the S-A-T also enables Deleuze to foreground the differences between a "theorematic" and a "problematic" regime of film thought[34] leading him to rethink completely cinema's relation to its language and its objects. Indeed, armed with the S-A-T, Deleuze easily shows that the cinema of Eisenstein or Godard, for example, refers not only to an ideological or aesthetic difference but more pointedly to a prior difference of position vis-à-vis the nature of the "problems" posed by cinema and its way of resolving them. Thus, from one filmmaker to another, from one aesthetic to another, there exist not only two confronting or opposing aesthetics, but two new signifying regimes and two new regimes of thought: the problematic regime and the theorematic regime— two regimes that affect the way we treat time and the way time affects us.

This analysis also reveals—thanks again to the S-A-T—the fundamental aspect of "new cinema" as being not necessarily linked (only) to some technical or historical particularity, but as linked to a "formal" characteristic of cinema in general, which alone can "make (a) difference": what is the nature of the existing link between the film-image, or better, the film-*thought*, and the world? Deleuze discovers that separating them is not so much any particular *worldly disagreement* as a "break in the *sensorymotor link* (action-image) and *more profoundly* in the link between man and the world (great organic composition)."[35] We have here an archaeological or even a "transcendental" discovery that "makes a difference" because it is no longer a question now of negotiating the relationship of cinema to the world in psychological or practical terms, but is one of opening up a new field of thought: a pure "psychic" field and situation and the specific modes of agency of op-signs and son-signs that must be mobilized by filmmakers if they are to be up to the task of facing a vision that will carry them off into an indefinite, like a becoming that is too powerful for them: the unthinkable![36] "It's too beautiful! Too hard to take!" (Rossellini). "Impossible to say! To formulate!" (Godard). Cinema of the seer!

In such conditions—and this is the contribution of the S-A-T—the work of an Eisenstein is characterized less by any formal "tic" or "ideologeme" than by the primacy he grants to a thought in which "the internal relationships from principle to consequences" would prevail.[37] By contrast, the work of a Godard or a Pasolini is characterized by the "problematic" character of the encounter of images (op-signs) and sounds (son-signs) with the "world" that is to be privileged. This is brought about by the intervention of "an event [this time] from the outside—removal, addition, cutting—which constitutes its own conditions and determines ... the cases."[38] Thus cinema is no longer conceived of as a "device" or an "apparatus" allowing us to represent the world in a more or less realist or adequate way, but as an "automaton"—in this it is called 'spiritual'—that allows us to "bring the *unconscious mechanisms of thought* to consciousness."[39] These premises result in the radically different "forms" or "types" achieved according to the orientation—or "choice"— one makes. A multiplicity of "forms" corresponding to a variety of new "beliefs" are presented; not necessarily in opposition to, but in addition to the Eisensteinian "types": the "*unsummonable*" of Welles, the "*inexplicable*" of Robbe-Grillet, the "*undecidable*" of Resnais, the "*impossible*" of Duras, or again, the "*incommensurable*" of Godard, each accompanied by its own sensitivity to time.[40] So many variations would have been impossible to bring to light, as Deleuze likes to put it, without the *scanning* that made the S-A-T possible. They now appear as the *forms* or the effects of the intrinsic *noetic* power of cinema as "spiritual automaton."

Thanks to his operator, Deleuze would subsequently be able to show that the theoretical demand to ascribe a new status to the image in modern cinema corresponds to the necessity of reworking or re-evaluating the "*rhetoric*" that had prevailed in film theory before the discovery of the S-A-T. Indeed, at the same time that he tears the cinematographic image from the "Narrative-Representative" field that held it the prisoner of an abstract or simply "logical" thought, Deleuze discovers that what connects cinema to the outside of all representation could not have been intuited had not the logic presiding at the production of its objects remained unaffected.

If the *first aspect* of the revolution that altered cinema was the break in the "sensory-motor link" and that between "man and the world," the *second aspect* of this break "is the *abandoning of figures, metonymy as much as metaphor, and at a deeper level the dislocation of the internal monologue as descriptive material of the cinema.*"[41] No more metaphors, no more metonymies, and still fewer "interior monologues," not only because cinema would have become amorphous or undifferentiated or even insensible to "poetry," but more profoundly, "because the necessity which belongs to relations of thought in the image has replaced the contiguity of relations of images (shot-reverse shot)." For example, the shot-reverse shot of classical cinema would henceforth be replaced by depth of field, the high-angle or low-angle shots of Welles or Astruc, the "model" of Bresson, or the "irrational cuts" of Godard or Pasolini, or even by the "hyper-spatial figures" that no longer refer cinematic images to the allegedly "familiar" representation of the world, but that refer instead to "an outside which makes them pass into each other, like conical projections or metamorphoses."[42]

When perception is made up of pure op-signs and sounds, it no longer enters into relation with simple movement or action alone, but with a virtual image, "a mental or mirror image," says Deleuze. The new "automatism" would make the actual image and the virtual image blend to produce the "crystal-image," always double, always intensified such as we find it in Renoir, Ophüls, Fellini. As Maurizio Grande has aptly shown in the fine study he devoted to Deleuze's work on cinema, "the crystal-image is a kind of *mirror-time*. In it, the real is always a present, but the present is the real image with, *in addition*, its own past rendered contemporaneous."[43] As "spiritual automaton," cinema gives us an image that will no longer be "cut off only from the thing and the body," "not only *something else* with respect to representation, memory, and recognition, which maintain a physical relation to the sensory-motor schemes of action," but an image—hallucinatory if you will—"grasped in the very instant of its dissolution, in the instant of its crystallization in an immediate temporality, directed and without connection to any other thing having to do with the image formed in crystal-time."[44] This means that only the "automatism" can enable us to think of cinema's contribution to our apprehension of time as the "unhinging of images from the body and from reality," or "time as *immediate image without possible body*, which translates as *Seeing* and as *Hallucination*."[45] The mode of crystallization changes in each instance, but in each instance a new quality of Time and its "layeredness" [*nappel*] is experienced (as argued by Roland Barthes). Deleuze situates the revolution that touched modern cinema in its essence in this "unhinging" related to the body and to consciousness—as the "originally synthetic apperception" of a "Me-present-to-itself." For ever since it was raised to the power of the "spiritual automaton," cinema reversed the relation of the subject to its body—in particular to its "vision"—and its memory, because "the image no longer derives from a perceiving (sleeping, memorizing...) body, nor from a brain-archive of data; the image sets the subject adrift, *sucking it into a trans-perceptive and 'falsifying world.'*"[46]

Having become "spiritual automaton" (non-dialectical "machine"), cinema must also conquer a new force, one that will still make it an automaton, but this time, as an a-grammatical and a-rhetorical machine, a machine with the power to "carry the image to the point where it becomes deductive and automatic, to substitute the formal linkages of thought to sensory-motor representative or figurative linkages."[47] For Deleuze, modern cinema is (or became) henceforth a "spiritual automaton" in that it can make the unrolling of film a true *theorem* instead of merely a pure association of images—"it makes thought immanent to the image."[48] A direct product of the new "automatism" traversing cinema, only this "immanence" actually permits an understanding of the veritable "mutation" that would come to affect other concepts in cinema and to change its economy.

Depth of field, for example, would no longer be situated in relation "to obstacles or concealed things"—a still entirely "mechanical" conception that reduces it to a technical feat or a simple aesthetic feature—"but in relation to a light which makes us see beings and objects according to their opacity."[49] Because depth of field is an integral part of an open "totality," it also has the "mental effect of a theorem, it makes the unrolling of the film a theorem rather than an association of images, it makes thought immanent to the image." Similarly, the sequence shot would no longer be merely one instrument among others for producing an action-image dominated by movement and the displacement of objects and beings in neutral space, but the "instance" or "viewpoint" of a *problem*. It is again due to the S-A-T and "false continuity" that the notions of "out of the field" ['Hors-Champ'] and "false continuity" can be seen to adjust their new status in relation to a "whole" that likewise undergoes a mutation, because it has ceased to be the "One-Being", in order to become the constitutive 'and' of things, the constitutive "between-two" of images ["*Entre-images*"]. Henceforth, the material automatism of images and sounds would no longer refer to the given world nor to a preformed psychological interiority, but would provoke from *outside*—an outside no longer homogeneous to exteriority—"a thought which it imposes, as the unthinkable in our intellectual automatism." The Whole would no longer be confused with a flat structure or "model," but with what, referring to Blanchot, Deleuze calls "the force of 'dispersal of the Outside'" or "the vertigo of spacing": cinema as the generator of a new "chaosmos" and of half-actual, half-virtual crystal-images capable of letting us see once more a world that had itself become a "hallucination."

In the end, the S-A-T enables us to understand better the nature of the mutations that condition the eruption of an image and a thought no longer having anything to do with actual things or beings, but that relate, rather, to a purely optical and sonorous world that refers to virtual things and beings: a *world to come*, a world where the actual image and the virtual image have fused, giving birth to "crystals" of unified time and space. In mobilizing the noetic force of the S-A-T, these are the different *modes of the crystallization of time* that Gilles Deleuze gave us to rethink so that we might better understand and better see (through) cinema. Yet, what we can "see" thanks to the S-A-T—or thanks to "the Mind's Eye," to cite Deleuze once more—"is Time, layers of time, a direct time-image that makes us able to grasp the mechanisms of thought" and thereby establish new links with the world—and to believe again in this world.[50]

But "to *believe*" here is not to rediscover the virtues of faith; no, it is, rather, to "return discourse back to the body and thereby to reach the body before discourse, before words, before the naming of things."[51]

Translated by Denise L. Davis

5

The Singularity of the Event: Gilles Deleuze, Paul Virilio, François Jullien

If the singularities are veritable events, they communicate in one and the same Event which endlessly redistributes them, while their transformations form a history.

Deleuze, *Bergsonism*, p. 53

What History grasps of the event is its effectuation in states of affairs or in lived experience, but the event in its becoming, in its specific consistency, in its self-positing concept, escapes History.

Deleuze and Guattari, 1994, p. 110.

Transformation is global, progressive and situated in duration, resulting from a correlation of factors. Since "everything" within it transforms itself, it is never sufficiently differentiated to be perceptible ... We do not see the wheat ripen, but we do notice the result: when it is ripe and should be cut.

François Jullien, *The Silent Transformations*, p. 8 (emphasis added)

The sudden stereoscopic highlighting of the event, accident or attack, thus well and truly amounts to the birth of a new type of tragedy, one not only audiovisual, but binocular and stereophonic, in which the perspective of the real time of synchronized emotions produces the submission of consciences to this "terrorism in evidence"—that we see with our own eyes—that further enhances the authority of the media. ACCIDENT or ATTACK? From now on, uncertainty rules, the mask of the Medusa is forced on everyone thanks

> to Minerva's helmet, or rather, this visual headset that endlessly shows us the repetition (in a mirror) of a terror we are utterly fascinated by.
>
> Paul Virilio, *The Original Accident*, pp. 20–1

No philosopher has conferred as much importance to the notion of singularity as Gilles Deleuze. We could even hypothesize that it is impossible to understand some of the fundamental tenets of his philosophy of sense as a *sui generis* event without analyzing the importance that he grants to a notion, which, from a mere noun designating what is one of a kind, is rapidly transformed into a central concept of his ontology. For Deleuze, *thinking* means first and foremost being able to free the singularities from what traps them in a supreme I, a unified subject, or a person endowed with an individual consciousness. And it is this that explains one of Deleuze's main objectives, as seen for example in *The Logic of Sense* and *Difference and Repetition*: to liberate philosophy from a transcendental field whose singularities are always already "enclosed" in empirical figures, things, or individuals. In *The Logic of Sense*, Deleuze even goes so far as to state that "singularities are the *true transcendental events*."[1]

It is true that the notion of singularity as Deleuze employs it owes nothing anymore to the traditional definition of this term as it was used in classical philosophy.[2] Stripped of the psychological connotations that "good sense" and "common sense"[3] conferred, singularities for Deleuze designate that which precedes any formation of *substance* and transcends any apodictic assertion of essence. According to Deleuze, the *singular* is what resists the establishment of the grand hypostases of representational thought: a subject that says "I," an individual who conceives of him/herself as "one," an always already established Self. As Pierre Montebello has convincingly suggested, "from below the individual and the personal, which refer to God and to the Self, Deleuze unearths *the much deeper reality of the singular*, neither individual, nor personal, but pre-individual and pre-personal."[4] This is the case because, far from being chaos, the singular "is the Real itself, *sub-psychic, sub-organic, sub-material*" on the basis of which "thought necessarily begins to sketch out a primordial image of nature."[5]

As I want to propose here, it is by investing in an updated concept of singularity—wrested from both "good" and "common" sense—that Deleuze is capable of giving the notion of the event the specific shape that it adopts in his philosophy. Deleuze seeks, as he writes, "to determine an impersonal and pre-individual transcendental field, which does not resemble the corresponding empirical fields"—a conscious subject, an individual answering to an I, or a unified and self-reflexive self—"and which nevertheless is not confused with an undifferentiated depth."[6] What is first and foremost the central concern of Deleuze's philosophy—and his understanding of singularity—is the liberation of thought from the false dichotomy imposed by metaphysics and classical transcendental philosophy (Kant, Sartre, Husserl, and, for Deleuze, even Heidegger): "*either* an undifferentiated ground, a groundlessness, formless nonbeing, or an abyss without differences and without properties, or a supremely individuated Being and an intensely personalized form," because of the assumption that "without this Being or this Form, you will have only chaos."[7] This is the kind of narrow dualism that Deleuze sought to eliminate from philosophy. That is to say: for Deleuze, it is only once we have given ourselves the means to access "the world, teaming [sic] with anonymous and nomadic, impersonal and pre-individual singularities" that precede and determine "the synthesis of the person and the analysis of the individual as these are (or are made) in consciousness" that we are finally able to enter the field of the transcendental properly speaking, which allows us to experience "a 'potential' which admits neither Self nor I, but which *produces them by actualizing or realizing itself.*"[8]

Beyond these veritable hypostases that the person and the individual, inherited from metaphysics, are (or were), this new mode of philosophy is one of exploring *singular points*—composed of differential forces, intensities, colors, tones, materials, and *singular* words—which traverse "men as well as plants and animals independently of the matter of their individuation and the forms of their personality."[9] This is an unprecedented freeing of singularities; it resembles a release of particles which, although they have not yet been imprisoned in a thing, a person, or an individual, each nevertheless possess their own characteristics, as well as the power to affect the world in which they "participate." It is, however, a strange kind of "participation," and one that no longer owes anything to Platonic Idealism: far from referring to eternal "Essences" or transcendental "Ideas," these particles open up a transcendental field that is traversed by nomadic singularities which take over for consciousness and create the conditions for the genesis of individuals and persons. As Pierre Montebello observed, after having highlighted what Deleuze owes to the work of Gilbert Simondon, especially in *L'Individu et sa Genèse Physico-Biologique*,[10] the individual is not "a concrete being, a complete being," an entity that is always already embedded in an "I," but rather "*the result of a process that allows singularities to communicate*."[11] This is what makes the Deleuzian concept of the event entirely original, as it is no longer a question of thinking of the event—any event worthy of its name—as something that happens (as if) from the "outside" to an autonomous subject, autarkic and free from any involvement in what happens to it. On the contrary, as Claude Romano pointed out, it is a question of "thinking *subjectivity itself* … as that which can only arise *from the event* in other words,[12] as the result of a throw of dice whose occurrence no "Idea" or concept could have subsumed or foreseen. From this point on, we no longer deal with an always already existing individual, fully formed from "head to toe," but with a "subject" that is the "fallout" or result of a gamble where one must "double down" or "counter-effect"[13] the singular points that had been employed in the previous "game." This is why in *What is Philosophy?* Deleuze and Guattari write that "the subject *now* appears as an 'eject,' because it extracts elements whose principal characteristic is distinction, discrimination: *limits, constants, variables, and functions*, all those functives and prospects that form the terms of the scientific proposition."[14] Working from such premises and from a phenomenological point of view, it becomes necessary to distinguish between two kinds of "worlds," two radically different ways of "being in the world" that refer back to two differentiated concepts: one qualified as evental [*événementiel*], concerning innerworldly facts insofar as these are only comprehensible and make sense *within a given context*; and one concept qualified as evential [*événemential*], relating to the event insofar as it escapes from any horizon of prior meaning. Both are events that, as Romano remarks, "in their anarchic bursting forth, make themselves manifest with their meaning only *on their own horizon*."[15]

Thus arising "*beyond any measure of prior possibilities*"[16]—namely, into a world in the true sense of the word—the evential [*événemential*] event becomes "world-establishing" [*instaurateur-de-monde*] for the subject that experiences it. In this sense, the event in fact becomes that which elucidates its own context and in no way garners its meaning from it: the event [*événement*]

The Singularity of the Event: Gilles Deleuze, Paul Virilio, François Jullien 73

is not a consequence, easily explainable due to pre-existing possibilities, but it rather *reconfigures the possibilities that precede it* and signifies, for the subject, the advent [*avènement*] of a new world. Thus, not only has the old world, as such, entirely disappeared, but its *meaning* now appears radically altered, the sum of the projects and purposes that had inhabited it and had granted it its signifying structure now appears so changed that it is not, strictly speaking, the *same* world anymore. By occurring, the event rendered the old world *in*significant, because it is no longer comprehensible *according to its context*. Once it becomes insignificant, the world loses "the fundamental phenomenological trait that precisely determines it as context—its significance. It is *abolished* as world. Going beyond every forecast and anticipation, the event has *reconfigured my intrinsic possibilities articulated among themselves*—my world—it has opened a new world *in and by* its bursting forth."[17]

What seems to best characterize this approach to the event is, according to Erwin Strauss, whom Claude Romano cites, its "inaugural character [*Erstmaligkeit*]" or "first time character" for the subject.[18] And yet, Deleuze understands the event as that which repeats (itself) and which endlessly returns without ever exhausting itself in a substance, a repetition, or a return that only takes place to inscribe a difference that displaces and transfigures (one's) being. From this point of view, if we really want to think of such an event, and think of it in its being, we must account for the active difference between intensive or qualitative—or "virtual"—multiplicities, and extensive, quantitative multiplicities that all belong to concrete entities.

If we wished to "illustrate" this thesis with an analytical example, we could point to the relationship that psychoanalysis established between the system of consciousness and that of the Unconscious: what is *actualized* and differ-en*ciated* [*différencié*] by consciousness is not consistent with what remains differen*tiated* [*différentié*] (virtual) in the unconscious. According to Deleuze, *differentiated* does not mean unreal or devoid of its own "logic" and mode of functioning. In this sense we can say that for Deleuze, the *evential* space—the site of the event—always refers back to the virtual conditions of existence of that which is actualized in the form of concrete entities. As Deleuze says, there are virtually always more "beings"—ideas, forms, figures—in one's thought than in one's consciousness! Or, to put it another way, events happen because the actual is always paired with the virtual.

In fact, for Deleuze, the virtual is the name of the being and the condition of the event. In order to give substance to this "view" of things and wrest the concept of the virtual from abstraction, Deleuze often referred to the work of Joë Bousquet who, for him, expressed most clearly the fact that all events owe their occurrence to the power of the virtual. Deleuze liked to cite the following passage from Bousquet's *Les Capitales*: "Everything was in order with the events of my life before I made them mine; to live them is to find myself tempted to become their equal, as if they had to get from me only that which they have that is best and most perfect."[19] This is why Deleuze argued that "the event is not what occurs (an accident), it is rather inside what occurs, the purely expressed. It signals and awaits us."[20] The "purely expressed" is none other than the inherent "power" [*dunamis*] of the virtual and the multiplicities that constitute it. Consequently, for Deleuze philosophy is first and foremost a theory of multiplicities if we keep in mind that all multiplicity involves actual elements and virtual elements and that there is no such thing as a purely actual object.

According to Deleuze, the perception of any object is always surrounded by a cloud of virtual images. This "cloud" fosters more or less extensive coexisting circuits—a swarm of singularities: form, color, smell, size—"along which virtual images are distributed and around which they run."[21] This is how an actual particle emits and absorbs virtual ones of varying proximity and different order. These particles "are called virtual in so far as their emission and absorption, creation and destruction, occur in a period of time shorter than the shortest continuous period imaginable; it is this very brevity that keeps them subject to a principle of uncertainty or indetermination."[22]

Everything actual is encircled by always renewed virtualities, each one emitting another, and all of them surrounding and reacting to the actual.[23] By virtue of this dramatic dynamism of each entity (physical, psychological, aesthetic), a mere perception is like a singular particle, intense and insistent: an actual perception surrounds itself with a cloud of virtual images, distributed on increasingly remote, increasingly large, moving circuits which both make and unmake each other. These are, for example, memories, images, phantasms of different orders: they are called virtual images or singularities because their speed or their slowness, their duration or their brevity, subjects them to a principle of the unconscious:

The Singularity of the Event: Gilles Deleuze, Paul Virilio, François Jullien 75

> With every event, there is indeed the present moment of its actualization, the moment in which the event is embodied in a state of affairs, an individual, or a person, the moment we designate by saying "here, the moment has come." The future and the past of the event are evaluated only with respect to this definitive present, and from the point of view of that which embodies it. But on the other hand, there is the future and the past of the event considered in itself, sidestepping each present, being free of the limitations of a state of affairs, impersonal and pre-individual, neutral, neither general nor particular, *eventum tantum* ... It has no other present than that of the mobile instant which represents it, always divided into past-future, and forming what must be called the counter-actualization. In one case, it is my life which seems too weak for me and slips away at a point which, in a determined relation to me, has become present. In the other case, it is I who am too weak for life, it is life which overwhelms me, scattering its singularities all about, in no relation to me, nor to a moment determinable as the present, except an impersonal instant which is divided into still-future and already-past.[24]

The same line of thought can be found in Virilio and Jullien, whose works I place in dialogue here with the Deleuzian concept of singularity. If I have given here first of all priority to the Deleuzian concept of the virtual and singularities over those of other contemporary philosophers, it is because Deleuze's seemed best suited to account for some of the theoretical fallout that others have experienced with regard to the status of the event in modernity, its political consequences, and its relation to the fate of humanity. Moreover, this is what prompted me to read Deleuze alongside two other writers who were clearly inspired by him, and who at times also attempt to widen the parameters of his thought.

This is certainly the case with the work of the urban planner and theorist Paul Virilio, for whom the notion of the virtual plays an essential role in his analyses of contemporary art, of cities and urban spaces, of speed and the impact of new technologies on modern ways of life. For example, Virilio notes in an essay entitled "The Revolutions of Speed," published in *La Pensée Exposée*:

> Most of all, I believe that we have to consider *the reality of the world* that we experience simultaneously as *virtual and actual*. The virtual is not in contradiction with the actual; that is to say, with the shift towards action. In the old world, virtuality was of minimal importance. Today, on the contrary, in the

dromoscopic world in which we swim, *virtuality prevails over actuality* ... This is equally true for representations: *the virtual image prevails in real time over the actual image.*[25]

What I find interesting in this new interpretation of the Deleuzian paradigm of the virtual and the actual is the displacement that these two concepts allow Virilio to perform. Following in the tradition of what Jean-Pierre Dupuy termed "enlightened catastrophism"—a catastrophism that Dupuy defined as "a ruse, which consists of separating humanity from its own violence by making the latter into a kind of fate, devoid of intention but capable of destroying us"[26]—Virilio went on to give "accidents" an entirely different ontological status. For him, what we call "accidents"—e.g., Chernobyl, Fukushima—should no longer be seen as marginal phenomena in relation to other human phenomena, but as constitutive of a world whose horizon has become the self-destruction, or perhaps even the annihilation, of humanity. (Virilio does not hesitate to consider man-made phenomena like Hiroshima, Nagasaki, and even September 11 as part of the same cocktail of disasters.) Whereas "risk managers" and other "insurance economists" are outraged at the idea that, in a kind of vast catastrophic cocktail, we can mix environmental pollution, climate deterioration, the depletion of fossil resources, risks tied to advanced technologies, and so many other present or future catastrophes[27]—when we do not have the means to see the singularities defining an empirical transcendental field in the Deleuzian sense—Virilio in turn grants these "accidents" the value of major events. According to him, it is "urgently necessary" to inverse the tendency that consists in seeing the facts as *contingent* phenomena. Instead, he introduces an approach which strives to "expose the accident" as the major enigma of (so-called) "modern progress." And consequently, the notion of the event itself changes in nature and ontological status: it will no longer be seen as what occurs—occurs to us—*accidentally, spontaneously, by chance or misfortune,* but as a "global" phenomenon, so to speak, which is an *integral part of a virtual world of announced catastrophes* that Virilio terms, in a chapter in *La Pensée Exposée* entitled "The Expectation Horizon," the "integral accident":

> The feeling of insecurity that has crept up over the last dozen years or so in the city is not only linked to the discourteous acts of so-called "incivility" currently

plaguing city-dwellers. It is, it would seem, a symptom of a *new expectation horizon,* a third kind of horizon after "revolution" and "war," the Great War, the "war to end all wars." I am talking about the expectation of the *integral accident,* this Great Accident *that is not merely ecological.* The latter has been part of our general mindset for the last thirty years or so. The integral accident is also, and above all, *eschatological.* It is the accident of a world now foreclosed in what is touted as "globalization," this internationalization at once desired and dreaded, now the subject of endless debate, as though the anthropological horizon of ideas and ideals suddenly felt blocked off, both by the foreclosure represented by a geographical lock-down and by *the suddenness of worldwide interactivity of exchange.*[28]

It is of these kinds "catastrophic" and "eschatological" concerns that drove Virilio to advocate for the promotion of what he called *"geopolitical ecology,"* a form of ecology that would entail *"facing up to the unpredictable,* to this Medusa of technical progress that literally exterminates the whole world."[29]

As we can see, we have moved a considerable distance away from the conception of the event as an existential epiphany as touted by phenomenologists, or as an "interruption" or "subtraction" in being, or even "destruction" for the philosophers of the so-called linguistic turn. It is no longer solely "birth," "death," "love," or "illness" that is at the source of an *evential* experience—as phenomenologists believed—but rather all the events which, much like what happened after Chernobyl, Fukushima, or September 11, force us to give *more ontological force and credibility* to the powers of destruction (of the future) that human "genius" has been able to generate, in order to potentially prevent the occurrence of the "integral accident" as described by Virilio. According to Svetlana Aleksievich, a Chernobyl survivor, ultimately, everything unfolds "as though the global nature of this catastrophe was manifested in the total *destruction* of the human world *according to ancient laws.*"[30]

But what are these "ancient laws"? What can they refer to in this context other than the *precepts, ideas, and values* that allowed humans to understand and live in a world that was "familiar" to them?[31] As Dupuy aptly observed, when responding to American philosopher Susan Neiman's *Evil in Modern Thought: An Alternative History of Philosophy* on the subject of Lisbon, Auschwitz, and September 11: "When moral evil reaches its apex, as at Auschwitz, moral categories are blown to smithereens."[32] The same situation occurs when certain technological forces of destruction have consequences that turn out to be irreparable. What becomes of the discourse—so often nonchalant or downright irresponsible or self-serving—on the impact of these *imperceptible and yet so real singularities* such as the greenhouse effect on planetary ozone layers or, even closer to home, the impact of GMOs on human and animal health? What about nuclear deterrence or chemical weapons? It is thus not *only*, as Dupuy suggests, the "cautionary principle" that needs to be challenged—the principle according to which we would need more time, more knowledge, and more research in order to know how to act—but more radically the way in which we *conceive* of our relationship to the earth and the endless and increasingly catastrophic transformations that we subject the latter to. Hence the necessity of giving ourselves the means to no longer see phenomena such as Chernobyl or Fukushima—regardless of their manmade or natural causes—as mere *epiphenomena*, but rather as veritable singularities that all contribute to what Deleuze calls "haecceity," wherein the "integral accident" is imperceptibly taking shape. Like sense for Deleuze, this accident is *unimaginable* because it is still enveloped by singular "events" that do not appear to be connected; but it is also *unrepresentable* and *immemorial* because no image is yet capable of presenting it as such.[33] This is precisely what Deleuze stated eloquently in a chapter of *The Logic of Sense*, devoted to the "ideal game" of thought:

> Just as the present measures the temporal realization of the event—that is, its incarnation in the depth of acting bodies and its incorporation in a state of affairs—*the event in turn, in its impassibility and impenetrability, has no present. It rather retreats and advances in two directions at once, being the perpetual object of a double question*: What is going to happen? What has just happened?[34]

What is also at play, and *at the same time*, is perhaps the nature of "knowledge" and of the information that we mobilize to *think* of our place on earth as human beings, as well as our relationship to our immediate surroundings—which also means thinking of the "essence of technology" and its impact on human life on earth. This has led many philosophers and environmental activists to ask the more radical question of whether "we can find better suited conceptual resources"—aside from those we have inherited from Western traditions—to understand and, if possible, to prevent [*pré-venir*] ("come before") the integral accident articulated by Virilio.[35]

From an entirely different perspective, but one which complements the ideas put forth by Virilio and Dupuy, the philosopher and sinologist François Jullien has examined the notion of the event by playing upon what he termed "the Chinese gap." In fact, in his work *The Silent Transformations*, Jullien analyzes a number of changes that are currently underway in a wide variety of areas—from mountain erosion to cellular degeneration—as the result of *slow, imperceptible, and invisible* transformations which we are unable to know or observe, but which are nevertheless constantly at work. This lack of awareness [*insensibilité*] explains why it is generally only in the form of a (fortunate or unfortunate) rupture that we become conscious of these changes and experience them as an "event," or, depending on our preferences and value systems, as "a sign of 'fate.'"[36]

For our line of inquiry, what is interesting is the importance that Jullien grants to these small nothings, these singular points, to all the "accidents" that are part of our lives and that we do not see, that we do not even notice when everything is changing around us. We see nothing, we are aware of nothing even though things are constantly changing in us and around us. The flowers of a pretty bouquet wilt, the body ages, the climate changes, the mountains erode, a relationship is falling apart, but we do not see any of these things, we do not feel them, *perhaps we do not want to know about them*.[37] According to Jullien, these tiny, uninterrupted changes, rarely noticed, constitute the very fabric of our existence. They unfold slowly and silently, everywhere present and yet invisible due to their gradual and unobtrusive nature. But "one fine day," so to speak, something unheard of happens, taking the shape of an unprecedented and absolutely new event: the flowers must be thrown out, yesterday's love has turned to ashes, the planet is in danger, I have aged. How did this come about? What changed? Or, to ask one of Deleuze's questions: *What just happened?* Where did *this* come from? It is generally only *after the fact* that we finally become aware of these singular points—too singular, too small—and of what was *always* there, without us being able to take them into consideration or observe their constant, silent transformations.

Working from this at first sight perhaps banal postulate, Jullien shows that although the Western metaphysical tradition has had difficulties with such a mode of thinking, Chinese culture has, on the contrary, granted it much attention and an essential place. According to Jullien, ever since Ancient

Greece, the West has first and foremost favored *definitions*, precise edges, "clear and distinct" ideas in Descartes's words, or "stratifications" in Deleuze's terms, which has ultimately prevented Western philosophy from understanding *transitions, the gradual shift* from one form of being to another, from one tone to another, from one state to another. It is important to note here that for Jullien, no change in nature or in ourselves marks an unpredictable and irreversible break: no more so than a fortunate and definitive thing gained. Drawing inspiration from the ideas of the Chinese philosopher Wang Fuzhi, Jullien concludes that far from being a rupture or an individual's sealed fate, the event is first and foremost a "continuous becoming" [*avènement continu*] that is no longer of the order of effraction, but rather of the order of emergence. Consequently, he writes, "instead of causing another possibility to appear," the event "is understood only as the consequence of such a subtle *maturity* that it has not ordinarily been possible to follow and observe."[38] Much like the changing of the seasons, our ageing process, or the natural outcome of general erosion, everything fluctuates, everything silently transforms itself. The "brutality" or suddenness of what we call an "event" surprises us, because we are unable to perceive the silent transformations that have led to a failure, an illness, or a discovery, because, in short, we have never been attentive to the *singularities working silently on our individuation*. According to Jullien, the "event" has been fetishized; there is a need, for any subject caught up in metaphysics, to believe in the event as an "ecstasy" or a form of escape from the ordinary "ecstasy." This *emprise* (drive to mastery or *Bemächtigungstrieb*) spares no one, not only because our "need" for events is contagious, but even more so because the "silent" presence of nomadic, transient, and imperceptible singularities is ignored [*méconnue*], despite the fact that they are constantly at work in our psyches, in our acts, and on the earth.

For Jullien, the merit of the concept of "transformation" (compared, for example, to a Hegelian scenario, which would still see the event as a form of *hidden progress* that is only revealed *retrospectively* after we have moved beyond it) is that "it sets us free from theo-teleological constructions and otherwise recomposes, in a non-metaphysical way, the relation between the visible and the invisible"[39]—or the virtual and the actual, to use Virilio's and Deleuze's terms. "Transformation," writes Jullien, "is gestation and stands for a condition; the event ... emerges on the surface."[40] Without transformation, there is no event. Consequently, the event will no longer appear to be a phenomenon that just "falls from the sky," so to speak, but as the "outcrop" of what has been "brewing" below the surface, maturing during a long and "silent" transformation. Since it refuses to separate the evental from the tendencial—"*l'événementiel du tendanciel*" in Jullien;[41] or in other words: 'what "happens" from what carries it along (rather than what "causes" it), or the chronological from what underlies it' (Jullien 2011: 142)—the concept of silent transformation allows us to follow the evolution of a phenomenon without leading to the hypostasis termed "event," that is to say: without turning the event into an anticipated occurrence or "expected Advent" [*avènement attendu*].[42] To be clear, for Jullien "[t]his concept will moreover no longer allow History to be split up according to a difference of scale or domain, but for the histories of the 'greatest' and the 'smallest,' the individual and the collective, and nature, climate, species, people and each of them to be linked under its aegis."[43]

We can, thus, imagine some of the consequences that such an approach could have on art history or on scientific, artistic or philosophical creation, depending on the analytical tool used. In the realm of the arts, a *true typology of artistic styles and perspectives could arise from this*. What impact could the choice of a theory of the event have on the way in which an artist views his or her work? What political consequences could stem from the choice of one of the theoretical "operators" that we have access to today regarding our relation with the world we live in? What consequences would it have on our conception of art history, or on our definition of "taste" or of "beauty"? And finally, how might a better understanding of the status of singularities and the new transcendental field that they create help us to avoid the advent of the "integral accident"?

Translated by Sarah-Louise Raillard

6

The Kafka Effect: Considerations on the Limits of Interpretation in Deleuze and Guattari's Book on Kafka

Writing is born from and deals with the acknowledged doubt of an explicit division, in sum, of the impossibility of one's own place. It articulates an act that is constantly a beginning: the subject is never authorized by a place, it could never install itself in an inalterable cogito, it remains a stranger to itself and forever deprived of an ontological ground, and therefore it always comes up short or is in excess, always the debtor of a death, indebted with respect to the disappearance of a genealogical and territorial "substance," linked to a name that cannot be owned.

Michel de Certeau, *L'Écriture de l'histoire*, p. 327.

As for us, that is why we were unable to posit any difference in nature, any borderline, any limit at all between the Imaginary and the Symbolic, or between Oedipus-as-crisis and Oedipus-as-structure, or between the problem and its solution.

Deleuze and Guattari, *Anti-Oedipus*, p. 106

In December 1934, the *Judische Rundschau* published an important text on Kafka by Walter Benjamin, in which we can read these decisive words: "There are two ways to miss the point of Kafka's works. One is to interpret them naturally, the other is the supernatural interpretation. Both the psychoanalytic and the theological interpretations equally miss the essential points."[1] In 1974, when Gilles Deleuze and Félix Guattari devoted a book to Kafka's work, they took their point of departure from the same principle: one misses the mark in Kafka either by putting him in the nursery—by oedipalizing and relating him to mother–father narratives—or by trying to limit him to theological-metaphysical speculation to the detriment of all the political, ethical, and ideological dimensions that run through his work and give it a special status in the history of literature. At the least, this initial convergence between Benjamin's approach and that advanced by Deleuze and Guattari seems worthy of note.

When we read each of the studies carefully, we cannot help being struck by the care taken in each case to avoid what might be called a political-ideological *recuperation* of Kafka or, perhaps, to avoid falling back upon what Deleuze and Guattari call a *hard segment*: the binary machine of social classes, sexes, neurosis, mysticism, and so on. In both cases, we find ourselves face to face with the same attempt to avoid making Kafka just another great "*littérateur*." Both pinpoint the need to make way for new philosophical, literary, and even psychological categories to come to terms with this unique work and to lead readers out of the impasse created by so many readings of exegesis.

First, let us read and consider what Benjamin would have us think about Kafka: What is the substance of what he says? What is he attempting to have us experience, and not simply interpret or read? What writing machine—already!—does he want to connect us to? Recall that the study begins with a *political* apologue: Potemkin was having a crisis and was therefore inaccessible, but affairs of state were pending. There was a stack of documents that urgently needed to be signed, and the high officials were at the end of their rope; but a junior clerk named Shuvalkin who was informed of the problem took hold of the documents, impassively marched into Potemkin's bedroom, presented the papers to him, and pressed him to sign them. Without blinking—at least, so it seemed—Potemkin signed all the documents presented to him one after the other. Everyone knows what happened: when the high officials finally had the famous documents in hand, they were stupefied to decipher in each instance the name Shuvalkin. Benjamin continues in a way that is highly significant for us:

> This story is like a herald racing two hundred years ahead of Kafka's work. The enigma which beclouds it is Kafka's enigma. The world of offices and registries, of musty, shabby, dark rooms, is Kafka's world. The obliging Shuvalkin, who makes light of everything and is finally left empty-handed, is Kafka's K.[2]

The "reading" that Benjamin proposes for Kafka's work is clear from the outset and is characterized—no less than that of Deleuze and Guattari—by never trying to find archetypes that claim to have "qualified" Kafka's "imaginary" or to "interpret" his work by moving from the unknown back to the known: the Castle is God, the world of the father, power that cannot be grasped; the cockroach is anxiety, castration, the dream world and its multiple metamorphoses, and so forth. But what is still more striking, neither does Benjamin try—he doesn't consider it useful or necessary—to relate Kafka's work to a *structure* with preformed formal oppositions and a signifier of the kind in which "after all is said and done, *x* refers to *y*"! Not at all. The reading of Kafka both in Benjamin and in Deleuze and Guattari is determined by the prominence they give to a *politics of* Kafka; but, as Deleuze and Guattari go on to articulate, this politics is "neither imaginary nor symbolic."

In characterizing the horde of messengers, judges, assistants, intermediaries, and lawyers who haunt Kafka's text, Benjamin never takes refuge behind a symbolic, allegorical, or mythical interpretation: he considers Kafka's ancestors to be the Jews and Chinese of ancient or contemporary history, or even the Greeks, rather than considering Kafka to be the descendant of "Atlas" who would carry the globe of the world on the back of his neck. Refuge behind myth, recourse to myth as the last hope, is radically rejected:

> Even the world of myth of which we think in this context is incomparably younger than Kafka's world, which has been promised redemption by· the myth. But if we can be sure of one thing, it is this: *Kafka did not succumb to its temptation*.[3]

Nor would Benjamin have yielded to the temptation to take refuge behind myth; to do so would be to inject mythical meanings into Kafka's work—to say that Kafka is to modernity what classical myth was to traditional society. Benjamin was one of the first "readers" of Kafka to see and then try to show—to *demonstrate*—that Kafka's work was, from a certain point of view, to be taken literally: in a word, that it functioned on the surface of its signs and that the issue was not—at least, not *only*—to try to "interpret" it but, above all, to practice it as an experimental machine, a machine for effects, as in physics. Of course, it is a writing machine or a group of writing machines that are made of assemblages of nouns and effects, of heterogeneous orders of signs that cannot be reduced to a binary structure, to a dominant or transcendental signifier, or ultimately to some phantasm (originary or not).

Benjamin (who was very well-acquainted with Freudian psychoanalysis) was able to avoid at every step the "dreary psychoanalytic interpretations" that Gilles Deleuze and Félix Guattari mention in their essay. When he evoked the well-known texts in which Kafka addresses the Father, Benjamin immediately showed how close the link is between what Kafka foregrounds about the relation to the Father and a juridical-political "assemblage" that exceeds and determines the father–son relation since time "immemorial" (as he liked to say):

> The father is the one who punishes; guilt attracts him *as it does the court officials.* There is much to indicate that the world of the officials and the world of the fathers *are the same to Kafka.*[4]

Thus, no matter how we approach it—and this is Benjamin's "lesson"—Kafka's work does not lend itself to domestication. It cannot be made into literature in the way one enters into religion. It resists on all levels, and it demands—at every obstacle and disruption that one simultaneously invents and experiences in its unfolding—not merely a new *rhetoric* or a new mode of *reading* but a genuine "traversal of its writing"[5] from which one does not emerge unscathed. It goes without saying that such a change of perspective—not satisfied with reading, one experiences, travels, concretely transforms oneself—cannot be conceived without a radical change in the very nature of the order of signs that is at work in the text. Benjamin had more than an inkling of this decisive aspect of Kafka's work when he attempted to account for the "economy" of his short stories (for example, the "undecidable," "unfinished" character of his work). Benjamin introduced the important notion of *gesture*. He may have borrowed the notion from Brecht, but for him it referred above all to a space where the subject of the statement and the subject of enunciation can no longer be separated. Benjamin showed that Kafka could well have adopted Montaigne's phrase: *"Mon livre et moi ne faisons qu'un."* It is impossible to separate the tool from the artisan, the reader as *lexeograph*[6] from the scriptor as *subscriptor*: they are together as machine and rhizome, a network, an entangled knot of movements and stops, of impulsions and immobilizations to experience interminably. They constitute what Deleuze and Guattari call a "Body without Organs," to experience and to deploy, according to the procedures and "methods" that are always new. Concerning the Kafkaesque gesture (in the medieval sense of the word), Benjamin says:

Kafka could understand things only in the form of a *gestus*, and this *gestus* which he did not understand constitutes the cloudy part of the parables. Kafka's writings [*Dichtung*] emanate from it.⁷

Nevertheless, Benjamin does not hesitate to advance hypotheses about the "origin" of Kafka's literary "creation" [*Dichtung*]. But rather than ascending to some singular transcendent figure or signifier, it is a matter of defining a "space," a *metastable* force that does not refer to a subject but designates a *vection*, a movement of translation that belongs to pre-individual forces. These forces seem to have already been traversed by an immemorial forgetfulness that makes it impossible to reduce the saying to the said and that refers to an experience for which only a collective enunciation can take responsibility. Recall the passage in which Benjamin brings out that aspect of things:

> What has been forgotten—and this insight affords us yet another avenue of access to Kafka's work—is *never something purely individual*. Everything forgotten mingles with what has been forgotten of the pre-historic world, forms countless, uncertain, changing compounds, yielding a constant flow of new, strange products. Oblivion is the container from which the *inexhaustible intermediate world* in Kafka's stories presses toward the light.⁸

The reader of Deleuze and Guattari's book on Kafka will readily perceive that they took it upon themselves to pick up the analysis of Kafka's work where Benjamin—not because of a lack of perceptiveness but, perhaps, because of the epistemological anchoring of his text—seemed to have reached an insurmountable barrier, a dead end. Despite his efforts, Benjamin was not always able to avoid the stumbling block that he calls Kafka's "failure" and that he ultimately characterizes in terms of a shortcoming (thereby being too quick to take literally what was merely one threshold of Kafka's work):

> This document [the testament that orders the destruction of his works upon his death], which no one interested in Kafka can disregard, says that the writings did not satisfy their author, that *he regarded his efforts as failures*, that he counted himself among those who were bound to fail. He did fail in his grandiose attempt to convert poetry [*Dichtung*] into doctrine, to turn it into a parable and restore it to that stability and unpretentiousness which, in the face of reason, seemed to him to be the only appropriate thing for it. No other writer [*Dichter*] has obeyed the commandment "Thou shalt not make unto thee a graven image" so faithfully."⁹

Without reading too much into the text, we can see a hint of nihilism that tilts Kafka's work—otherwise very positive—in the direction of the literature of failure: not far removed from Camus and his philosophy of the absurd and of the futility of every human work. Too human! But in writing *Kafka*, Deleuze and Guattari propose an experimentation of Kafka that refrains from—even in the name of a solemn *gestus*—referring to any idea of failure, of shortcoming, or "immemorial" guilt. This book represents a watershed and is invaluable for the modern reader of Kafka: instead of seeking to capture his work in one of the "segments" that constantly draw it toward some "black hole," Oedipus, or failure (in short, nihilism), Deleuze and Guattari do their utmost to resist. They successfully show that although the different diabolical machines—letters, novellas, so-called unfinished novels—that Kafka created throughout his life do derive in a *gestus* that is constantly running the risk of annihilation, destruction, or regression, it is nonetheless wholly impossible to reduce the specific *effects* to nihilistic figures that we have enumerated in reference to Benjamin. For Deleuze and Guattari, Kafka's work is characterized by the total absence of negation: above all, by a total absence of complacency (even in his journals), and consequently a rejection of every problematic of failure. Those who read this book carefully will perceive that the authors tried to show that Kafka's work is in no way susceptible to an anthropological or psychological explanation but is essentially the bearer of an affirmation without reserve.

Without seeming to deal with the question at all, Deleuze and Guattari begin by detaching Kafka from what the academic institution calls "Literature." It quickly becomes obvious that Kafka has been misinterpreted and, from a certain point of view, "misunderstood" only because he has for a long time—too long, according to the authors—been judged to be the embodiment of a concept of literature (and of the "*Law-of-Genre*,"[10] of "Desire") that is totally inapplicable to his work. Deleuze and Guattari do not simply say that Kafka was unconcerned with literature or that he was not a writer by occupation. Instead, they break down the complex mechanism whose operation—because one is driven to "categorize" it—leads precisely to failure: an always excessive reduction of his work.

By proposing the concept of "minor literature"—a concept that opens so many new avenues of research in postcolonial countries and also in Europe and the United States—Deleuze and Guattari give the modern reader a means by which to enter into Kafka's work without being weighed down by the old categories of genres, types, modes, and style (in the "linguistic" sense of the term, as Barthes would say). These categories would imply that the reader's task is at bottom to *interpret* Kafka's writing, whether the interpretation take the form of parabolism, negative theology, allegory, symbolism, "correspondences," and so on. The concept of minor literature permits a reversal: instead of Kafka's work being related to some preexistent category or literary genre, it will henceforth serve as a *rallying point* or *model* for certain texts and "bi-lingual"[11] writing practices that, until now, had to pass through a long purgatory before even being read, much less recognized.

Why has it been necessary to introduce this category of minor literature to account for Kafka's work? First, because Kafka, in his *Diaries* and "theoretical" texts, meditated at length on the type of "literature" that he believed himself to be inventing and that he saw certain of his contemporaries practicing. If we reread Kafka's *Diaries* in light of what the authors bring out in this book, it immediately becomes apparent how important it was for Kafka to situate the type of writing and rewriting he was practicing. Commentators have been too quick to label as mystical (neurotic?) or metaphysical meditations that always took the form of a radical questioning of classical or traditional literary writing. Kafka does not read and admire Goethe and Flaubert to imitate them, much less to move beyond (*aufheben*) them according to some teleological schema like that of Hegel, but to determine and appreciate the incommensurable distance that separates him from their ideal of depth or perfection. Writing against the current and from a linguistic space that is radically heterogeneous with respect to his great predecessors, Kafka appears as the *initiator* of a new literary continent: a continent where reading and writing open up new perspectives, break ground for new avenues of thought, and, above all, wipe out the tracks of an old topography of mind and thought. With Kafka—at least with the Kafka that Deleuze and Guattari think through anew—one has the feeling that literature has been given a new face: it has changed both its addresser and its addressee.

The new category of minor literature is also essential because it allows one to dispense with dualisms and rifts—whether linguistic, generic, or even political—that have ultimately constituted a sort of *vulgate* (a fortress, if you will) that, although not indisputable, has been at least sufficiently restricting to impede access to what has been characterized as Kafka's "epoch": Einstein and his deterritorialization of the representation of the universe; the twelve-tone Austrians and their deterritorializations of musical representations (Marie's death cry in Wozzeck or that of Lulu); expressionist cinema and its double movement of deterritorialization and reterritorialization of the image (Robert Wiene of Czech origin, Fritz Lang born in Vienna, Paul Wegener and his use of themes from Prague); the Copernican revolution of Freud; and finally, the so-called linguistic revolution carried out by the Prague circle. All the elements are brought together for a radical change of *episteme* that Kafka contrives to transcribe with the most diverse means, the most complex methods. The readers of this book—if they are not in a hurry—will certainly be impressed by the extreme care that Deleuze and Guattari have taken first in describing, and then in analyzing, the variety of those methods. Whether it is a question of the relation of Kafka's texts to the German language or to the economy of writing, the authors emphasize the procedures that Kafka sets to work to produce the effect(s) that are linked to his name today: what one might call the *Kafka effect*.

It will come as no surprise to readers familiar with Deleuze and Guattari's work that the idea of the machine producing effects is not used metaphorically or symbolically but always in the most concrete sense. In his *Dialogues* with Claire Parnet, Deleuze makes it more precise:

> Machine, machinism, *machinic*: it is neither mechanical nor organic. The mechanical is a system of gradual connections between dependent terms. The machine, on the other hand, is a clustered "proximity" between independent terms (topological proximity is itself independent of distance or contiguity). A machinic assemblage is defined by the displacement of a center of gravity onto an abstract line.[12]

From this perspective, we can more easily understand that there will always be a "primary" social machine in relation to human beings and animals (within the limits of what Deleuze calls its *phylum*): a gesture coming from the East will always presuppose an Asiatic machine that without preceding it in time will condition the situations in which it can be concretely effected. But in the same way that every mechanical element presupposes a social machine, the organism in turn presupposes a *Body without Organs* that, by means of its lines (of flight), its axes of intervention, and its "gradients," will largely exceed the ectodermal limits of the human body as well as the psychological representatives of its identity.

For Deleuze and Guattari, if Kafka still occupies the place granted him in the history of Letters, it has nothing to do with the fact that he renewed its "themes" or transformed its style. Instead, they see him as important because he figured out a mode of writing that allows us to account for the different "machines" that condition our actual relation to the world, to the body, to desire, and to the economy of life and death. And even if he has *paredre*—brothers of blood and affection—he has no predecessor. Deleuze and Guattari are especially interested in foregrounding some of the effects produced in relating ("classical") literature and the *minority machine* in Kafka's work. It is not only a question of tapping libidinal energy but also one of opening up new registers of thought and action of speed:

> This question of speed is important and very complicated as well. It doesn't mean to be the first to finish; one might be late by speed. Nor does it mean always changing; one might be invariable and constant by speed. Speed is to be caught in a becoming that is not a development or an evolution. One would have to be like a taxi, a waiting line of flight, a bottleneck, a traffic jam, green and red lights, slight paranoia, difficult relations with the police. Being an abstract and broken line, a zigzag that slips "between."[13]

Thus, Kafka's work is revolutionary in the way it affects the language in which it is effected. A language that is a "major" language is affected by a strong deterritorialization factor and is subjected to a series of displacements that make it slow down to a crawl in certain texts (contexts) (see, for example, "The Metamorphosis") or send it into a panic, unfolding at a vertiginous pace (see one of the short texts, like "The Cares of a Family Man"[14]). For Kafka, therefore, it is never a matter of "trafficking" in language or of mishandling it—how many writers and poets have supposedly "subverted" language without ever having caused the slightest ripple in comparison with the language of Kafka, Joyce, or Kleist?—but of essentially proposing a new *way of using it*. This new usage in effect short-circuits the appeal—within and by means of the "paper language" that for Kafka is German—to a higher, dominant reality (transcendent or transcendental) that would function from within as a principle of subjectivization. In Deleuzian terms, that new "language" (of a "*Logothete*," or creator of new languages, as Barthes would say[15]) performs an "absolute deterritorialization of the cogito" by the processes that it sets to work.[16] If, according to Deleuze and Guattari, the principal strata that bind and imprison the human being are "the organism, meaningfulness, interpretation, subjectivization, and subjection"[17] then "minor" language is the instrument *par excellence* of that destratification.

We can see now what separates Benjamin's "interpretation" from the "course" taken in Deleuze and Guattari's book. What in Benjamin gives way in a (blind? asymbolic?) gesture that refers to failure here takes the path of an experimentation of life: the setting into place of a "field of continuous intensities" and of an "emission of sign-particles" that can no longer lead to failure because the security of a subject is no longer necessary. The authors show that referring Kafka's work to an idea of failure necessarily implies the full-fledged return of literary and philosophical categories that presupposes a logical, even ontological, priority of content over form: since the content is given in a given form, one has to find, discover, or see the form of expression appropriate to it. But with Kafka it turns out that this schema and this vection, which seem so "natural," are radically put into question.

In other words, if Kafka's watchword was really "Thou shall not make unto thee a graven image," it was certainly not in the manner of the "Turks" or "Muslims" that Hegel describes in his *Aesthetics*—those people who "forbid the painting or reproduction of the human being or any living creature"[18]— and even less like Plato—who in *The Republic* condemns art as the "greatest danger" or as *simulacrum*: a simulacrum that leads those who do not possess the antidotes of reason and knowledge (that is, animals, children, and the ignorant) to lose track of the distinction between the sophist and the philosopher, between truth and illusion.

According to the authors, it was because he liked children, animals, and the "ignorant" that Kafka understood how to effect the strongest challenge to the wall of censure erected by the history of literature. Like the animal that could never really have a thought because it would simultaneously forget what it was on the verge of *thinking* (a process Nietzsche discussed in his *Untimely Meditations*), "minor" literature as reinvented by Kafka "begins by expressing itself and doesn't conceptualize until afterward."[19] With Kafka we are no longer confronted by a "dialectic" or a "structural" correspondence between two kinds of "forms"—forms of content, on the one hand, and ready-made forms of expression, on the other—but, in the authors' words, by *a machine of expression* that is capable of disorganizing its own forms, of disorganizing the forms of content, so as to free up *an intense material of expression* that is then made of pure content that can no longer be separated from its expression:

> Expression must break forms, encourage ruptures and new sprouting. When a form is broken, one must reconstruct the content that will necessarily be part of a rupture in the order of things. To take over, to anticipate, the material.[20]

Thus, the art (*modern* art in this sense) that Kafka tried to introduce is effectively no longer an art that proposes to "express" (a meaning), to "represent" (a thing, a being), or to "imitate" (a nature). It is rather a method (of writing)—of picking up, even of stealing: of "double stealing" as Deleuze sometimes says, which is both "stealing" and "stealing away"—that consists in propelling the most diverse contents on the basis of (no signifying) ruptures and intertwining of the most heterogeneous orders of signs and powers. The familial triangle, for example, is connected to other triangles (such as commercial, economic, bureaucratic, and juridical ones), and thus the "individual concern" finds itself linked directly to the political. According to Deleuze and Guattari, the second principal characteristic of minor literature is that it is always political, not only in the sense in which one speaks of politics, but specifically in the sense in which further activity is no longer related to a unified instance, to an autonomous subjective substance that would be the *origin* of the choices we make, of the tastes we have, and of the life we lead.

In that sense, each and every gesture takes on a quasi-cosmic dimension. Benjamin says it well:

> Kafka does not grow tired of representing the *gestus* in this fashion, but he invariably does so with astonishment. Experiments have proved that a man does not recognize his own walk on the screen or his own voice on the phonograph. The situation of the subject in such experiments is Kafka's situation; this is what directs him to learning, where he may encounter fragments of his own existence, fragments that are still within the context of the role. (p. 137)

But it is with regard to the apparently "fragmentary" character of Kafkaesque exegeses that Deleuze and Guattari once again differ from Benjamin. Although Benjamin never tried to relate Kafka's work to a previous text or record that would allow one to "explain" it, his text does remain tacitly saturated with considerations that refer more or less directly to Jewish theology. Did Benjamin not write to Scholem in 1939 that "anybody who could see the comic sides of Jewish theology would at the same time have in hand the *key to Kafka*"?[21]

In fact, at the end of his dense study of Kafka, when it is a matter of accounting for the "law" of the work and bringing to light the internal principle that Kafka himself followed, Benjamin refers to the loss of the Holy Writ. Kafka's work somehow remains enigmatic, his life and attitude incomprehensible and mysterious: "Kafka, however, has found the law of his journey—at least on one occasion he succeeded in bringing its breathtaking speed in line with the slow narrative pace that he presumably sought all his life" (p. 139).

Seen from a certain angle, Deleuze and Guattari's book on Kafka represents the annulment of such a question because—as they do their best to show—if there is one thing that should be avoided besides the natural (psychoanalytic) explanation and the supernatural (theological) one, it is the temptation to draw Kafka toward the "individual concern," the tragic (that is, toward personal psychology, neurosis, or an author's individual tastes). Neither allegory, metaphor, nor theology will sum up a work that has explored them all without letting itself be taken over by any single one. But, above all, neither the transcendence of the law, the internalization of guilt, nor the subjectivity of the enunciation can ever give an adequate account of the intrinsic force of Kafka's work.

Far from relating this work to an interior drama, an intimate tribunal, or something else drawn from the same old grab bag, Deleuze and Guattari ask us to be attentive to the labor of the "dismantling" or demolition of forms and categories that determine the "great literature" in Kafka. A calm dismantling—one would be tempted to say "pacific"—that first takes the form of an "*a priori* elimination of every idea of guilt": there are certainly many "guilty" characters in Kafka, and with an extremely strong and deleterious guilt, but Kafka never takes that guilt for granted. On the contrary, it appears at each moment as the effect of an assemblage, of a machine if you will, that indirectly takes up lawyers, judges, *and* the victims in the same movement. As Deleuze and Guattari write: "culpability is never anything but the superficial movement whereby judges and even lawyers confine you in order to prevent you from

engaging in a real movement—that is, from taking care of your own affairs."²²
So much for culpability!

The dismantling mentioned above has a second aspect, and this one is decisive in confronting the reading proposed by Deleuze and Guattari with that of Benjamin: "even if the law remains unrecognizable, this is not because it is hidden by its transcendence, but simply because it is always denuded of any interiority: 'it's always in the office next door, or behind the door, on to infinity.'"²³ It is very easy to see the implications that such a hypothesis entails in regard to theology (whether Jewish or another). The law is not stated in accord with its ("sham") transcendence, but the opposite occurs: "it is the statement, the enunciation, that constructs the law in the name of an immanent power of the one who enounces it—the law is confused with that which the guardian utters, and the writings precede the law, rather than being the necessary and derived expression of it."²⁴ Transcendence of the law, the interiority of guilt, and the subjectivity of enunciation are the three "themes" that, according to Deleuze and Guattari, have misled readers and made access to Kafka's work difficult if not impossible, for it becomes inevitably a matter of relating the complexity to his "genius," to the "mystery" of his existence, as in the relationship of the *Hagadah* to the *Halaka*, which Benjamin mentions in his text on Kafka.²⁵ In delving into the "methods" and the processes that Kafka uses to revoke the law's mystery and relate it to the places of its enunciation, and in describing them with precision, Deleuze and Guattari make way for—perhaps for the first time—a 'joyous' reading of Kafka: a *Gaya Scienza* of Kafka's work.

Free of the "three most tiresome themes" of the interpretation of the law, Deleuze and Guattari are led to propose a conception of the relation of law to desire that allows them to call into question all the ambiguities and semi-obscurities that weigh down all the commentaries on Kafka's work. For them, since the law that is constantly referred to in Kafka no longer lends itself to an anthropological or theological explanation, the entire economy of that strange "work," and in particular its relation to desire (of writing, reading, and loving), has to be reinterpreted. And not only has the nature of the law been "misinterpreted," but the status and role of desire in Kafka's work have not fared any better. Deleuze and Guattari are the first to underscore the importance and force of desire in Kafka. As they reveal, this desire cannot be placed in a relation (of dependence) with a lack or even with the law in general, with a localized "natural" reality (the substantial "object" of my desire), or with worldly pleasure (above all the "carnivalesque"). As Deleuze and Guattari say in an essential passage in this book: "*where one believed there was the law, there is in fact desire and desire alone. Justice is desire and not law.*"[26]

One can guess the consequences they will draw from such premises: since desire is the effective "operator" of an assemblage where everybody—officials, judges, lawyers, artists, men, women, and so forth—is held, it becomes obvious why neither a lack nor a privation (of a transcendent meaning, for example) *gives* or causes desire; on the contrary, one can *lack* something only in relation to an assemblage from which one is excluded, but one *desires* only as a function of an assemblage where one is included: if only, as Deleuze says, in an "association of banditry or revolt."[27]

Thus, we can better understand what was lacking in Benjamin's attempt to reach an interpretation by means of *"gesture" à la Kafka* or the *Talmud*: by making law into a substance and desire (for justice) into an exigency that, if not transcendent, is external to the assemblage where every subject is only one piece of a complex montage, he has to hypostatize a nature of justice and of the law. He also has to derive desire from a lack or a law that transcends the subject or, if you will, from a law that the subject has "forgotten" and that is waiting to reemerge into the light.[28] According to Deleuze and Guattari, conversely, if justice doesn't lend itself to representation, it is not because justice is inaccessible or mysteriously hidden, but because it is desire:

> Desire could never be on a stage where it would sometimes appear like a party opposed to another party (desire against the law), sometimes like the presence of the two sides under the effect of a superior law that would govern their distribution and their combination.[29]

Thus, the following conclusion is drawn:

> If everything, everyone, is part of justice, if everyone is an auxiliary of justice, from the priest to the little girls, this is not because of the transcendence of the law but because of the immanence of desire.[30]

This last version—very "Kafkaesque" indeed—of the avatars and metamorphoses of desire reveals that for Kafka there is never any need for a representative to intercede between him and his desire, just as there is no need for an intermediary between the "work" of the text and the reader. Because it is *immanent*, the desire that traverses Kafka's work doesn't even require what Benjamin, in referring to Father Malebranche (!), claims for Kafka himself: for instance, the possession of *attentiveness*, "the natural prayer of the soul." On the contrary, Kafka knew that to find justice—the justice that he was seeking, that traversed him—it was necessary to move, to go from one room to another, from office to office, from language to language, and from country to country, always following his desire.

To find the "key" to Kafka's work, Deleuze and Guattari haven't sought to *interpret it*; they didn't seek to relate it to some single, transcendent law. Like K., the man of the immanent quest following the line of infinite flight, they have tried to grapple with the extraordinary machine of expression that Kafka set to work and have taken up the task of rewriting the quest to infinity, interminably. In reading this short but very dense book, we find, in place of infinite *exegesis*, a reading of Kafka's work that is *practical*: "continuum of desire, with shifting limits that are always displaced."[31] It is this procedure in action, this continuous process, and this field of immanence that Deleuze and Guattari have tried to help us traverse with a Kafka freed from his interpreters.

Translated by Terry Cochran

7

On the Concept of "Minor Literature": From Kafka to Kateb Yacine

> *We would call this a blur, a mixed-up history, a political situation, but linguists don't know about this, don't want to know about this, since, as linguists, they are "apolitical; pure scientists."*
>
> Deleuze and Guattari, *Kafka: Toward a Minor Literature*

In 1975, when Gilles Deleuze and Félix Guattari presented their short book on Kafka, many critics thought that the thesis defended in it could be chalked up to the militant "schizoanalysis" of *Anti-Oedipus*. For such critics, as for other skeptical readers of Deleuze and Guattari, this book was merely a more popular way of defending the ideas that they had previously put forward: linguistic pragmatism, desiring-machines, lines of flight, and other deterritorializing "Bodies without Organs."[1] With the benefits of hindsight, it is much clearer now that this seemingly marginal book was not based on a need for publicity or propaganda; rather it was a book that ushered in a sound, new way of thinking and writing, and—more importantly—it was a text that discovered a new theoretical "continent": that of "minor literature." Indeed, before Deleuze and Guattari took on the task of bringing to light what is at stake (politically and ideologically, but also pragmatically and experimentally) in Kafka's work, Kafka still enjoyed a secure place in the hierarchy of "great authors"; and one could hardly have thought it possible to discover such a theoretical time bomb within his "canonized" texts. If there were critics who dared broach the question of whether or not it was necessary to "burn Kafka" for the heresy of not conforming to genre codes or to the laws of narratology, no one was truly prepared to disclose the fact that Kafka's work had sufficient resources to allow it to be no longer liable to the sort of questioning to which it had been subjected until that point. Kafka's name was still inextricably connected to a conception of literature according to which Flaubert, Goethe, Hegel, Marx, and Freud called the shots; only by invoking all these names in relation to Kafka could one claim access to his work and become one of the "initiated." Later, undoubtedly because Kafka's polymorphous work—somewhat in the sense in which Freud speaks of "polymorphous" sexuality—continued to resist the psychological analyses to which it was subjected, it was even to be pushed in the direction of theology and the Kabala.

All this commotion would undoubtedly have continued or even escalated— has Kafka not been imagined as visiting professor at an American university in a short story by Philip Roth?![2]—had not Deleuze and Guattari intervened with their gentle jolt. This jolt was the result not of a new attempt to enrich Kafka's work artificially by trying to "swell it up through all the resources of symbolism, of oneiric, of esoteric sense, of a hidden signifier,"[3] nor from a new attempt at a totalizing interpretation of Kafka's work; on the contrary, the break that Deleuze and Guattari brought about came from the radical reversal of this "perspective." For Deleuze and Guattari, the revolution that Kafka introduced is not the outcome of any particular philosophical proposition; neither does it stem from this or that thematic invention or rhetorical *dispositio*, but rather from the enactment of new operational principles for literature: in Kafka's hands, literature refuses to play the game of what people call "literature (with a capital L)"; for him literature becomes experimental, but in a new sense. Indeed, for Kafka literature is no longer related to the desire to tell extraordinary and edifying stories; nor is it a question of inventing a new style or improving upon what the "masters" did, in the hope of relieving what Bloom calls the "anxiety of influence." It is the creation of a new regime of writing that enables us to account for what the writer currently apprehends as a situation of "underdevelopment" with which he or she experiments as if it were an extreme solitude or desert. The Kafka that Deleuze and Guattari give us anew is no longer seen as a writer preoccupied with the question of deciding in which language he should write, but rather as the writer who for the first time radically throws open the question of "literature" to the forces and the differences (of class, race, language, or gender) that run through it.

As we discussed in the previous chapter on Kafka, creating the concept of "minor literature" with respect to Kafka's work, Deleuze and Guattari have brought about not merely a simple reterritorializing revaluation of literature, but a drastic change of the entire economy of "literature" itself as a compendium of hierarchically ordered literary genres or as a center of subjectification. Literature no longer begins with man in general—*Der Mensch uberhaupt*—but rather with this particular man or that particular woman: here a Jew, a Czech, one who speaks Yiddish and Czech but writes in German in a Prague ghetto; later on a Berber, but of Algerian nationality, who speaks French and Arabic but who must write in French for an illiterate public; or again, a Mexican American who speaks Spanish at home but writes in English. "How many people," Deleuze and Guattari ask forcefully, "today live in a language that is not their own? Or no longer, or not yet, even know their own and know poorly the major language that they are forced to use? This is the problem of immigrants, and especially of their children, the problem of minorities, the problem of a minor literature, *but also a problem for all of us*: how to tear a minor literature away from its own language, allowing it to challenge the language and making it follow a sober revolutionary path? How to become a nomad and an immigrant and a gypsy in relation to one's own language? Kafka answers: *steal the baby from its crib, walk the tightrope*."[4]

In this short passage, we already have enough to go on to submit without fear of going astray that in the effort to reread Kafka, to tear him away from high literature and make him the precursor of a radically new political literature, there is not the least desire—not even a repressed one—to rediscover a canon or to canonize literature all over again.[5]

From such a perspective, writing quickly acquires a network of overcoming determinations that will prohibit the writer from ever assuming a preexisting identity, language, or even subjectivity. Being a "minor" writer, in the sense that Deleuze and Guattari give the expression on the basis of Kafka's work, is no longer a matter of a simple aesthetic choice, but the result of an exigency—no longer seen as dependent on the mere will of a subject felt as transparent to itself but on an existential situation, as it were. However, having no standard or canonical means of expression at its disposal—no abstract universal in the form of *a single* national language, *a single* ethnic affiliation, *a single* prefabricated cultural identity—this existential situation calls into being a new economy of writing and of reading. The utter uniqueness of this situation is what shapes the three principal characteristics that Deleuze and Guattari identify in what they will henceforth include in the category of "minor literature."[6]

The first fundamental characteristic has to do with the forces that determine the relationship that the writers concerned have with the languages involved. "'A minor literature doesn't come from a minor language; it is rather that which a minority constructs in a major language," write Deleuze and Guattari, who proceed to elaborate as follows: "The first characteristic of minor literature in any case is that in it language is affected with a high coefficient of deterritorialization."[7] This characterization clearly describes the situation of a writer such as Kafka "himself" as a Jew living in Prague who, with no other language than German really available as a cultural medium, will have to leave behind his mother tongue and begin to write in a foreign language. Whence the "impasses," the series of "impossibilities" that will confront him: the "impossibility of not writing, ... the impossibility of writing other than in German, the impossibility of writing in German."[8] I have said that this is clearly Kafka's "himself," but it is easy to see that such also is the situation of the Algerian, Moroccan, or Tunisian writer—or, more generally, that of the *non-French* Francophone writer: one from Canada, for example, from the Antilles or Senegal, or from Mauritania. These writers will experience the same "impossibility" of not writing, because "national consciousness, uncertain or oppressed, necessarily exists by means of literature."[9]

The second characteristic of "minor literatures," according to Deleuze and Guattari, is that "everything in them is political."[10] Referring to Kafka's work, they have no difficulty in showing that, contrary to the many *psychological* interpretations that had accustomed us to the idea of an "individualist" and/or "intimist" Kafka, or again, of Kafka as a fitting psychoanalytic subject (Marthe Robert), everything in Kafka is political—but not at all in the sense that he speaks of *nothing but* politics (in the politician's usage of the term); rather in the sense in which what takes precedence and governs the economy of daily life is no longer a "private affair," as Kafka says, but rather the concern of the political instance [*le politique*]. Here, the individual no longer appears as the product of a particular isolated consciousness (even an "unhappy" or "split" one), but rather as an arrangement ["*Agencement*"] of *n* elements—in other words a "machine" that functions only because it is always already connected to other "machines." Most of the time these are stronger and more efficacious machines—both more efficient and productive, to be sure—but also more "determinant": commercial machines, economic machines, but also the horde of bureaucratic and judicial machines.[11]

The third characteristic of minor literature that Deleuze and Guattari discuss and which, from a certain perspective, is derived directly from the first two "is that in it everything takes on a 'collective-value.'"[12] Indeed, because it is not the product of agents participating in a dominant culture or language and feeling themselves to be part of an always already constituted and transparent whole—because it results from a situation "where there are no possibilities for an individual enunciation"[13]—minor literature will appear as the literature in which every statement, however slight, refers to a collectivity, or even a community that is no longer *actual*, but essentially *virtual*. It is this state of affairs that gives minor literature its specific status and worth.[14] To speak in Althusserian terms, it is as if the system of "interpellations" that works fully in the regime of so-called great literature no longer works. We must not forget that the regime of high literature is an essential system because it constitutes the transparency of the subject and its adhesion to the great symbolic subject of French and German language and nationality. As Kafka says, and as Deleuze and Guattari aptly repeat, "What in great literature goes on down below, constituting a not indispensable cellar of the structure, here takes place in the full light of day, what is there a matter of passing interest for a few, here absorbs everyone no less than as a matter of life and death."[15]

Although recognizing here a founding and revolutionary theory—not only for "popular" literature and for literatures referred to as "marginal" but also for "literature" in general—a number of modern theorists have not failed to notice the limits or blind spots that, according to them, must be analyzed if the ruts of classical bourgeois literature are to be avoided.[16]

In Louis A. Renza's view, Deleuze and Guattari, in writing their book on Kafka and the concept of minor literature, had attempted to introduce an antiauthoritarian and anti-"great-author" conception that would also be "third-worldly." Such a conception would finally open up a space and give voice to the literatures that escape "totalizing formulations of formalist, oedipal, bourgeois or Marxist modes of organization."[17] In fact, according to Renza, for Deleuze and Guattari, minor literature exemplifies the type of relation to and practice of literature that they had already problematized in their *Anti-Oedipus*; as such, minor literature would be seen as inscribed squarely within the rather anarchist problematic that involved replacing the preformed formal entities of yesteryear—subject, author, representation, history, science—with a theory of "desiring-machines," of "deterritorialized flows," and/or of "bodies without organs." This change in perspective, moreover, is in Renza's eyes the best index of the distance separating Deleuze and Guattari's conception of literature—a conception that the notion of "minor" literature enables them to radicalize—and a Marxist conception, for example. In fact, Renza believes, because it has tended to deny the impact of desire on the economy of social exchanges—a denial effected by "fetishizing the discourse of labor"[18]—Marxism itself, despite its sensitivity to the question of oppressed minorities, has missed the revolutionary dimensions of desire and become liable to a schizoanalysis according to the rules. Moreover, it is the same logic that, according to Renza, allows Deleuze and Guattari to erect a guardrail around the oedipalizing intervention of Freudian psychoanalysis, and which leads them to criticize the Marxist regimentation (through labor) and domestication (through the "Oedipal nursery" [*la mise en pouponnière*]: "daddymommy-me"!) of the deterritorializing forces of desire. This critique of Freudo-Marxism is, in Renza's view, what causes Deleuze and Guattari to define an antibourgeois counterculture and to isolate a certain number of artistic works as characteristic examples of the new literature, i.e., of minor literature as a set of desiring-machines whose task it is to "short-circuit social production ... by introducing an element of dysfunction."[19]

From such a perspective, minor literature—or, more precisely, the work called "minor"—would be *the ideal anti-Oedipal text*, which would conform to the theoretical exigencies of schizoanalysis, and which would come to illustrate somehow the parameters that schizoanalysis has formally assigned to it. In other words, for Renza, it is not the case that the "minor" text with its own formal and ideological characteristics made it necessary to remodel the genres and to reshuffle the cards; on the contrary, it is that a prior theoretical demand assigned a revolutionary role and function to a text *singled out arbitrarily*. From this perspective, Deleuze and Guattari are not seen as truly innovative, nor as having helped free us from the hermeneutic circle in which we were caught; rather, by setting out to challenge the validity of the criteria assigning to literary texts their place within the hierarchy of genres and (bourgeois) values, but ignoring those elements that do not fit *their* theory, Deleuze and Guattari end up establishing a system of values as rigid and dogmatic as the previous one and bringing about a return to the ideal of a literary canon. The minor literature that is then mobilized will appear simply as one kind (of literature) among others and will therefore lose its specificity.[20]

If Renza's criticism gives food for thought and calls us to vigilance, it seems nevertheless not to take into account the *politico-historical mooring* from the vantage point of which Deleuze and Guattari have attempted to develop their analysis. For, if it is indeed true that the works of Kafka or of Edgar Allan Poe have been effectively coopted by the dominant bourgeois culture and strongly integrated into the literary canon, it is not automatically the case that they were predestined to suffer this fate. Quite the contrary, this recuperation could be one more indication of the potency of the majoritarian literary model, whose force derives precisely from the fact that it makes possible both the deflection of the destabilizing power [*dunamis*] of what can now be identified as minoritarian flows of texts, and their inscription after all as texts in the mainstream, the canon. In this sense, pulling Kafka onto the side of minor literature, or using his work as an occasion for a reshuffling and a new theoretical deal, may be conceived as a strategy enabling a new literary theorist to kill two birds with one stone: first, to reevaluate the criteria for the definition of what "literature" is and, second, to wrest from the grip of "literature" works that would not have been integrated into the canon without having their critical (political and ideological) force *neutralized*. From such a standpoint, to appropriate Kafka or to claim his authority for the sake of minor literature would not so much reinforce the established system, as show its boundaries suggesting a map of these at the same time as pointing to a way out of them.

It seems to me that David Lloyd understood these dynamics very well when, instead of focusing on the adequacy (or inadequacy) of any formal criterion of definition *in abstracto*, he set himself the task of providing us with new vital leads. In fact, as Lloyd sees it, while Renza may have succeeded in bringing out dramatically the contradictions inherent in all attempts to define the concept of minor literature—from Northrop Frye through Harold Bloom and Fredric Jameson, to Deleuze and Guattari—he nonetheless failed to assess correctly two fundamental elements: (l) the political function of the evaluations that he criticized and (2) the ideological function of the canon to which he referred without really managing to keep the necessary distance from it.[21] According to Lloyd, one of the touchstones for the questions posed in this debate is less the different conceptions of the subject or of subjectivity in general, less the redefinition and redistribution of literary genres for the sake of promoting a new canon, than it is the historico-political causes of the emergence of what we call, for the moment and for lack of a better term, "minor literature":

> Rather than shore up the notions of subjectivity that underpin canonical aesthetics, and rather than claiming still to prefigure a reconciled domain of human freedom in creativity as even surrealism does, *a minor literature pushes further the recognition of the disintegration of the individual subject of the bourgeois state, questioning the principles of originality and autonomy that underwrite that conception of the subject.*[22]

And in fact, as soon as we begin to analyze the intrinsic value of what is played out in texts that integrate the criteria proposed by Deleuze and Guattari—namely, deterritorialization of language, connection of the individual to political immediacy, collective arrangement of utterance—it becomes much easier to measure the scope of the changes that have occurred and to evaluate their nature. But the fact is that at this point the literary canon is no longer conceived in terms of an apolitical and ahistorical institutional norm concerning only the university and the school, or the ("individual") affair of the critics, but rather *as a normative institution* whose fate is linked to the nature of the *states* that are its counterparts. In such a context, minor literature can no longer be considered as just another *Genre category*, but must be seen as a concept that makes it possible to orient thought in completely different directions. If, for the time being, the literary canon fails to impose itself as a necessary and sufficient system of values, it is not only because literature has changed, but also because the institutions that used to present literature as eternal are in the process of disintegrating. There are minor literatures because peoples, races, and entire cultures were in the past reduced to silence. Minor literature appears, therefore, as the practical manifestation of that very voice: the voice of Algerians, for example, men and women who can begin to speak not only of the violence of colonization, but also of their own differences—the difference between what the state wants them to be and what they themselves want to experiment with; differences between, on the one hand, imperial conceptions of a "New World Order" that takes into account only the well-understood interests of affluent countries and, on the other, the "minor" conceptions that naturally belong to peoples continuing to struggle against the underdevelopment that is the legacy of years and sometimes decades of slavery; differences, finally, between East and West and, more recently, between North and South. These are some of the differences beginning to be heard *in literature* but also elsewhere, on the political scene, for example—at the price, most often, of the most costly sacrifices.[23]

In order to substantiate my claims, I would like to devote the rest of this chapter to the analysis, illustrated by the theatrical experience of the writer Kateb Yacine, of certain theoretical and practical difficulties that Francophone Algerian literature has encountered in its effort, despite the obstacles it faces, to create a language of its own, to elaborate a terrain, and to find an audience.

What is the situation of a country like Algeria at the time of independence? What terrain is available for getting a cultural life off the ground? What conditions confront Algerian writers? On the one hand, Algeria inherits a state of rampant mass deculturation, in view of which the very notion of an audience seems to be a luxury or, in the best of cases, a difficult objective to reach; on the other, the number of writers, artists (including filmmakers), and intellectuals is woefully insufficient in relation to its needs, and, for the most part, these writers and artists are wholly acculturated (almost all of them have, in the best of cases, been formed in the French school system). Not only, therefore, are (cultural) products and producers lacking, but the terrain itself is missing in which these products may take root and acquire a certain significance. That is to say that at the time of Algeria's independence, cultural problems in general, and those of literature in particular, were being posed not *in universal and abstract terms of expression*, but, first and foremost, in terms of regional and concrete territorialization. In other words, we were faced with an attempt to create from scratch—but not casually—on the ruins of a social community that escaped disaster and dislocation only *in extremis* a new collective subject, or even a national subject. It is evident here that every decision and every engagement was, to borrow one of Kafka's expressions, a question "of life or death": To create or recreate a terrain or to define something as a national characteristic sounds natural enough—but out of what? Out of the forgotten, obliterated past? Out of the ruins of popular memory? Out of folklore? Tradition? Which folklore, which tradition? In fact, not one of these instances was strong enough and cohesive enough to anchor a national culture. And in any case, even when raised in this way, the questions are not very clear and the problems remain abstract because, whether by means of folklore, the past, tradition, or anything else of that ilk, the creation of a specific, authentic culture requires first of all a solution to the problem of the medium through which it must—or can—be accomplished: specifically, the problem of language. In which language should one write? In which language should one communicate? Which language should be used on the radio, on television, in films? French—this "paper language" that only intellectuals and lettered people speak and read? Arabic? But which Arabic? The language of the educated or that of the street? Or again: What does one do with the Berber language? Prohibit it? Ostracize it?

These are the concrete and vital problems that explain the crucial tensions, contradictions, and difficulties encountered by every artist in Algeria and in any other former French colony: to write for the writers, or to make films for the filmmakers, becomes an urgent question because, as we understand very well by now, every one of the choices they make is a *founding* choice; each one of their words carves out the very flesh of the nation to come. In all cases, it is a matter of creating the missing terrain—for the terrain is indeed missing—though from a certain point of view what is missing is also the people itself.[24] It is a matter of finding a way out from the labyrinth of languages: a matter of staking one's territory like an animal, of never leaving one's *Umwelt*—with the understanding that this declaration of a missing people is not a renunciation, but rather "the new basis on which it is founded."[25]

We know today that this "lack," as well as the movements of deterritorialization that accompany it, is inseparable from the problem of language: the situation of Francophones in a country that opts very rapidly for Arabization in schools and administrative bodies; the situation of Arab-speaking writers in a country with an illiteracy rate of over 8.5 percent, and with French still the dominant language everywhere; the situation of the Berbers in the mountains and the Tuaregs in the Sahara, forced to abandon their own languages as they leave the desert or the rural areas. What is to be done with this blur of languages? For Algerian writers, there have been only two possible paths to take. One has been to enrich the French language artificially, to "swell it up through all the resources—of symbolism, of oneirism, of esoteric sense, of a hidden signifier,"[26] an approach resulting in some of the texts of writers such as Mohammed Dib, Rachid Boujedra, and, to a certain extent, Nabile Farès. But such efforts have implied once more "a desperate attempt at symbolic reterritorialization based in archetypes"[27]—sexuality, blood, or death—that have only accentuated the break from the people. The alternative has been to move toward a greater "sobriety," a poverty of means, a "white writing" out of which have come texts such as Boujedra's *L'escargot entêté* or the poems and later novels of Dib.

Faced with these limitations, Yacine very soon leaves off writing novels and poetry in order to give himself entirely over to theatrical production. This was a "minor" genre in Algeria when Yacine laid hold of it at the beginning of the 1970s, but he made it into an extraordinary instrument of metamorphosis, transforming a situation of extreme cultural poverty and stagnation into a revolutionary process. Having understood very early on the importance of the linguistic element in the situation/circumstances Algeria was going through during that period, Yacine quickly seized on the advantages to be gained by exploiting the resources of the popular theater. He understood at any rate that it made no sense to promote a theater limited to spoken Arabic—be it the "vernacular" Arabic—in order to produce plays in a country with not one spoken language but rather several vernacular languages (Arabic, French, and Berber), each with its own temporality and its own terrain. Yacine understood as well that if independence had emancipated Algeria from its politico-administrative tutelage, it had not solved the problem of its relation to French as a vehicular language (of commercial exchange and bureaucratic transmission) and as a referential language (the instrument of politics and of *Gesellschaft*)! His understanding of this complex interplay, it seems to me, is what explains the affinities between his theater and the minor literature that Deleuze and Guattari present as emerging with Kafka. Yacine's theater, with the capacity to take all these elements into account, is able to function as a *practical* sociolinguistics and to fill the prevailing void. Because his work takes off from the same politico-historical premises as Kafka's, it is no surprise that it shares in the principal traits that characterize minor literature: Yacine has spontaneously transposed these features into his work.

The first thing that strikes the reader or the viewer of his plays is the treatment to which he subjects the languages he mobilizes. Yacine found a way to transform French in order to bend it to the needs of the cause he was defending: in order to speak to the people, to address the people, to lend it a voice when it was foreign to itself. He accomplishes this by means *of underdeveloping*—developing from below—French, in order to bend it to the political and ideological demands of his people, through the elimination of syntactic and lexical forms. We should not forget the taste for "innate genitality," as Antonin Artaud would have called it, in the semantic overload of words—an overload that often reaches the pitch of a cry, or of the popular song of Sheikh Mohammed el Anka and of Rai music.[28] Having said this, we must also acknowledge that Yacine was never oriented toward a cultural reterritorialization through spoken Arabic or Berber, and even less through a hyper-cultural usage of French or classical Arabic. On the contrary, since *both* French *and* Arabic were themselves deterritorialized in Algeria as in the entire Maghreb, Yacine chose to push ever further in the direction of an increasingly *intensive* use of French. Indeed, although in his novels French syntax was still more or less respected, in his theater Yacine definitely dismisses "standard" French in order to draw the language nearer to the most disarticulated usages, which are also the closest to popular practice. Thus, besides the common vernacular languages used (Arabic, Berber), the knowledgeable public could also recognize the French of the immigrant worker, the French of the Berber speaker, or the French of a particular town (Algiers, Oran, or Constantine) mixed with the different accents that correspond to these. This mishmash helps explain the "becoming" that Yacine has his characters undergo: not only Tunisian president Bourguiba's becoming "short neck,"[29] but also the general's becoming "killer consonants" ["Q qui tue!"].[30]

The other characteristic feature of this theater is obviously its political dimension. Here, as well, we are faced with a theater that is political not because of the political themes it mobilizes, but essentially because it is a theater where every individual concern is always and immediately connected with politics. In Yacine's theater, if an individual concern is necessary, it is, above all, insofar as it is always another story, a much larger and more complex one—the story of colonization, most definitely, but also the story of racism, of the prison and the psychiatric asylum, of the French school system, etc.—all of these stories are vibrating within the private affair that stems from them and is played out in them. It is thus that the familial triangle will always find itself broken and exploded: in Yacine, one always abandons one's mother (the motherland) and one's father at one remove, a phony father or a stepfather. The fact is that family ties were historically subordinated to many other laws besides those of an "integrated" society: when it is not the father who emigrates, leaving his offspring to a brother or a cousin, it is the sons who leave never to return, and who end up inventing their own genealogy.[31] Familial relations will then be replaced by *blocks of alliance*, and the Algerian will find more affinity with a Portuguese immigrant in France or an African-American than with a compatriot who has accepted the "new deal" with one race, one language, and a single religion, Islam. In Yacine's universe, neither race nor religion, nor even language, sufficiently accounts for the mental world (affects and percepts) of a North African.

And it is in this context that one could say that Yacine's theater is a *political theater*, even a theater of grand politics, and not only a politicized theater. Whereas in dominant nations the family, the couple, and even the individual carry out their affairs as *private affairs*, in the theater of Yacine "the private affair merges with the social—or political—immediate."[32] Thus, as is also the case in the films of Glauber Rocha or in the novels of Gabriel Garcia Marquez, "the myths of the people, prophetism and banditism (and, I would add, emigration and the impossibility of return) are the archaic obverse of capitalist violence, as if the people were turning and increasing against themselves the violence that they suffer from somewhere else out of a need for idolization."[33] It is this violence that Yacine, without knowing or even caring about what Kafka may have done, mobilizes in his theatrical work, which he transforms into the largest imaginable arena of *agitprop*, which "is no longer a result of a becoming conscious, but consists of *putting everything into a trance*, the people and its masters, and the camera (in Yacine's case, the *mise-en-scène*) itself, pushing everything into a state of aberration, in order to communicate violence as well as to make private business pass into the political, and political affairs into the private."[34] For Yacine and for many writers and filmmakers from former colonies, as for Kafka, it is no longer a question of invoking myths in order to discover their archaic sense and structure, "but of connecting archaic myth to the state of the drives in an absolutely contemporary society, hunger, thirst, sexuality, power, death, worship."[35] As Yacine puts it, "plans are constantly being turned upside down!" Once again, it is not a matter of opposing "reality" (which one?) to myth, but, on the contrary, given the existing circumstances, of extracting from the myth a "lived actual" that would make it possible to account for the impossibility of living in the conditions that people have inherited. Such an impossibility could certainly drive people to madness but it can also be transformed into a revolutionary instrument for attending to first things first—for example, to the need to give life and voice to the people. But, for Yacine, defending the people no longer means hunkering down and retreating into oneself, but, on the contrary, showing that the people are never one but always plural: a multiplicity of peoples with intersecting destinies.[36]

In this way, popular theater takes over a potential revolutionary machine, not only for short-term ideological reasons, but rather because only this machine is able to fulfill the conditions of collective utterance that are nowhere else to be found. One must be blind therefore, or irresponsible, to accuse Deleuze and Guattari of not being political enough, or of being shortsighted from a historical point of view. One must be deaf not to hear the shout of joy let out by all writers living and writing in the conditions that they describe the day that they were able to count Kafka as one of their own and to add the multiple resources of his "minor" art to the instruments that they had created against the silence and the indifference of the literary *establishment*. Minor literature had long since made its *practical entry* into the history of literature; but its *theoretical entry* had yet to be made. Thanks to the work of Deleuze and Guattari, and judging by the renewed interest it is currently receiving and, above all, by the rich debates it has provoked, one can say that this theoretical entrance has taken place and all to the good of literature.

Translated by Jennifer Curtiss Gage

8

Becoming-Animal, Becoming-Political in Rachid Boudjedra's *L'escargot entêté*

Fantasies are never pregnant forms, but border or frontier phenomena ready to cross over to one side or the other. In short, Oedipus is strictly undecidable, it can be found everywhere all the more readily for being undecidable, and in this sense it is correct to say that Oedipus is strictly good for nothing.

Deleuze and Guattari, *Anti-Oedipus*, p. 149

Portrait of an illusion: one of the most striking phenomena for critics—and perhaps for literary critics in particular—is indeed the critical fecundity and pertinence of Deleuze and Guattari's concepts pertaining to literary texts and, more generally, of their artistic concepts (painting, cinema, music). We marvel at the fact that a certain text by Kafka, Döblin, Blanchot, Proust, or Mozart seems to have been written in the wake of what we find in conceptual form in the work of the two philosophers. But even more interesting and disturbing in certain respects is the existence of the reverse phenomenon in another "species" of critics. For these latter, it was not the philosophical and critical work of Deleuze and Guattari that unearthed an analytic or critical gem (on the quality of a musician's pulsed timing, intuition relating to an event, a line of flight, or the capture of a "haecceity," the singularity of an author's "becoming-animal," etc.) but, on the contrary, the perspicacity and poetic genius of the authors and creators "elected" by the two philosophers that led them to develop their theoretical problems and refine their concepts. If critics base their arguments on such premises, what is, perhaps sadly, missed in both cases is the specificity of the philosopher's work in relation to that of the creator of a work of art. Both are, in my opinion, empirical approaches which remove from the "encounter" between philosopher and artists everything that makes such an encounter a crucial moment in the creative process—in the process of the creation of concepts on the part of the philosopher, and in the process of the creation of percepts and affects on the part of artists. But let us not be mistaken: sending the former back to his concepts and the latter back to their "percepts" or "affects" does not imply in the least that both do not ride the same tide. A "real" concept carries as much affect as a literary text. And reciprocally, what Deleuze and Guattari define as "percepts" are never without critical or theoretical implications. The poetic force of a verse by Celan or Hölderlin does compel one to think.

It seemed important to signal some of these problems raised by the relation between Deleuze's critical texts and the works he interprets, in order to lay bare a number of risks or pitfalls: the "empirical" pitfall, as it was called earlier, of reducing the unknown and the new to the known; but most importantly the risk of missing the real nature of the "encounter" between a philosopher's thought and that of a writer, painter, or musician. What deceives us here and leads to this paradoxical situation is the fact that the Deleuzian approach itself seems very often to go in the direction of the illusion I am describing: the illusion that it would be from the reading of an admired author or a particular work that a certain concept is "born." We can even find a reason for such a misunderstanding, for example, in the first chapter of *The Logic of Sense*, which invites us to believe that Deleuze merely "extracted" his "logic" of sense from the works of Lewis Carroll and the paradoxes the latter created in *Alice in Wonderland*. Indeed, the preface of *Logic of Sense*, entitled "From Lewis Carroll to the Stoics," argues that "the privileged place assigned to Lewis Carroll is due to his having provided the first great account, 'the first great *mise en scène* of the paradoxes of sense.'"[1] If in this text Lewis Carroll is hailed as the first in the initial discovery of paradoxes of meaning, and more precisely of their "staging," then it seems necessary to highlight the conceptual terrain of this—which is precisely what Deleuze sets out to do in *The Logic of Sense* in what he calls an "attempt to develop a logical and psychological novel."[2]

Thus, when reading Deleuze too hastily and with too little care, we risk overlooking the fact that, despite appearances, the Deleuzian concepts and the properly Deleuzian philosophical problematic are not induced from the works he admires, but above all deduced by means of *prior theoretical labor*, which at the start owes nothing to the works that are elected. Moreover, Deleuze himself declared that this "new image" of sense found in Lewis Carroll or in the Stoics "is already closely linked to the *paradoxical constitution of the theory of sense*" and that it took this "logical and psychological novel" to draw this out.[3] As Anne Sauvagnargues has shown in her fine study of the Deleuzian conception of art, for Deleuze "art cannot be the subject of hermeneutic interpretation" since, "with Spinoza, [he] undertakes to critique all attempts that reduce art to the expression of a meaning which needs to be derived from the material of the piece."[4]

This implies that in his analyses, Deleuze never simply formalizes *in retrospect* what he "discovers" (by chance, or by accident?) in the writers he examines, but that he rather proceeds by way of inference according to his own method. It is as an experimenter in new theories, which he "draws" from his critical reading of the history of philosophy, psychoanalysis, and linguistics, that Deleuze shortlists, so to speak, the writers who will become part of his universe. We, thus, have to overthrow our traditional assumptions of the relation of art and philosophy: literature and art (cinema, painting, music) never function as an "illustration" or a confirmation of the validity of a Deleuzian concept. On the contrary, it is the newness of the concepts Deleuze creates (on the subject, on language, time, becoming, etc.) which allows us to "discover" the play of intensities in the works of art, as well as the ideas and the virtual images they contain. In this way, we can avoid saying that a novel, a film, or a musical piece is "Deleuzian," unless it has been directly inspired by Deleuze's work. To say that a work is "Deleuzian" would mean falling prey to what Bergson called the "retrospective illusion of the truth": I attribute an intuition or an idea to the author I am reading, which I have only been able to identify because I already held the concept that allowed me to decipher that intuition or idea. When under the spell of such an "illusion" one fails to see the true nature and effective critique of a philosophical concept worthy of its name.

By not acknowledging this situation, we run the risk of reducing the analysis of a text or œuvre to the mechanical "application" of the concepts at hand, instead of experimenting, instead of opening up new fields of investigation and exploration. Ultimately, we risk missing that which makes the encounter between a work of art and a philosophical analysis an experimental process, and not only (or not at all) a process of interpretation.⁵ And indeed, when we move from the simple "application" of concepts to an experimental mode which, for example, in Deleuze implies a becoming-animal, a becoming-imperceptible, or a becoming-woman, "everything changes" because, without warning, one finds oneself on the plane of consistency or immanence, which is necessarily perceived in its own right in the course of its construction: "experimentation replaces interpretation, now molecular, nonfigurative, and non-symbolic, the unconscious as such is given in micro-perceptions ... The unconscious no longer designates the hidden principle of the transcendent plane of organization, but the process of the immanent plane of consistency as it appears on itself in the course of its construction."⁶

As can be seen very well in this passage, Deleuze always insists on the moment of construction: the construction of adequate concepts, the construction of one or more planes of consistency on which one begins an analysis, and which in turn always goes back to determining the conditions of a problem. I have permitted myself this small theoretical detour for one rather simple reason: if one wants to put Deleuzian concepts to work in the analysis of texts, one should be less concerned with emphasizing what Deleuze has done in this or that "case" or with trying to find more texts which support still "better" the legitimacy and/or productivity of the concepts he created; one should rather ask oneself what newness these concepts allow us to discover in the texts under analysis.⁷

Let us take for example a text like *L'escargot entêté* (*The Stubborn Snail*, 1985 [1977]) by the Algerian writer Rachid Boudjedra. What, for example, would a classic psychoanalytic reading of the text yield? It would quite quickly become the banal story of a civil servant, a professional ratter, who dreams of ridding the city for which he is responsible of the five million rats that infest it and endanger the health and security of its inhabitants. In addition, the character (who happens to be also the story's intradiegetic narrator) is slightly perturbed—he notes down all the thoughts that cross his mind on small bits of paper which he hides in the twenty-two pockets of a jacket he never takes off, he still lives with his mother despite being in his fifties, and he is obsessed with the presence of a snail that he comes across in his garden every day. We have all the ingredients to seal the text off in a psychoanalytic line of interpretation.

Rachid Boudjedra does not exclude such a "line" by making his narrator an obsessive character who lives with a timer in his hand and a calendar in his pocket, a sexually repressed individual who moans constantly about his indulgence for onanism, an unrepentant misogynist, who notes that:

> The civil service has difficulty recruiting people. Young people have prejudices. Not to mention women! They don't stay in their job. They get jaundice and, after a few weeks, go and work elsewhere or get married. They like to be wed. Even if it's just the one time. Why this obsession? Reproduction! The only thing of real interest to them. Like rats and mice.[8]

A character who, to top it all, has an infamous authoritarian personality, telling anyone who will listen that "blind obedience is the essential quality of a civil servant,"[9] someone who does not hesitate to loudly proclaim his "infallible devotion to the state,"[10] and that he fears he might "transfer his affection"[11] onto the rats for whose extermination he is responsible.[12] Other elements reinforce the pertinence, to a certain extent, of a psychoanalytic reading of Boudjedra's text: beyond (or in addition to?) the fascination with rats, there is, of course, the ubiquitous presence of the mother, as obsessive and disquieting as the presence of the snail that haunts and taunts the narrator. Furthermore, there is also the memory of the castrated father upon which a hysterical mother—who has become "phosphorescent" by repeatedly pushing aside the father, and who is "daubed coarsely on the inside,"[13] as the narrator suggests—has imposed her will; and, last but not least, we have the handicapped sister whose only dream is to marry a brother steeped in frustration and in repressed feelings of all kinds, misogynist, asocial, and a misanthrope who would never consider the idea of marriage.

As we can see, nothing is missing from this nosographic portrait in order for us to read the story's protagonist as a very banal neurotic, and to complement such a reading by recourse to intertextual references, which would allow us to better situate Boudjedra's text in the literary field. In this case, we would summon the debt that the text owes, for example, to Gregor Samsa's "becoming-cockroach" in Kafka's *The Metamorphosis*, or to Beckett's *Molloy* whom Boudjedra's narrator calls to mind. While Molloy never ceases to pass the stones he sucks on from one pocket to another, the protagonist of Boudjedra's novel multiplies the number of pockets that absorb the innumerable notes he endlessly takes—on the mood of the day, on the poisons he feeds to the rats, on onanism, snails, labyrinths, on his subordinates at the office, on the morals of his fellow citizens, and, finally, on his psychological "emotions." Even his proximity to and interest in the rats and his obsession with this "perverse" *Stylommatophora* that the snail represents can be interpreted in psychoanalytic terms. Also in this regard, Boudjedra makes it easy for us by constantly establishing the link between the relationship the narrator sees between rats, faith, the State, history, war, and migrations on the one hand, and the links that connect the snail to sexuality, desire, sexual difference, and generally to everything that relates to the morals of a so-called modern society on the other hand. While for the narrator the rat "is a seismograph,"[14] for the reader the narrator is, despite his denials and reactionary conservatism, in his own way, a philosopher as well as a well-informed political analyst and a sociologist. For is he not constantly mindful of the ills of the society in which he lives? And is it not also true that through his observations we discover the damaging effects of "nepotism," urban sprawl, the abuse of power, state censorship, and of the intolerance of anticommunism and religious dogma?

It is interesting to note at this point that, from a Deleuzian–Guattarian point of view, nothing is missing from this portrait because "it is all there":[15] "a becoming-animal not content to proceed by resemblance and for which resemblance, on the contrary, would represent an obstacle or stoppage."[16] Indeed, the narrator never "takes" himself to be a rat, nor does he take on any of their traits. He does not imitate them and he never gives up on his desire to exterminate them. He declares that he knows them well, which shows that he never leaves the firm ground of his "human" identity. The thought of acting the rat or of abandoning his ambition to be the greatest ratter never crosses his mind. In his own way, he is a Doctor Frankenstein:

> At dawn, I mix my poisons, while the rats I keep in my cellar are sound asleep, gorged with treats. I know them well. There is always one of them that keeps guard to alert the others, whenever I come close. I know what to do. I know their psychology. My dosages are renowned among specialists ... The tranquility of the city is at stake, if not its economic prosperity. But I do not want words to be interpreted as an attempt to politicize a merely zoological phenomenon.[17]

We can see that the line separating human beings from animals is clearly marked. That is to say, if there is a becoming-animal, and particularly a becoming-rat, it will have to occur by way of a very different process than imitation or resemblance. No analogy or representative series could lead from human to rat. Rats, we are told, have "their psychology" and many other characteristics which give the narrator's becoming-animal its own specificity.

At the same time, what this short novel also shows is a becoming-molecular: "the proliferation of rats, the pack"—there are over five million in the city, the narrator claims—"that undermines the great molar powers of family, career, and conjugality."[18] Here too, "it is all there," everything that Deleuze and Guattari tell us about becoming-animal seems to apply word for word to this novel. As shown above, the protagonist may be presented as a profoundly perturbed human being, and yet it is through him, through what he experiences on a daily basis, that it becomes clear that something is rotten in the city—is it Algiers, or Oran, or Constantine? He is our intercessor, our negotiator, our night watch: his phobias, his fears, his anxieties, his repulsions as well as his most personal tastes serve to reveal what is dysfunctional in the family, disorganized in the work sphere, broken in so-called romantic relationships. As the narrator says, "large networks of multiple interferences … Another labyrinth under crystal."[19] Although he claims to have no interest in politics, every gesture, every judgment he passes on the society in which he lives, has political implications.

It appears as if his incapacity to live like everyone else, so to say his neurosis, and the ignoble character of his profession—he lives more among rats than humans—become the conditions for the appearance of certain haecceities which give the city that he lives in its tonality and substance: the revolting squalor covering the streets, the din of the mosques' loudspeakers calling to prayer, the inhabitants' ignorance of the dangers posed by hordes of rats that engulf the city, their inability to hear what is being said and done in their name by the State, by the muezzin, by civil servants, and also their lack of sensitivity to what proliferates around them, mirroring what goes through the confused mind of the narrator, and risking destroying the population in the most terrible ecological catastrophe:

> murmurs of mute syllables which fall back on my skull like soft snow. Shimmering itch. Hatchings. Stripes. Cracks. Partial sentences tainted with saffron. Residues of crushed dreams. Nauseous gulps. Salivated burps. Alkaline rigidities. Purplish caking. Vinous macerations.[20]

But having arrived at this point, we have to ask if all the dimensions which play a role in a becoming (still in a Deleuzian–Guattarian sense of the term) have been accounted for. It seems that at least three other stages are still missing in the truly initiatory journey of a becoming.

(1) The stage of what Deleuze and Guattari call the "evil" or "baleful choice." As we know already, Boudjedra's narrator lives among rats, but he cannot disregard the snail that stubbornly crosses his path every day and seems to question everything he believes in. It seems as if at a certain point he does not know any more to which saint he should devote himself: the rat or the snail. Everything in his head becomes confused, everything in his body becomes muddled, and he finds himself gradually caught up in a metabolic metamorphosis which erases all human "borders."

(2) We also cannot but attend to the particular assemblage that is formed, "a war machine or criminal machine," which can also here "reach the point of self-destruction."[21] (As is apparent, I am simply following step-by-step Deleuze and Guattari's determinations of what plays a part in a becoming-animal in general.) The narrator in *L'escargot entêté* notes that "[all] my poisons and all my mixtures will be useless. Sexual hormones are the future in this deadly fight. Only they can strike at the root of evil. That is to say, diminish reproduction until the species has entirely disappeared."[22] If we know of the narrator's deep disdain for what he calls "the masses" and that he tends to assimilate them with rats—saying that "[t]he masses like to be taken care of. So do rats"[23]—we can better take measure of the type of genocidal or eugenic assemblage he may have entered.[24] Clearly, another parameter of what characterizes the becoming-animal according to Deleuze and Guattari has full hold here. We have something of the order of a destructive and criminal war machine here, which leads to the narrator's self-destruction. This significantly means that becoming-animal does not necessarily imply a liberation or an enrichment for the "subject" who undergoes it, but rather an experimentation that one must know how to manage. Hence also the numerous warnings by Deleuze and Guattari against hazardous experiments and improvisation with drug use.[25]

But how can we explain such a play of correspondences between what originates in theory and what is found in a work of art? Is this purely accidental or something entirely different? The demonstration undertaken in the previous sections of this essay shows that what is at stake is not an empirical description of this strange thing that Deleuze and Guattari call becoming-animal, but rather a haecceity, that is to say, "a mode of individuation very different from that of a person, subject, thing, or substance ... A season, a winter, a summer, an hour, a date."[26] In this sense, *L'escargot entêté* is a text that lends itself well to a Deleuzian–Guattarian analysis of becoming-animal, not because the main character is obsessed with the reproductive capacities of rats, snails, or pigs, but because the author has managed to find the mode of individuation that displays the relation of movement and rest between humans and animals—but also among humans themselves—of which life in the unnamed city of ... is made.[27]

> The city no longer reaches me ... She comes to me, unreal, blurry, almost obliterated. Nevertheless she does not cease to flourish with constructions and convulsions. Her excess of fat will kill her. Urban sprawl! I had noted down somewhere: she is a splattering sprung from the materials that made her, accumulated in an incredible bric-à-brac. A miracle of balance and the sea that gnaws at her! But, I confess, she carries her leprosy like a blue lace.[28]

What a magnificent, dark description of a city which one can barely discern. It will take the madness and passion of a ratter to uncover the haecceities that shape it. Our impression that we are dealing here indeed with a becoming-animal as a means to capture a haecceity is further reinforced by the correspondences we can see with the two other determinations at stake in a becoming-animal, as Deleuze and Guattari define it. Indeed, as mentioned above, in Boudjedra's novel, the narrator is also the subject of (3) a "circulation of impersonal affects, an alternative current that disrupts signifying projects as well as subjective feelings, and constitutes a nonhuman sexuality."[29] He says and writes that he "no longer has contours, or borders," and his relation to genital sexuality is rather problematic. After all, he worships Onan and his practices.[30] We also know that he has no intention to marry, nor to have a romantic or sexual relationship with a person of the opposite sex. It is this, among other things, that pushes him to enter into "an irresistible deterritorialization that forestalls attempts at professional, conjugal, or Oedipal reterritorialization."[31] The omnipresent relation to his mother plays out in the proverbs he inherited from her and the disgust for sexual relations and sexual reproduction that she impressed upon him, and it is interesting to note that the proverb that comes back most often in the narrator's notes and memories alludes—surely neither innocently nor by chance—to a becoming-rat: "My mother used to say: the rat's son is a rodent."[32]

Like Deleuze and Guattari's little Hans in *A Thousand Plateaus*, Rachid Boudjedra's narrator is caught up in an assemblage that constantly makes him drift from one dimension of a becoming-subject to another, a becoming-subject that cannot be reduced to a totalizing transcendental signifier—the proverbs and moral sayings of the mother, the father's absence, the sister's expectations, the little schemes of the bus driver who drives him to work, the behavior of the employees at the ministry, as well as the narrator's sexual disorders, all of these constantly restart the attempts to identify with a unified self. But it seems as if the narrator is faced with two opposing metaphysics: one, as we saw, which his becoming-rat pulls in the direction of a (state) control of affects and the most rigid interiorization of the law, social rules, cleanliness, work, profitability, and sexual and moral taboos, all of which make him see himself (a little more every day) as an "agent of the state"; and another (metaphysics or "ontology") that is a result of his becoming-snail and incessantly shatters the politico-moral edifice he struggles to put in place as an obedient and untiring civil servant. Contrary to the rat, the snail, as a good *Stylommatophora*, spurs him toward a very different political economy and toward a morality that is opposed to the first one in every regard.

The snail's hermaphroditism ensnarls the narrator in a becoming—perhaps a spiral becoming if we consider what he says on myths relating to snails: "So the snail's spiral appears like the order at the heart of change, and like a balance in imbalance."[33] Or one might as well say that his becoming-snail enables him to discover dialectics, marking a becoming-Hegelian of the narrator, a becoming which radically puts into question the clean conscience he has in regard to the neat separation of genders: being both male and female, the snail invokes a non-human sexuality that greatly perturbs the narrator and causes him to experience emotions that overthrow his normal routine and tear his habitual value system to shreds. A moment comes when the narrator no longer knows whether he has a rat, mouse, or snail in his head: "Accumulated superimpositions. Conoidal series. But essentially: sticky threads *that get tangled around my head* and made of the mucus used by the snail to close off the holes it lives in at a slow pace, winter and summer. There are also *strange noises in my skull* that sound like mice gnawing."³⁴

Thus, even if the narrator appeared ambivalent toward rats at the start of the narrative, it quickly becomes clear that the attention he pays to them exceeds his professional duties: the rats become an object of fascination and, at the same time, an opportunity to discover and to acquire some of his (aesthetic, political, sexual) preferences. Indeed, he spends much time—despite being so frugal with it—studying rats meticulously, at first scientifically, then rapidly in historical, literary, and aesthetic terms:

> I like the mist and rain drops on top. They draw labyrinths in zigzags similar to the rats' itineraries described by Amr Ibn Bahr (166–252 of the Hegira) in his Book of Animals [*Traité des Animaux*]. Because the rat does not run, it zigzags. It ignores the straight line! It meanders.³⁵

One of the first instances of a convergence between the narrator and these animals he claims to abhor is the labyrinth. It occurs as the lifting of a repression: the narrator thought that only the straight line was the right choice, but he discovers affinities with the Rhizomatic trajectory of the rat. This is in any case the first form that his becoming-rat takes: a taste for "routes of escape," for the "capacity to take side roads," and the art of "beating dead ends."³⁶ In one of his secret notes, he writes:

> I have noted down everything … Know thy enemy. It's a common principle in strategy and tactics. Otherwise imprisonment beckons. Rats have their own way of circling objects. The labyrinth is a gradual imprisonment. It points to extremely rich symbolism and its history is fascinating.³⁷

As stated earlier, becoming-rat does not work by resembling a rat but rather by an a-parallel encounter of certain points that provoke a system of resonances *sui generis* in the subject that experiences it: here, a hitherto unknown interest in labyrinths and a taste for meandering paths.

Before, the narrator ran, but now he meanders, he walks, acts, and thinks in zigzags. While he used to concentrate solely on the science of poison, he now spends his time reading veritable "*Traités*" on war and becomes passionate about history. This means that his becoming-rat now also occurs by way of a becoming-historian and becoming-researcher which paves the way for a multiplicity of other "interests," such as, for example, the study of the nature of space, of strategic and tactical spatial assemblages of the human habitat, of labyrinths, and more generally of what he calls "the combinatorics" of different conceptions of space and time:

> Transcription wears me out and combinatorics fascinate me. A dream of lace. I fell asleep reading the Book of Animals by Abou Othman Amr Ibn Bahr (166–252 of the Hegira). I was just relishing in the description of the way in which a rat builds its labyrinths ... I could no longer go to the office. Strange dream, *with lines zigzagging along the meanders of my brain, worn out by transcription and combinatorics*.[38]

Later in the narrative we discover that the narrator's fascination with combinatorics does not stop at his interest in the rats' art of managing their habitat, but that it extends also to a fascination he has for another "combinatorics," namely that linked to myths relating to snails—or does it double, oppose, or complete his fascination for rats?

> If the Romans told fortune by reading animal entrails, ancient Mexicans read in the patterns on snail shells. Undoubtedly, Aztecs disappoint me. They worshipped said animal to the point of seeing, in the variation of its growth marks, a complex and fascinating combinatorics ... Indeed, myself, as worn out and fascinated as I am by transcription and combinatorics, I would have been the first to become passionate about the shells of Gastropods![39]

From one secret annotation to another, the reader discovers that, while the becoming-rat gives the narrator his sense of superiority vis-à-vis his employees and the "masses," this is always accompanied—or even doubled—by this border phenomenon of the snail. As soon as he has become an erudite and fine connoisseur of the complex architecture of labyrinths, he shows only contempt for those who ignore the labyrinth's importance in their lives: "Silas Haslam, a 19th century surveyor, dedicated a thick volume [to labyrinths]: A General History of Labyrinths. I tell this to my subordinates. They do not understand. They snigger."[40]

Once more, the ratter, the "exterminating angel" for rats, is transformed, gradually, into a historian fascinated with human civilizations and migrations in an a-parallel becoming to that of the rats. Although the narrator denies any interest in politics, by way of his movement through the intersecting history of humans and rats he comes to take a position and discovers that his becoming-rat throws him continually in the arena of political stakes and struggles and that he passes judgment on everything, including the politics of his country's leaders. The rats' zigzagging itinerary and their "combinatory" art lead him little by little to discover that he has always taken part and has always been a participant in political matters.

> One only needs to take a map of invasions to precisely trace the itinerary they [the rats] have taken. No matter how often I repeat this to my employees, they don't listen to me. They say it's politics and that they don't understand it. As if I was fascinated by politics. Not at all![41]

This is a handsome "Denegation" or denial which shows that, to some extent, the narrator knows very well that what he does and says is political, and that the rat "business" is a political matter in as much as it relates to the hygiene and health of a people, as well as to the responsibility of politicians and civil servants. And undoubtedly, this is also what enables an understanding of the other "game" which he is passionate about, and which he shares with the rats: the art of camouflage. The rats' art of escaping and of covering the tracks is all the more fascinating for the narrator as it corresponds perfectly to his own compulsion to cover his tracks, to hide his most intimate thoughts—his "emotions" as he likes to say—by multiplying the number of pockets where he hides what he calls his "little writings." Soon, this becomes an art of writing, an art of writing as camouflage or as Deleuze would say, a "power of the false" which slowly takes shape:

> Where did I read that a large city consumes five hundred tons of food every day? I must have noted it down on a piece of paper and transcribed it on an index card marked: economic misdeeds. Easy to check. My files are up to date. My little writings never stay more than twenty-four hours in my pockets. I sometimes get muddled but I quickly redress the situation.[42]

Rapidly, we realize that the narrator has (at least) two "writings" in stock: one is the writing of his daily notes which consists, he says, of "indescribable hieroglyphics" and castrations, and the other is the "assiduous" and "legible" writing, which even his secretary can easily decipher.[43] What seemed at first merely a question of orthography and diligence for the narrator turns out to be the execution of a true poetics. And we come to a moment when the art of camouflage and combinatorics that we perceived in the narrator must be to a certain extent transferred, so to speak, to the author himself. Does the author himself not proceed like our ratter? Does he not constantly displace his notes and hoard his index cards? What do we know of these cards of his? How many of them have been disclosed? Which pocket is still hidden from us? How many "pockets" are there in total? What are the links between the pockets?

As we can see, it is once more a (labyrinthine) question of combinatorics—that is to say of an assemblage of elements that first need to enter into a plane of composition, and then, if "all goes well," into a plane of consistency, which will allow the writer to transmit some of his ideas (on politics, morality, the social administration of a population's health, art, or religion) without being stopped by state censorship or self-censorship. We are, thus, not surprised to realize that the narrator's becoming-rat corresponds to the author's becoming-imperceptible, who will have needed to mobilize all the resources of the power of the false and of camouflage (the multiplication of pockets, the main character's neurosis, a pack of rats, a stubborn snail) to achieve this, precisely by way of erasing [*en raturant*] everything that may give him away to the authorities and to his superiors, and by avoiding political blunders as much as possible. "A life. A void. A useless word. To cross off. Or to hide in the twenty-first pocket so that no one comes to know what I really feel. Only my social role must emerge from my personality: chief officer of the city's pest control."[44]

Indeed, of Rachid Boudjedra's personality only his social role transpires: the writer's! The reason for this is that as a writer, he proceeds in disguise behind his "sinister" doubles: a civil servant who is obsessed with his work as a ratter, and a snail that stubbornly puts into question all of his preconceived opinions and beliefs. We then understand all the more clearly why Deleuze and Guattari have intimately linked every becoming-animal worthy of its name to a becoming-imperceptible. By slipping into the skin of a ratter who is fascinated by rats and obsessed with a snail, Boudjedra has been able to suppress everything "that prevents us from slipping between things and growing in the midst of things,"[45] in the midst of human—all too human—affairs by mobilizing the labyrinthine resources of a becoming-rat and by playing off the dialectical richness of the spiral that inspires him to the slow progression of a snail towards new shores.

These are a few lines of thought that one can draw from a Deleuzian–Guattarian reading of a text like Boudjedra's. The analysis hopes to have shown that *L'escargot entêté*—Boudjedra's novel—"is" not Deleuzian but that we have submitted it to a becoming-Deleuzian by choosing to abandon a psychoanalytic line of reading, and to move instead into the direction of a quest shared by both: that of the minimal conditions for the capture of a haecceity. In Deleuze and Guattari, this appears in the form of the concept of becoming, and in Boudjedra as the shadow that engulfs a city and soon after an entire country, like a lead weight.

Translated by Patricia Krus

Notes

Preface

1   Gilles Deleuze and Félix Guattari, *A Thousand Plateaus: Capitalism and Schizophrenia*, trans. Brian Massumi (Minneapolis: University of Minnesota Press, 1987), "Becoming-Intense, Becoming-Animal, Becoming-Imperceptible," p. 251 (emphasis added).
2   Gilles Deleuze, writing on Foucault, quoted in blog "*Le corps utopique de Michel Foucault – De la philosophie pratiquée comme 'sport extrême*'": http://labophilo.blogspot.com/2013/05/le-corps-utopique-michel-foucault-de-le.html; emphasis added. Where no published translation is cited, English versions of quotations from French are by Jennifer Curtiss Gage.
3   François Regnault, "La Vie Philosophique," *Magazine littéraire* 30, no. 257 (September 1988), special issue on Gilles Deleuze, *Un Philosophe Nomade*.
4   Gilles Deleuze, in *Lendemains, Études Comparées sur la France*, No. 53 (June 1989), ed. Bensmaïa. Deleuze's letter was written as a response to the question I had posed to him on the philosopher's relationship to "non-philosophers" and as a gesture of gratitude to the researchers who had contributed texts on Deleuze's work: Alexandre Zavadil, Jean-Pierre Dubost, Bruno Paradis, Monique Scheepers, Pascal Levoyer, Philippe Encrenaz, Jean-Louis Leutrat, Jacob Rogozinski, and myself. This is the passage of the letter I am referring to: "The *Ethics* is a book of concepts (the second kind of knowledge), but also of affects (the first kind) and percepts (the third kind) too. Thus the paradox in Spinoza is that he's the most philosophical of philosophers, the purest in some sense, *but also the one who more than any other addresses nonphilosophers and calls forth the most intense nonphilosophical understanding*. This is why absolutely anyone can read Spinoza and be very moved, or see things quite differently afterward, even if they can hardly understand Spinoza's concepts. Conversely, a historian of philosophy who understands only Spinoza's concepts doesn't fully understand him. We need both wings, as Jaspers would say, just to carry us, philosophers and nonphilosophers, toward the same limiting point. And it takes all three wings, nothing less, to form a style, a bird of fire." Deleuze's letter was republished, without precise reference to its context, in

Pourparlers, 1972–1990 (Paris: Minuit, 1990). The English translation of that letter is to be found in Gilles Deleuze, *Negotiations*, trans. Martin Joughin (New York: Columbia University Press, 1990), pp. 164–6.

5 As Robert Sasso and Arnaud Villani clearly note in *Le Vocabulaire de Gilles Deleuze*, the refrain (*Ritornello*), far from being a "musical phrase that is repeated" like the Italian *ritorno*, is above all linked to Kierkegaardian repetition and to Nietzschean repetition in the sense of the "eternal return." See: *Le Vocabulaire de Gilles Deleuze*, Les Cahiers de Noesis No. 3, Spring 2003, C.R.H.I./UMR 6045, pp. 304–5; cf. Deleuze's introduction to his *Difference and Repetition*, trans. Paul Patton (New York: Columbia University Press, 1994), pp. 6–7. "It is a matter of bringing back—through *an exchange of codes and the value accrued in passage*, in a rhythm like a *space between* that throws all measures off balance—the singular universal opposed to 'the particularities of memory' and 'the generalities of habit.' In the refrain, there is this invention of 'vibrations, rotations, whirlings, gravitations, dances or leaps which directly touch the mind'" (Deleuze, *Difference and Repetition*, pp. 7–8). It is in *A Thousand Plateaus* that we find the most direct treatment of the profound connection between refrain and territory or land, enmeshed in disjointed time: "the refrain is a prism, a crystal of space-time. It acts ... to increase the speed of the exchanges and reactions in that which surrounds it ... The refrain fabricates time (*du temps*). The refrain is the 'implied tense' (*temps*) ... the refrain is the *a priori* form of time" (*A Thousand Plateaus*, pp. 348–9). See also the "explanations" provided by Sasso and Villani in their *Vocabulaire*, pp. 306–7.

6 I allude here to Andrei Tarkovsky's film *Stalker* for its powerful evocation of a space referred to as the "zone." For those who are not familiar with the film, the zone in question is a region of the earth that has—perhaps in consequence of a meteorite or other cosmic catastrophe?—been rendered uninhabitable and perilous to human existence. Only the "stalker" of the title—a mysterious figure whose identity remains unclear—can enter into the zone without being killed or annihilated by what seems to be a threat invisible to the naked eye. Film critic Guy Gauthier wrote of Tarkovsky's film that, "Seen from the outside, the zone appears as a space *that has limits*. The proof is that it can be surrounded by police cordons. Seen from the inside, by whoever dares set foot within it, everything is different. All measures of time and space are inoperative, geometry is meaningless, and a triangle ABC has no possibility of being equal to the triangle A'B'C' or to any other triangle. The straight line is not only the longest distance between two points, but it is impassable. To travel 200 meters, one must pass through tunnels, navigate waterfalls, brave deserts, and

naturally—this being Tarkovsky's universe—wade through endless waters. The *'zone' controls movement, alters itineraries, issues commands, and punishes those who violate the rules.* The worst is that *there are no known rules*, and no one knows whether the zone accepts, repels, or condemns to death. According to the *Stalker*, only those who are heartbroken can traverse it; but even he doesn't seem very well informed. For anyone simply looking around, the zone is a verdant landscape littered with ruined houses, wreckage, and all the signs of desertion." (Guy Gauthier, *Andréi Tarkovsky*, Filmo-19 [Paris: Edilig, 1988], p. 106, emphasis added). It is difficult to read these lines, and even more difficult to consider Tarkovsky's film, without thinking of the place and status that Deleuze was to assign to the word "zone" as early as *The Logic of Sense* and, even more systematically and forcefully, together with Félix Guattari, in *A Thousand Plateaus* and *Anti-Oedipus: Capitalism and Schizophrenia*. Deleuze and Guattari took on the task of transforming the "word" *zone* into a concept of formidable operative power, first in the realm of analysis and soon after in the realms of philosophy and politics. With the advent of the zone as a schizo-analytic concept, the entire landscape of "classical" philosophy is transformed before our eyes into a "zone" to be negotiated via entirely new pathways, and the essential question of limits is reconceived afresh. No one has more fully grasped the importance of this "moment" in Deleuze's thought than David Lapoujade. It is true that he approaches the question not from the angle of the concept of *zone*, but from that of the limit. But his elaboration of the concept shows that he is tackling the same question: the "juridico-ontological" question of limits (of sexuality, of law, of reason, of madness, of life and death, of language): "In general, the question of the limit is inseparable from the question: *quid juris?* To trace a limit is not a neutral gesture; it is a decisive, law-giving act. This is what makes philosophy inseparable from a relation to the earth, as in Kant." Later in his text, Lapoujade goes somewhat further in defining the status of this concept in Deleuze: "For Deleuze the limit is no longer a wall, a Great Wall of China or Roman *limes*, but rather becomes a filter, a sieve, a membrane that topologically places an inside and an outside farther away than any external world." See David Lapoujade, *Deleuze, Les Mouvements Aberrants* (Paris: Minuit "Paradoxe" series, 2014), p. 292 and p. 294. In developing this line of thought, I am particularly gratified to discover Lapoujade's direct reference to Deleuze's "*côté arpenteur*," the image of the surveyor that I introduced in my preface to the special issue of *Lendemains* devoted to Deleuze's work in June 1989, certain elements of which serve as a springboard for the present analysis. Lapoujade writes: "The philosopher is a 'geographer of reason' or a surveyor who circumscribes the limits of conquered land. He is *Juris auctor*, the law-maker, like the surveyors of the Roman Empire" (*Deleuze, Les Mouvements Aberrants*, p. 292). See the first chapter of the present work for a discussion of the idea of "encounter" in Deleuze.

7   Deleuze, *The Logic of Sense*, trans. Mark Lester (New York: Columbia University Press, 1990a), p. 106, original emphasis. The reader is again referred to Lapoujade, *Deleuze, Les Mouvements Aberrants*: "To the classical alternative of *either … or* must be opposed the Deleuzian *neither … nor*: neither cosmos nor chaos, but *chaosmos as a new figure of the Whole*. No longer the Open, but the Outside" (p. 294)—the only way, as I have tried to show in these collected essays, to meet the challenge of entering into resonance with the "zones of presence" as places of inscription of what will embody an "event." See for example Chapter 1 below, *Postcolonial Haecceities*, or Chapter 5, *The Singularity of the Event: Gilles Deleuze, Paul Virilio, François Jullien*.

8   Deleuze and Guttari, *A Thousand Plateaus*, p. 249 (emphasis added).

9   Thanks to David Lapoujade's masterly study of these "movements," it is clear that they constitute one of the most preponderant problems of Deleuzian thought. And on this topic, "one can invoke haphazardly the aberrant movements of Difference and Repetition, the perverse behavior of the masochist and his 'twisted' contracts, Tournier's perversion of Robinson, the fissure that pervades Zola's naturalism and casts his characters into madness and death, the logical paradoxes of Lewis Carroll and Artaud's sigh-screams in *The Logic of Sense*, the positive figure of the 'Schizo' and his 'lines of flight,' his 'Body without Organs' [*Logic of Sense*, pp. 92, 188, 192–3, 199, 203, 224 plural, 342, 351, 371 …] and his blurring of social codes" (Lapoujade, *Deleuze, Les Mouvements Aberrants*, p. 9).

10 Deleuze and Guattari, *A Thousand Plateaus*, p. 250 (emphasis added).

11 See Deleuze's criticism of these notions in *The Logic of Sense*: "Paradox is initially that which *destroys good sense* as the only direction, but it is also that which *destroys common sense* as the assignation of fixed identities" (*The Logic of Sense*, p. 3, emphasis added). "It is here [within the paradox], however, that the *gift of meaning* occurs, in this region *which precedes all good sense and all common sense*. For here, with the passion of the paradox, language attains its highest power" (*The Logic of Sense*, p. 79, emphasis added).

12 What I am attempting to illuminate in each text are no longer simply recognizable "objects" or Platonic essences, but in each case a "truth" or "haecceity" that is different from Plato's. For here, in contrast to the essences that "exist *before apprenticeship*, that do not change, that do not move, that are

immutable, in and of themselves, always presupposed *before apprenticeship* itself or the experience of the real," "*apprenticeship* proceeds through *accidental* encounters, through signs that force us to think in order to glean their truths (or their meanings). Apprenticeship is possible because we are sensitive enough to be affected by the signs that we encounter *randomly*. At that moment, we seek the truth (or the meaning) of the signs by which we have been affected, and *we enter into a singular process of experimentation and creation*, for everyone is affected in a different way and everyone has her own way of seeking the truth" (emphasis added). For the first quotation, see Pierre Montebello, *Deleuze et Proust, Les mondes de l'art ni subjectifs ni objectifs* in https://www.academia.edu/1401245/Deleuze_et_Proust_les_mondes_de_lart_ni_subjectifs_ni_objectifs; for the second, Fabiana Fernandes Ribeiro Martins and Sergio Luiz Antunes Neto Carreira, "L'apprentissage chez Deleuze: l'un, l'autre, les signes et l'affection": http://www.sofphied.fr/MFCS.pdf (accessed March 2016), 1. See also Michael Hardt's *Gilles Deleuze: An Apprenticeship in Philosophy* (Minneapolis: University of Minnesota Press, 1993), Chapter 4, "Conclusion: An Apprenticeship in Philosophy," p. 112 seq.

13   Here one has to keep in mind that the parallelism of the series—those of language *versus* those of "experience," for example—*is not of a shared essence between the series* but rather a *mark of the series' differentiation*. As James Brusseau has beautifully demonstrated in his book, "Deleuze postulates that series begin with difference and come into relation as an expression of that difference. The name he applies to this counterfeit community is 'resonance.' The series' characterization as parallel and analogous arises from a preliminary distance across which *the two series resonate without coming into contact and thus without reducing into each other*. Again, the two series share no *a priori* essence, though their resonance subsequently produces what appears to be an identity or essence between them. From this premise of an ersatz community growing from primary and unconquerable difference, Deleuze can talk about experience while he talks about language without fearing that the one will cave into or undercut the other. *In brief, language and experience belong to different logics.*" See, James Brusseau, *Isolated Experiences: Gilles Deleuze and the Solitudes of Reversed Platonism* (Albany, NY: State University of New York Press, 1998), p. 204 (emphasis added). Though they don't address the same questions or mobilize the same concepts, the chapters of this book do "resonate" with each other without reducing to a totalizing whole or unifying center.

Chapter 1: Postcolonial Haecceities: On Deleuze's Names

1. Quoted in "Michel Foucault and Zen: A Stay in a Zen Temple," in J. R. Carette (ed.), *Religion and Culture* (Manchester: Manchester University Press, 1999), pp. 110–15.
2. Quoted by Claire Parnet in *Dialogues II* (2006: p. 24, trans. modified). Translator's note: *The Great Wall of China* was pieced together after his death. The quotation in question was translated into English as part of a fragment of "The Great Wall," under the title "An old manuscript," in Nahum N. Glazer, ed., *The Complete Stories* (New York: Schocken, 1983), p. 416: "They come like fate. Without reason, consideration, or pretext … In some way that is incomprehensible they have pushed right into the Capital. At any rate, here they are; it seems that every morning there are more of them." See also "A leaf from an Old Manuscript," in Franz Kafka, *The Metamorphosis and Other Stories*, trans. Malcolm Pasley (Harmondsworth: Penguin, 1992), p. 163: "By some means that is incomprehensible to me, they have penetrated as far as the Capital, although this is a very long way from the frontier. At all events, there they are; it seems that every morning there are more of them."
3. Deleuze and Guattari, *A Thousand Plateaus*, p. 268 (emphasis added).
4. Arnaud Bouaniche, *Gilles Deleuze, une introduction* (Paris: Pocket, 2006), p. 131.
5. Ibid.
6. Deleuze, *Negotiations, 1972–90*, trans. M. Joughin (New York: Columbia University Press, 1995), pp. 165–6.
7. Deleuze, G., *Two Regimes of Madness: Texts and Interviews, 1975–1995*, ed. D. Lapoujade, trans. A. Hodges and M. Taormina (New York: Semiotext(e), 2007), pp. 166–7.
8. François Cusset, *French Theory: How Foucault, Derrida, Deleuze & Co. Transformed the Intellectual Life of the United States*, trans. J. Fort with J. Berganza and M. Jones (Minneapolis: University of Minnesota Press, 2008), pp. 10–11.
9. See for example what Paul Patton and John Protevi write in their Introduction of *Between Deleuze and Derrida* (2003), p. 9: "While Deleuze's collaborative works with Guattari were rapidly translated—*Anti-Oedipus* (1972) appeared in 1977 and *A Thousand Plateaus* (1980) in 1987—the major works of the 1960s, *The Logic of Sense* (1969) and *Difference and Repetition* (1968) *had to wait twenty-one and twenty-six years respectively for their English translation in 1990 and 1994. The historical works of the 1960s on Nietzsche, Spinoza and Bergson endured similar gaps of at least twenty years for translation.* Thus it was

not until the mid-1990s that a reasonably complete corpus of Deleuze's work existed ..." (emphasis mine).

10 See Patton, P., "The Event of Colonisation," in I. Buchanan (ed.), *Deleuze and the Contemporary World* (Edinburgh: Edinburgh University Press, 2006). Patton opens his article with the observation that "Colonisation was not a topic that figured largely in Deleuze's work" (109). Other critics and commentators also note this.

11 Alain de Beaulieu, *Gilles Deleuze, héritage philosophique* (Paris: PUF, 2005), p. 10.

12 Bouaniche, p. 294ff. See also Beaulieu (2005). I am only summarizing here the examples which these two commentators provide of the impact made by Deleuze's work on artists, scientists, and critics.

13 See Beaulieu, p. 164.

14 Ibid., p. 161.

15 Roland Barthes, *The Pleasure of the Text*, trans. R. Miller (New York: Hill and Wang, 1975), p. 13.

16 Jean-Hugues Barthélémy, *Simondon ou l'encyclopédisme génétique* (Paris: PUF, 2005), p. 151.

17 Deleuze and Parnet, *Dialogues II*, new edition, trans. H. Tomlinson, B. Habberjam, and E. R. Albert (London: Continuum, 2006), p. 5.

18 The following is only a partial list of the works I am alluding to. French-language books: Alain Badiou, *Deleuze: La clameur de l'être* (Paris: Hachette, 1997); Alberto Gualandi, *Deleuze* (Paris: Les Belles Lettres, 1998); Manola Antonioli, *Deleuze et l'histoire de la philosophie, ou De la philosophie comme science-fiction* (Paris: Kimé, 1999); Alain de Beaulieu, *Gilles Deleuze, héritage philosophique* (Paris: PUF, 2005); François Zourabichvili, *Le Vocabulaire de Deleuze* (Paris: Ellipses, 2003); Suzanne Hême de Lacotte, *Deleuze, philosophie et cinéma: le passage de l'image-mouvement à l'image-temps* (Paris: L'Harmattan, 2001); Claude Jaglé, *Portrait oratoire de Gilles Deleuze aux yeux jaunes* (Paris: PUF, 2005); Monique David-Ménard, *Deleuze et la psychanalyse* (Paris: PUF, 2005); Jean-Claude Dumoncel, *Le Pendule du Docteur Deleuze: une introduction à L'Anti-Œdipe* (Paris: Cahiers de l'Unebévue, 1999); Stéfan Leclercq, *Gilles Deleuze, Immanence, univocité et transcendantal* (Mons: Editions Sils Maria, 2001); Christophe Fiat, *La Ritournelle: une anti-théorie* (Paris: L. Scheer, 2002); Éric Alliez, *The Signature of the World: What is Deleuze and Guattari's Philosophy?*, trans. Eliot Ross Albert and Alberto Toscano (London: Continuum, 2004 [1993]); Gilles Deleuze, "Immanence et vie," *Rue Descartes* 20 (2006); Gilles Deleuze, "L'Intempestif," *Rue Descartes* 53 (2008); John Rajchman, *The*

Deleuze Connections (Cambridge, MA and London, England: MIT Press, 2000); Eugene Holland, *Deleuze and Guattari's Anti-Oedipus: Introduction to Schizoanalysis* (London: Routledge, 1999); Ronald Bogue, *Deleuze on Literature* (London: Routledge, 2003); Paul Patton, *Deleuze and the Political* (London: Routledge, 2000); Gregory Flaxman, *The Brain is the Screen: Deleuze and the Philosophy of Cinema* (Minneapolis: University of Minnesota Press, 2000); David Norman Rodowick, *Gilles Deleuze's Time Machine* (Durham, NC: Duke University Press, 1997); Paul Patton, *Deleuze: A Critical Reader* (Oxford: Blackwell, 1996); and Keith Ansell-Pearson, *Deleuze and Philosophy: The Difference Engineer* (London: Routledge, 1997).

19 Gilles Deleuze, *Negotiations, 1972–1990*, trans. M. Joughin (New York: Columbia University Press, 1995), p. 88: "I don't know what Foucault meant, I never asked him. He was a terrible joker. He may perhaps have meant that I was the most naïve philosopher of our generation. In all of us you find themes like multiplicity, difference, repetition. But I put forward almost raw concepts of these, while others work with more mediations."

20 Deleuze, *Negotiations*, p. 6. To show that the question of names does not appear by chance in Deleuze's work, we could cite many other instances where this "theme" is broached. See, for example, the way he explores it in *Dialogues II* (2006: p. 5): "You *encounter* people (and sometimes without knowing them or ever having seen them) but also movements, ideas, events, entities. All these things have proper names, *but the proper name does not designate a person or a subject*. It designates an effect, a zigzag, something which passes or happens between two as though under a potential difference: the 'Compton effect,' the 'Kelvin effect'" (my emphasis).

21 This is how Deleuze characterizes the nature of "movement" in the modern world: "nowadays we see movement defined less and less in relation to a point of leverage. All the new sports—surfing, windsurfing, hang-gliding—take the form of entering into an existing wave. There's no longer an origin as starting point, but a sort of putting-into-orbit. The key thing is how to get taken up in the motion of a big wave, a column of rising air, to 'get into something' instead of being the origin of an effort" (Deleuze, *Negotiations*, p. 121).

22 Deleuze and Guattari, *A Thousand Plateaus*, pp. 343–4 (emphasis added). I have in mind here the warnings that Deleuze and Guattari give their readers every time an experiment (relayed by a concept) presents the risk of the disintegration of the subject or a danger to its survival. One "example" among hundreds of others in *A Thousand Plateaus* is: "A mistake in speed, rhythm, or harmony would be catastrophic because it would bring back the forces of

chaos, destroying both creator and creation" (ibid., p. 343). On this point, it is interesting to note the frequency with which Deleuze and Guattari use the (imperative? prescriptive? descriptive? preventive?) expression "*il faut*" ("it is necessary"/"one must"). This subrepetition of the phrase *il faut* could (erroneously, in my opinion) be interpreted as an example of "voluntarism" on the part of the authors. In my view we *must* rather interpret their use of this expression as a term of warning, of the following sort: "If you wish to avoid the danger that is represented by a becoming-animal or a BwO, you *must* avoid [*il faut éviter*]…" In this sense, the "*il faut*" is less of the order of a command than a warning sign or signal that serves either as an alarm (e.g., "wrong move," "no trespassing," etc.) or as a kind of "user's manual." Here are some "examples" drawn from the first chapter of *A Thousand Plateaus*: "The problem of writing: in order to designate something exactly, anexact expressions are utterly unavoidable" ["*il faut absolument des expressions anexactes…*"] (p. 22); "The multiple must be made, not by always adding a higher dimension, but rather in the simplest of ways" ["*Le multiple, il faut le faire…*"] (p. 7); "the tracing should always be put back on the map" ["*il faut toujours reporter le calque sur la carte*"] (p. 14); "To attain the multiple, one must have a method that effectively constructs it" ["*Pour le multiple, il faut une méthode…*"] (p. 24); and for the "user's manual" type of usage: "Go first to your old plant and watch carefully the watercourse made by the rain" (p. 12); "Make rhizomes, not roots, never plant! Don't sow, grow offshoots! Don't be one or multiple, be multiplicities!" (p. 27). There is no better way of saying that we are essentially dealing with a practical philosophy (or philosophy of practice). Deleuze himself said: "Truth is producing existence. It's not something in your head but something existing. Writers generate real bodies" (*Negotiations*, p. 134).

23 See Cusset's superb book *French Theory*, in particular, the chapter entitled "The Politics of Identity" (*French Theory*, pp. 131–65), in which he has no difficulty tracing the links that would be forged between French theoretical imports and postcolonial theory. Nevertheless, he struggles to force Deleuze's work into the "crusher" of postcolonial, subalternist, or "identity" theory: "The reception given to Deleuze and Guattari was more complex [than that given to Derrida], marked in this arena by twenty years of misunderstandings!" (ibid., p. 150). On the other hand, when Cusset is discussing the Deleuzean "theoretical machinations" of innovators and experimenters on the internet and in film— such as the DJ Paul Miller (DJ Spooky), the Lords of Chaos, the Legion of Doom, or the Wachowski brothers—he doesn't hesitate to add: "These French authors are presented, one after another, as prophets of the Internet—*with*

Deleuze and Guattari as the key voices, because their botanical notion of the rhizome, an underground and nonhierarchical network of laterally linked stems, appears to be a precise foreshadowing of the Web" (ibid., pp. 251–2, my emphasis).

24 As we shall see, many critics and commentators identify enormous contradictions between the Deleuze of *The Logic of Sense* and *Difference and Repetition*, for example, and the Deleuze who instigates a new theoretical advance in the works written with Guattari. For them, there is not simply a discontinuity between one of Deleuze's "avatars" and another, but a radical theoretical break. I'm thinking here of the way in which theorists such as Slavoj Žižek, Alain Badiou, Jean-Loup Amselle, and Christopher L. Miller tackle these questions in their books on Deleuze or specific aspects of his work. See Badiou, *Deleuze: La clameur de l'être* (Paris: Hachette, 1997); Jean-Loup Amselle, *L'Occident décroché: enquête sur les postcolonialismes* (Paris, Stock, 2008); and Christopher L. Miller, *Theories of Africans: Francophone Literature and Anthropology in Africa (1990)* (Chicago: University of Chicago Press, 1993).

25 Except the generalizing "post-structuralist movement," of course. But, as Archie Bunker, the ineffable character of *All in the Family*, would have said: "What (real) difference does it make?" How does it help in understanding what makes Deleuze's idiosyncratic way of thinking ... *different* (from Derrida's, Lyotard's, or Foucault's way of thinking)?

26 Badiou, *Deleuze*, p. 141. Does Badiou not show a keen awareness of the problem we are trying to tease out here—that of a certain "equivocity" of Deleuze's "names"—when he gives the title "Which Deleuze?" to one of the first chapters in his book, and when he remarks: "We can scarcely ... expect that this philosophy, in which the One is sovereign, in which the hierarchy of power is ascetic, and in which death symbolises thought, should be, as is commonly thought, devoted to the inexhaustible variety of the concrete." Rare indeed are the postcolonial theorists who take up the challenge thrown by Deleuze at any attempt to "dialectize" the relationship between being and the simulacra which are the different modes of its actualization. It is perhaps only in the works of Achille Mbembe that the sovereign One and death, theoretically at least, come into play. See the chapter "Out of the world," in *On the Postcolony* (Berkeley: University of California Press, 2001), p. 173ff.

27 Badiou, *Deleuze*, p. 141 (original emphasis).

28 Deleuze and Parnet, *Dialogues II*, p. 5 (emphasis added).

29 Deleuze, *Negotiations*, p. 122 (translation modified).

30 "Whenever it is in a fallow period, philosophy takes refuge in reflecting 'on,'" Deleuze declared in *L'Autre Journal*. "If it creates nothing itself, what else can it do but reflect 'on'? Then it reflects on the eternal, or on the historical, but it does not manage itself to set things in motion." Deleuze gives the same reaction in "Portrait of the Philosopher as a Moviegoer." To the question of how he made the leap from painting to film, he replies: "I didn't make a leap from painting to film. *I don't think of philosophy as a reflection on one thing or another—painting or film. Philosophy is about concepts, it creates them*" (Deleuze and Parnet, *Dialogues II*, p. 213 [emphasis added]).

31 Deleuze, *Negotiations*, p. 95.

32 Ibid., pp. 123–4 (emphasis added).

33 Ibid., p. 125 (emphasis added).

34 Ibid., pp. 125–6 (emphasis added). He later raises questions linked to the problems in New Caledonia: "On the Caledonian problem we're told that from a certain point onward the territory was regarded as a settler colony, so the Kanaks became a minority in their own territory. When did this start? How did it develop? Who was responsible? The Right refuses these questions" (ibid., p. 127).

35 I'm thinking less here of the studies, monographs, and critical readers "on" Deleuze, which have appeared all around the world, than of works such as Hardt and Negri's *Empire* (Cambridge: Harvard University Press, 2000) or Alliez's *Les Temps capitaux*, vol. 1: *Récits de la conquête du temps* (Paris: Éditions du Cerf, 1993), and studies whose goals are not so much to "explain" some aspect of Deleuze's thought than to put into practice certain theoretical or political "expectations" which run through it. The scope of the present article does not allow me to analyze such relations as they appear in the work of leading postcolonial thinkers like Homi K. Bhabha, Gayatri C. Spivak, Edward Said, etc. It is sufficient for our purposes here to have shown what has conditioned the "dissemination" of Deleuze's names.

36 Failure to pose such questions entails serious consequences, of course, since it inevitably tends to invalidate the "logic" of the mediation as Deleuze formulates it. What if, at the very moment he embarked on this new form of collaborative writing, Deleuze had continued to pursue a philosophical perspective that was *his alone*? And what if, in his "encounter" with Guattari, Deleuze was continuing to pursue and probe more deeply problematics he felt he had not "finished" in the texts that he wrote without Guattari. Last but not least, by considering only the texts that Deleuze wrote with Guattari, are we in a position then to understand how far Deleuze's contribution goes, or the point from

which it proceeds, in the Deleuzo-Guattarian "project"? The assumption that clearly underlies all these questions is that there is a Deleuzean agenda which is not analytically inscribed in the work he produces with Guattari. What is the contribution that the wasp makes to the orchid? See Chapter 8 for more specifications on these questions.

37 This expression refers to Patrick Chamoiseau's book entitled *Écrire en pays dominé* (Paris: Gallimard, 1997).

38 Deleuze and Parnet, *Dialogues II*, p. 379 (emphasis added).

39 I am thinking here of Deleuze's direct political "engagement" with the Palestinians and his unwavering defense of their struggles for their independence and rights. See the Special Issue of *Discourse* that Jalal Toufic and I have devoted to *Gilles Deleuze: A Reason to Believe in this World*. In that issue, one can find important texts written by Deleuze on the Palestinians including: "The Troublemakers", "The Indians of Palestine" (a conversation with Elias Sanbar), "The *Grandeur* of Yasser Arafat," and "Whenever They Can See It." See *Discourse, Journal for Theoretical Studies in Media and Culture*, 20.3 (Fall 1998), Jalal Toufic and Réda Bensmaïa (eds.). These texts show clearly how important the Palestinian question was to Deleuze. This is for example the opening remarks of the text he devoted to Arafat: "The Palestinian cause is first and foremost the set of injustices that these people have suffered and continue to suffer. These injustices are acts of violence, but also illogicalities, false reasonings, false guarantees that claim to compensate or vindicate them. Arafat needed only one word to describe the broken promises, the violated agreements, at the moment of the Sabra and Shatila massacres: *shame, shame*" (Deleuze's emphasis).

40 However, it should be borne in mind that, as Cusset has clearly demonstrated, the epicentre of this "conversation" is located in the United States, even for problems relating to postcolonial questions. It's true that this "conversation" has never really taken off in France. Cusset's rather pessimistic observation was outlined in a chapter bearing the revealing title "Meanwhile, Back in France …": "Following the developments in the United States, Lacanian-Derridean and *Foucauldian-Deleuzean* [sic] perspectives gradually began to occupy *the intellectual field in many countries*. But not only did these discourses gradually subside in France, the very possibility of discussing theory was virtually banished from the scene. As the authors passed away (Barthes in 1980, Lacan in 1981, Foucault in 1984, Guattari in 1992, Deleuze in 1995, Lyotard in 1995), their presence in the public sphere gradually shrank into obituaries and intellectual nostalgia, and their legacy became the monopoly of a few

isolated heirs and the official rights holders of their publications" (Cusset, *French Theory*, p. 309, my emphasis). It should be pointed out that Cusset makes this observation in a long chapter in which he tries to show how strong a hold postcolonial theory has gained in American universities. It is revealing to compare what Cusset says here and what he says at the start of the chapter entitled "The Politics of Identity." The description he gives of what is occurring in American universities contrasts starkly with what is happening *at the same time* in French universities: "*Following the investigation into cultural studies*, we must consider what lies at the heart of the new community-centred discourses in American universities: ethnic and postcolonial studies. It is here that the old concept of identity is called into question, or at the very least combined into two main components: first, the role of cartology is considered, where identity plays a central role in determining international relationships of power, revealing complex layers of historical battles; second, pluralisation is examined, along with the increasing complexity of identity that it entails, with so many composite narratives and interwoven journeys, and large numbers of diaspora identities and migrant descendants" (ibid., p. 138, my emphasis). And Cusset adds the following, which shouldn't greatly surprise us: "This combination can be said to have sprung from a *Foucauldian* line of thought—where the subject is constructed first through subjugation by institutions of control and their dominant discourse, and from the Deleuzean motif of a subject that has been de-composed over the course of passages of nomadic flight" (ibid., p. 138). Here also the reference to Deleuze as one of the leading theoretical figures of postcolonial theory, in one or other of his manifestations, is presented as self-evident. It is as though one of the conditions of the possibility of his emergence was inseparable from this "reference."

41 Deleuze, *Negotiations*, p. 125 (emphasis added).
42 Gilles Deleuze, "*The Method of Dramatization*," in *Desert Island and Other Texts: 1953–1974*, ed. David Lapoujade (New York: Semiotext(e), 2004), p. 60 (emphasis added).
43 Deleuze, 2004, p. 60 (emphasis added).
44 Gilles Deleuze, *Logic of Sense, Series 15: "On Singularities"*, p. 123.
45 Ibid.
46 See also ibid., p. 130: "Only when something is identified between divergent series or between incompossible worlds, an object = x appears *transcending individuated worlds, and the Ego which thinks it transcends worldly individuals*, giving thereby to the world a new value *in view of the new value of the subject which is being established*" (my emphasis). This text, dating from 1969,

highlights the enduring nature and the importance of the problematics of divergent series and of their "encounter" due to the (esoteric and atopic) object = x. It is the problematic of the philosopher as "dark precursor" of the protocols to come that is outlined in this "informal" or "modal" definition of the subject (of the utterance).

47 Slavoj Žižek, *Organs without Bodies: Deleuze and Consequences* (New York: Routledge, 2004), p. xi.
48 See: Robert Sasso and Arnaud Villani, *Le Vocabulaire de Deleuze, Les Cahiers de Noesis* 3 (Spring 2003).
49 Žižek, *Organs without Bodies*, p. xi (emphasis added).
50 Ibid. (emphasis added). Žižek cites many other metamorphoses of Deleuze's incarnations and reincarnations which all tend to show that Deleuze has "misread" or "misunderstood" Hegel, whom he apparently parrots, clumsily and partially, without being aware of it. A detailed study could be undertaken to show how ignorance of the "logic" of the Snark, brought into play by Deleuze, can create a great deal of critical harm. It should be conceded though that Žižek claims to attack Deleuzeanism rather than Deleuze. Our theory about the multiplication of Deleuze's names finds confirmation later in the same text, in a chapter entitled "A Yuppie reading of Deleuze": "There are, effectively," writes Žižek, "features that justify *calling Deleuze the ideologist of later capitalism*" (ibid., p. 183, my emphasis).
51 See Badiou, *Deleuze*.
52 Ibid., p. 9.
53 Ibid., p. 96.
54 Gilles Deleuze, *Logic of Sense*, p. 146. The fact that Deleuze once again uses in almost the same terms the "logic" of "esoteric words" in his definition of the "dark precursor" and its efficacy in intensive systems says much about the continuity of his thinking on this point. This "insistence" shows just how important Deleuze considered the vicariance of the "subject" in the system of differences.
55 Gilles Deleuze, *Difference and Repetition*, p. 147 (emphasis added).
56 See Chapter 2 here for more developments on the question of the subject (of art) in Gilles Deleuze's work.
57 Deleuze and Parnet, *Dialogues II*, p. 68. He adds: "One such plane is that of the Law, in so far as it *organises and develops forms, genres, themes, motifs, and assigns and causes the evolution of subjects, persons, characteristic features and feelings: harmony of forms, education of subjects*" (my emphasis).
58 Ibid., pp. 68–9.

59 Deleuze, G. and Claire Parnet (2006), *Dialogues II*, new edition, trans. H. Tomlinson, B. Habberjam, and E. R. Albert (London: Continuum), p. 118.
60 Deleuze and Parnet, *Dialogues II*, p. 69.
61 I am rereading this passage at the moment our world seems to be stricken by what Jacques Derrida would have called an "auto-immune malady": the war and the deteriorating situation in Syria, Iraq, Libya, Egypt, the so-called "refugee" crisis in Europe, and the incapacity of the European community to unite and do something.
62 Not because they relate exclusively to questions concerning the postcolony, but in as much as they refer to questions which took shape only after the end of the process of decolonization. But they can be called "haecceities" in that they widely "overflow" any determination of nation, race, culture, or even history.
63 I am referring here to the powerful reflection on the status of the witness in Robert Harvey's *Witnessness: Beckett, Levi, Dante and the Foundations of Ethics* (London: Continuum/Bloomsbury, 2010).
64 Deleuze, 2006, p. 345, emphasis added, trans. modified.
65 Ibid., p. 347, emphasis added.
66 Gilles Deleuze, *Spinoza, Practical Philosophy*, trans. R. Hurley (San Francisco: City Lights Books, 1988b), p. 129.

Chapter 2: The Subject of Art: Prolegomena to a Future Deleuzian Aesthetics

1 This text is the development of a lecture I gave on October 15, 2004 as part of a seminar organized at Paris VIII by Marie-Claire Ropars-Willeumier, Pierre Sorlin, and Christian Doumet on the theme of "Art without Subject." I made substantial modifications for this book on Deleuze, but I was not able to eliminate all traces of the oral style that I originally gave to the text. My intention was to share with the participants some elementary analyses on the question that brought us together that day, starting from some texts of Deleuze that I had to work through again, but also from the texts of critics who are interested in some of the problems posed by the question of the "subject" in Deleuze's work. Thus what I advance here is a kind of reflection to the second degree, which presupposes some familiarity with the commentaries and criticisms of Alain Badiou, Éric Clemens, Alberto Gualandi, René Schérer, and others. All of those who have made the same journey will easily recognize what my reflection owes to their work.

2   Gilles Deleuze, *Kant's Critical Philosophy: The Doctrine of the Faculties*, trans. Hugh Tomlinson (Minneapolis: University of Minnesota Press, 1985). Hereafter KCP.
3   Philippe Lacoue-Labarthe and Jean-Luc Nancy, *The Literary Absolute: The Theory of Literature in German Romanticism*, trans. Philip Barnard and Cheryl Leser (Albany: State University of New York Press, 1988), p. 30. Hereafter LA.
4   Gilles Deleuze, *The Logic of Sense*, trans. Mark Lester with Charles Stivale (New York: Columbia University Press, 1990a), p. 260. Hereafter LS.
5   Lacoue-Labarthe and Nancy, LA, p. 30.
6   Deleuze, LS, p. 105.
7   Ibid.
8   Éric Clemens, *La fiction et l'apparaître* (Paris: Albin Michel, 1993), p. 183. Hereafter FA. Cf. the fine chapter titled "La dépense de la fiction," and in particular pp. 171ff devoted to the "transcendental imagination." The clarification I propose in the following paragraphs depends to a great degree on this analysis.
9   Immanuel Kant, *Critique of the Power of Judgment*, The Cambridge Edition of the Works of Immanuel Kant, ed. Paul Guyer, trans. Paul Guyer and Eric Matthews (Cambridge: Cambridge University Press, 2000), p. 63 [5: 176]. Page numbers in brackets refer to those of the Akademie Edition. Hereafer CPJ.
10 Ibid., p. 66 [5: 179].
11 Ibid., p. 71 [5: 184].
12 Gilles Deleuze, *Difference and Repetition*, trans. Paul Patton (New York: Columbia University Press, 1994), p. 167. Hereafter DR.
13 Ibid., p. 161. Emphasis mine.
14 Kant, CPJ, p. 125 [5: 241]. Italics mine.
15 Ibid., pp. 125–6 [5: 241–3]. Italics mine.
16 On this aspect of Kant's thought, see Florence Khodoss' commentaries in Emmanuel Kant, *Le jugement esthétique*, trans. Florence Khodoss (Paris: PUF, 1970), p. 97ff. Hereafter JE.
17 Kant, CPJ, p. 77 [5: 192].
18 Here again I owe the clarity of these specifications to Clemens, FA, p. 180ff.
19 Kant, CPJ, p. 114 [5: 230]. Italics mine.
20 "[…] the method of vice-diction," write Niamh McDonnel and Sjoerd van Tuinen, "is the method of a machinic thought that says only 'AND': is 'neither a union, nor a juxtaposition, but … the outline of a broken line which always sets off at right angles, a sort of active and creative line of flight … AND … AND …

AND'" (*D* 10). Cf. *Deleuze and the Fold, A Critical Reader*, Niamh McDonnel and Sjoerd van Tuinen (eds.) (London: Palgrave-Macmillan, 2010), p. 27.

21 Gilles Deleuze, "The Method of Dramatization," in *Desert Islands and Other Texts: 1953-1974*, ed. David Lapoujade (New York: Semiotext(e), 2004), p. 99.

22 Pierre Zaoui, "La grande identité Nietzsche-Spinoza, quelle identité?," *Philosophie* 47 (1995): 64-84.

23 Gilles Deleuze, DR, pp. 189-90.

24 Gilles Deleuze, "The Idea of Genesis in Kant's Esthetics," in *Desert Islands and Other Texts: 1953-1974*, ed. David Lapoujade (New York: Semiotext(e), 2004), p. 56. Hereafter IG.

25 For more details on these questions and on the following paragraphs, I refer once again to Clemens, FA, 97ff, which I adapt here for my own purposes.

26 Kant, CPJ, p. 67 [5: 180].

27 It is perhaps worthwhile to recall in passing—and to avoid any confusion—that for Kant, what is "subjective" in the common sense of the term comes from the taste of the senses and is consequently only "agreement!"

28 See the explanations given by Khodoss in Kant, JE, pp. 105ff.

29 Kant, CPJ, p. 122 [5: 237-8]. Italics mine.

30 Ibid., pp. 160-1 [5: 279-80]; pp. 168-9 [5: 287-9].

31 Ibid., p. 134 [5: 250]. Italics mine.

32 Cf. Clemens, FA, pp. 185ff. "The homology of imagination and aesthetic judgment comes first from their *non-relation* to the object. In the two cases, if there are two, the object remains in the background in favor of the pure form. The 'object' of art is useless, both for knowing and for acting, even more than the pure *a priori* form of time: and neither of the two is anything objective."

33 Deleuze, IG, p. 60.

34 Alberto Gualandi, *Deleuze* (Paris: Les Belles Lettres, 1998), p. 92. Hereafter D.

35 Deleuze, DR, p. 136.

36 Alain Badiou, *Manifesto for Philosophy*, trans. Norman Madarasz (Albany: State University of New York Press, 1999), p. 61. Hereafter MP.

37 I have in mind here, for example, the way in which Deleuze and Guattari "transform" Bergsonian "fabulation" into a "visionary faculty," an operation which "consists in creating gods and giants, 'semi-personal powers or effective presences'" which come to be added to the imagination and to the other faculties. Gilles Deleuze and Félix Guattari, *What is Philosophy?*, trans. Hugh Tomlinson and Graham Burchell (New York: Columbia University Press, 1994), p. 230, n. 8. Hereafter WP.

38 Gualandi, D, p. 95. Italics mine.

39 See Deleuze, KCP, Ch. 3, "The Relationship of the Faculties in the Critique of Judgement."
40 Deleuze, IG, p. 69.
41 Ibid., pp. 69–70. On the dangers represented by the hasty "dialecticization" of the Kantian "schematism" (in Panofsky, for example), one will refer with interest to the fine analyses that Georges Didi-Huberman devotes to the status of the notion of "schema" in *Confronting Images: Questioning the Ends of a Certain History of Art*, trans. John Goodman (University Park: The Pennsylvania State University Press, 2005). See in particular Ch. 3, "The History of Art within the Limits of its Simple Reason." "To require of artistic forms themselves a kind of reciprocity congruent with the form of knowledge, this was to require of symbolic forms that they realize, in their essence, the movement *from concept to image*" (p. 132). It is this type of "transfer," from schematism to the conceptual *without another form of process,* that Deleuze—in analyses that have a certain consonance with those of Didi-Huberman—categorically refuses.
42 Gilles Deleuze and Félix Guattari, WP, p. 166.
43 René Schérer, "Subjectivités hors sujet," *Chimères* 1, no. 21 (1994): 2. Hereafter SHS.
44 Ibid.
45 Deleuze, LS, pp. 102–3.
46 Deleuze and Guattari, WP, p. 197.
47 Ibid., pp. 202–3.
48 Deleuze, LS, p. 103. Translation slightly modified.
49 Éric Alliez, *The Signature of the World: What is Deleuze and Guattari's Philosophy?*, trans. Eliot Ross Albert and Alberto Toscano (London: Continuum, 2004), p. 56. Hereafter SW.
50 Badiou, MP, pp. 66–7.
51 Ibid., p. 93. Italics mine.
52 Deleuze, DR, p. 188.
53 Ibid., p. 189.
54 Ibid.
55 Ibid., p. 191.
56 Ibid., pp. 191–2.
57 Gualandi, D, p. 51.
58 Cf. Gualandi, D, pp. 100ff. "According to Deleuze, art is neither an activity of representation nor, as the Kantian doctrine of the beautiful contends, an intersubjective activity of enjoyment and of free judgment. Art is a true practice

of experimentation and of the problematization of the real, of its pre-individual and ideal domain, of its fields of individuation and individuating factors" (p. 102).
59 Deleuze, DR, p. 194.
60 Ibid.
61 Deleuze and Guattari, WP, p. 203.
62 Cf. Schérer, SHS, which gives an excellent description of this thematic.
63 Deleuze and Guattari, WP, p. 210.
64 Ibid., p. 211.
65 Ibid., p. 212. Italics mine.
66 Ibid., p. 211. See the development of this aspect of Deleuze's thinking in Ch. 3: *Cineplastic(s): Gilles Deleuze Reader of Élie Faure.*
67 Alliez, SW, pp. 75–6.
68 Deleuze, DR, p. 293.
69 Schérer, SHS, p. 3.
70 Deleuze and Guattari, WP, p. 182.
71 Alliez, SW, p. 70.
72 Gualandi, D, p. 103.
73 Deleuze and Guattari, WP, pp. 202–3.

Chapter 3: *Cinéplastique(s)*: Deleuze on Élie Faure and Film Theory

1 Gilles Deleuze, *Cinema 2: The Time-Image*, trans. Hugh Tomlinson and Robert Galeta (Minneapolis: University of Minnesota Press, 1989). Hereafter C2. Italics mine.
2 Élie Faure, *The Art of Cineplastics*, trans. Walter Pach (Boston: The Four Seas, 1923), p. 20. Hereafter AC.
3 Ibid., p. 22.
4 Ibid., p. 15.
5 Ibid., p. 20. Italics mine.
6 Deleuze, C2, pp. 171–2. Italics mine.
7 Faure, AC, p. 24.
8 Ibid., p. 27.
9 Ibid., p. 29.
10 Ibid., p. 27.
11 Ibid., p. 25.

12 Élie Faure, "Introduction à la mystique du cinema," in *Fonction du cinéma* (Paris: Editions Gonthier, 1963), p. 51. Hereafter IMC.
13 Cf. Réda Bensmaïa, "Les *Transformateurs-Deleuze* ou le cinéma comme 'automate spirituel,'" *Quaderni di Cinema/Studio* 7–8 (1992): 89–117. This article is reproduced here with some changes: see Chapter 4. In this chapter I attempt to give an account of the place Deleuze gives to the notions of "automaton", "automatism," and what he calls the "spiritual automaton" in his conception of cinema.
14 Faure, IMC, p. 56.
15 Deleuze, C2, pp. 265–6: "Clockwork automata, but also motor automata, in short, automata of movement, made way for a new computer and cybernetic race, automata of computation and thought, automata with controls and feedback ... And in frequently explicit forms, the new automata were to people cinema, for better and for worse (the better would be Kubrick's giant computer in *2001*), and restore to it, particularly through science fiction, *the possibility of huge mises-en-scènes* that the impasse in the movement-image had provisionally ruled out. But new automata did not invade content without a new automatism bringing about a mutation of form ... In *all these senses, the new spiritual automatism in turn refers to new spiritual automata.*" It is, as we know, this "mutation of form" that determines in Deleuze's work the plastic transformations and innovations: the "new image" will have no more interiority than exteriority and will refer to "reversible and non-superimposable" spaces; it will lose its directional dimension in favor of an "omnidirectional" space which "constantly varies its angles and coordinates, to exchange the vertical and the horizontal." And the screen "itself" will no longer refer to the human posture, like a window or a painting, but will constitute rather "a table of information, an opaque surface on which are inscribed 'data,' information replacing nature, and the brain-city, the third eye, replacing the eyes of nature" (ibid., p. 265).
16 Gilles Deleuze, *Foucault*, trans. Séan Hand (London: Continuum, 1999), p. 55.
17 Deleuze, C2, p. 253. Italics mine.
18 Ibid., p. 256. Italics mine.
19 Faure, IMC, p. 60.
20 Cf. Pierre Zaoui, "La grande identité Nietzsche-Spinoza, quelle identité?," *Philosophie* 47 (1995). Hereafter "Grande Identité."
21 Élie Faure, "La Prescience du Tintoret," in *Fonction du cinéma* (Paris: Editions Gonthier, 1963), p. 9.
22 Faure, AC, p. 33.

23 Cf. Faure, IMC, p. 57: "I said as many foolish things as the others. We were for a long time accustomed to fixing our modes of expression into very defined forms—painting, sculpture, music, architecture, dance, literature, theater, even photography—and each of us tended to reduce cinematography to those forms that he had previously devoted himself to. Most, at the beginning, made it dependent on theater, while others linked it to music, and others to *the plastic in general*. I was among the latter. I still believe, incidentally, that since cinema reaches us through the intermediary of vision, it is plastic education that best prepares us to understand it. But that is all. Cinema is neither painting nor sculpture, nor architecture, nor dance, nor music, nor literature, nor theater, nor photography. It is simply cinema. And cinema is at least as different from each of these eight languages as each is from the others."

24 Ibid., p. 49.

25 Faure, AC, p. 22.

26 I am thinking here of what Faure proposed in *Fonction du cinéma* in the short text—one could say the "short treatise"—titled "La Danse et le cinéma" where we can read the following, which is unequivocal and full of lessons concerning Faure's "prescience": "Dance is a neglected art, cinematography a nascent art. And yet it seems to me that cinema and dance could deliver to us the secret of the relations of all the plastic arts with space and with the geometrical figures that give us at once the measure and the symbol." He adds immediately that "dance, in every era, like the cinema tomorrow, is charged with joining the plastic to music, by the miracle of a rhythm *at once visible and audible*, and to make the three dimensions of space enter vividly into duration" (p. 11). What this test shows nicely is that Élie Faure already had a very clear idea—one could say "concept"—of the "plasticity" of cinema, a dimension that he does not confuse with the "plastic arts." Faure was in this sense, along with Jean Epstein, the first theorist of the plasticity of cinema.

27 Immanuel Kant, *Critique of Pure Reason*, The Cambridge Edition of the Works of Immanuel Kant, ed. and trans. Paul Guyer and Allen W. Wood (Cambridge: Cambridge University Press, 1998), pp. 193–4 [A51/B75]. Page numbers in brackets refer to those of the Akademie Edition.

28 Just as it was thanks to the "conceptual persona" of the "idiot" that Descartes was able to create the concept of the *cogito*, it is thanks to the "conceptual persona" of the "cineplast" created by Élie Faure that Deleuze could begin to demarcate in a way the "plane of immanence" specific to cinema. Cf. the fine article by Isabelle Ginoux, "Rapports entre des types psychosociaux et le personnage conceptual," in *Gilles Deleuze*, ed. Isabelle Stengers and Pierre

Verstraeten (Paris: Vrin, 1998): "Only an idiot (as private thinker provided only with his natural thought and determined to think for himself) is capable of traversing the test of doubt which makes a *tabula rasa* of all the understanding that takes up so much space in the heads of scholars and public professors, in order to reach the evidence of the clear and distinct idea and finally to pronounce his own 'idiocy': *Cogito ergo sum, I think, therefore I am*. In a movement that will have constituted in itself *a new image of thought, a new way of turning oneself toward the true and of orienting oneself in thought, in short, the outline of a new plane of immanence leading to the creation of unprecedented concepts*". (p. 97 n.1). As "conceptual persona," the "cineplast" opens the way to a new way of thinking of the cinema and of bringing to the surface the outline of this new "plane of immanence" which is the "plastic" dimension of cinema.

29 Gilles Deleuze and Félix Guattari, *What is Philosophy?*, trans. Hugh Tomlinson and Graham Burchell (New York: Columbia University Press, 1994), p. 177. Hereafter WP.

30 As we know, these are not the representatives of the philosophers who employ them or of their philosophy, but rather the "agents of enunciation" that enable the philosopher to distinguish himself from some putative subjectivity, to put his discourse in perspective, and to traverse the plane of thought on the basis of which his philosophy becomes *possible*. Cf. Zaoui, "Grande Identité": "Conceptual personae, on the other hand [in contrast to the simple figurehead] perform the movements that describe the plane of immanence of the author …"

31 Élie Faure, "Vocation du cinéma," in *Fonction du cinéma* (Paris: Editions Gonthier, 1963), pp. 72–3.

32 Ibid.

33 Here I pastiche and transpose for my own purposes what Deleuze says of "life" in Bergson: "Life as movement alienates itself in the material form that it creates; by actualizing itself, by differentiating itself, it loses contact with the rest of itself [i.e., with the virtuality that is the ground of its existence]. Every species is an arrested movement; it could be said that the living being turns on itself and closes itself." Gilles Deleuze, *Bergsonism*, trans. Hugh Tomlinson and Barbara Habberjam (New York: Zone Books, 1991), p. 104.

34 As regards the problem of "interferences" between disciplines, we look with interest to the distinction that Deleuze establishes between the three types of interference that exist between art, science, and philosophy. One of these, the second in the order of exposition, and which he qualifies as "intrinsic" (and which he differentiates from "extrinsic" interferences and from interferences

"that cannot be localized"), enables us to better understand the kind of relation Deleuze maintains with the texts of his paredros: "But there is a second, intrinsic type of interference when concepts and conceptual personae seem to leave a plane of immanence that would correspond to them, so as to slip in among the functions and partial observers, or among the sensations and aesthetic figures, on another plane; and similarly in the other cases." Deleuze and Guattari, WP, p. 205.

35 Deleuze, C2, p. 280. Italics mine.
36 Cf. Zaoui, "Grande Identité," p. 83.
37 Deleuze, C2, p. 280. Italics mine.
38 Cf. the fine little book by Hélène Sarrazin, *À la rencontre d'Élie Faure: Première approche et tentative de compréhension* (Périgeux: Pierre Fanlac, 1982).

Chapter 4: On the "Spiritual Automaton," or Space and Time in Modern Cinema According to Gilles Deleuze

1 The conceptual persona has nothing to do with an abstract personification, a symbolic or an allegorical figure, because it lives, it insists (in us). The destiny of the philosopher is to become his conceptual persona or personae, at the same time that these personae themselves become something other than what they are historically, mythologically, or commonly (the Socrates of Plato, the Dionysus of Nietzsche, or the "idiot" of Cusa). The conceptual persona is the becoming or the subject of a philosophy, on par with the philosopher (see Deleuze and Guattari, *What is Philosophy?*, p. 64).
2 Colombat, 1991, pp. 10–24.
3 Ibid., p. 14.
4 Gilles Deleuze, *Expressionism in Philosophy: Spinoza*, trans. Martin Joughin (Brooklyn, NY: Zone Books, 1990c).
5 Colombat, 1991, p. 14.
6 Deleuze and Guattari, 1987, pp. 149–66.
7 Colombat, 1991, p. 14.
8 Spinoza, 1992, pp. 255–6.
9 Deleuze, *Expressionism in Philosophy*, p. 115.
10 Ibid.
11 Deleuze, *Expressionism in Philosophy*, p. 140.
12 "When he shows that our ideas are causes of one another, he deduces from this that all have as cause our power of knowing or thinking. It is above all the

term 'spiritual automaton,' which is to say: 'In thinking we obey only the laws of thought, laws that determine both the form and the content of true ideas, and that make us produce ideas in sequence according to their own causes and through our own power, so that in knowing our power of understanding we know through their causes all the things that fall within this power'" (Deleuze, *Expressionism in Philosophy*, p. 140).

13 This "moment" occupies the greatest part of the analyses in the first book and is presented as a rereading of Bergson as a philosopher of movement.

14 See the magisterial study that David Lapoujade has produced in *Deleuze, Les Mouvements Aberrants* (Les Éditions de Minuit, 2014). For Lapoujade, Gilles Deleuze's philosophy presents itself as a "kind of encyclopedia of aberrant movements" which can be found in Francis Bacon's deformed figures, Lewis Carroll's non-sense, schizophrenic processes of the unconscious, crack up of thinking, line of flight of nomads through history, etc. ... At some point, David Lapoujade doesn't hesitate to write: "Aberrant movements constitute the *signs* of Gilles Deleuze's general problem" (ibid., p. 15, my emphasis).

15 Deleuze, *Cinema 2*, pp. 156–7.

16 Ibid. (my emphasis).

17 Ibid., p. 159 (my emphasis).

18 Ibid., p. 158.

19 Which means, for Deleuze, as we will see below, non-grammatical, non-dialectical, and non-rhetorical.

20 Deleuze, *Cinema 2*, p. 161 (my emphasis).

21 I refer here to the fine analysis Deleuze proposed of the audio-visual complex as it works in Michel Foucault's thought (see Deleuze 1988a, pp. 94–123). David Rodowick shows the importance of the theoretical stakes for film theory of the confrontation between the regime of "visibilities" and the regime of énoncés in Foucault:

> Rather than closing in on itself, enunciation obeys a centripetal force derived from the accelerated orbit of the expressible with respect to the increasing density of the visible. The velocity of regimes agitates énoncés like atoms in a particle accelerator. But what new elements—as concepts or possibilities of thought and imagination—will be created? What possibilities of liberation or alienation will they herald? (David Rodowick, *Gilles Deleuze's Time Machine* [Durham: Duke University Press, 1990], p. 33)

Olivier Dyens' paper on "cyberspace" and "morphism" (2001) and Edmond Couchot's work on the "virtual" image (1998) give us an adequate idea of the new possibilities offered to cinema for thinking of the relation of cinematographic images to the "real."

22 I will henceforth write S-A-T in order to keep its operative, that is "machinic," dimension in mind: the "spiritual automaton" as "accelerator"... of concepts!
23 Deleuze, *Cinema 2*, p. 165.
24 Ibid., p. 166 (translation modified).
25 Or as this "dismantled," paralyzed, petrified, frozen instance which testifies "the impossibility of thinking that is thought" (ibid.).
26 Ibid.
27 Ibid.
28 Deleuze, 1983, p. 40.
29 Ibid.
30 Ibid. In *The Time-Image*, we find another "formula": "The Whole can only be thought, *because it is the indirect representation of time which follows from movement*" (Deleuze, *Cinema 2*, p. 158, my emphasis).
31 Deleuze, *Cinema 2*, p. 40.
32 Ibid. (my emphasis).
33 Ibid.
34 For a theoretically pointed discussion of these two regimes, see *Cinema 2*, pp. 173ff. and specifically on p. 174: "The problematic is distinguished from the theorematic (or constructivism from the axiomatic) in that the theorem develops internal relationships from principle to consequences, while the problem introduces an event from the outside—removal, addition, cutting— which constitutes its own conditions and determines the 'case' or cases."
35 Deleuze, *Cinema 2*, p. 173 (my emphasis).
36 "It is the material automatism of images," writes Deleuze, "which produces *from the outside* a thought which it *imposes*, as the unthinkable in our intellectual automatism" (*Cinema 2*, pp. 178–9, my emphasis).
37 Ibid., p. 174.
38 Ibid.
39 Ibid., p. 160 (my emphasis).
40 Ibid., p. 182 (my emphasis).
41 Ibid., p. 173 (my emphasis).
42 Ibid.
43 Grande, (1992).
44 Ibid., p. 61.
45 Ibid. (my emphasis).
46 Ibid., p. 60 (my emphasis).

47   Deleuze, *Cinema 2*, p. 174.
48   Ibid., p. 173.
49   Ibid., p. 176.
50   Deleuze, 1983, p. 38.
51   Ibid., p. 38.

Chapter 5: The Singularity of the Event: Gilles Deleuze, Paul Virilio, François Jullien

1   Deleuze, *The Logic of Sense*, pp. 102–3 (emphasis added). For the historical and theoretical background of the concept of singularity, see Birgit M. Kaiser, "The Singularities of Postcolonial Literature: Preindividual (Hi)stories in Mohammed Dib's 'Northern Trilogy,'" in *Postcolonial Literatures and Deleuze: Colonial Pasts, Differential Futures*, ed. Lorna Burns and Birgit M. Kaiser (London: Palgrave Macmillan, 2012), pp. 123–44, in particular the section entitled "The Singular as the Non-Substitutable and Intensive (Deleuze)."

2   Right off the bat, and in order to avoid any later misconceptions, let us state that for Deleuze singularities must never be associated or confused with actual or empirical objects, as they are first and foremost *potentials*. As we shall see below, we must similarly not confound the "virtual" and the "possible." As Stéphane Lleres wrote, "[t]he possible is a neutralized tracing of the actual or the empirical; the virtual, however, *does not resemble the actual, the singular points [dy/dx] do not resemble the (actual) curve that integrates them*" (*La Philosophie Transcendantale de Gilles Deleuze* [Paris: L'Harmattan, 2011], pp. 149–50). In the same fashion, we could also say that these singular points—the sensations, daydreams, hopes, wishes, hesitations, questions, and uncertainties that cross an individual's mind—do not resemble the (actual) subject which *integrates* them or which *results* from their interactions and conflicts. This explains why, for Deleuze, the actualization of the virtual—always composed of heterogeneous or incompossible singularities—is always presented as the solution to the problem it constitutes. We find the same perspective on the process of individuation in the issues addressed by Paul Virilio in *La Pensée Exposée* and François Jullien in *The Silent Transformations*, to which I will turn below.

3   In *The Logic of Sense*, Deleuze says the following about these two notions: "Paradox is initially that which destroys good sense as the only direction, but it is also that which destroys common sense as the assignation of fixed identities" (p. 3). In *Difference and Repetition*, he goes so far as to say that good sense and

common sense "constitute the two halves of the *doxa*" (p. 134)—"[f]or while common sense is the norm of identity from the point of view of the pure Self and the form of the unspecified object which corresponds to it, good sense is the norm of distribution from the point of view of the empirical selves and the objects qualified as this or that kind of thing (which is why it is considered to be universally distributed)" (pp. 133–4).

4 Pierre Montebello, *Deleuze* (Paris: Librairie philosophique J. Vrin, 2008), p. 112.
5 Ibid.
6 Deleuze, *The Logic of Sense*, p. 102.
7 Ibid., p. 106.
8 Ibid., p. 103 (emphasis added).
9 Ibid., p. 107.
10 See Simondon, *L'Individu et sa Genèse Physico-Biologique* (Paris: Presses Universitaires de France, 1964), p. 37 and passim. See also the excellent description of Deleuze's relation to Simondon in Kaiser, "The Singularities of Postcolonial Literature," pp. 132–4.
11 Montebello, *Deleuze*, p. 115.
12 Claude Romano, *Event and World*, trans. Shane Mackinlay (New York: Fordham University Press, 2009), p. 75.
13 "The event," write Deleuze and Guattari, "is actualized or effectuated whenever it is inserted, willy-nilly, into a state of affairs; but it is counter-effectuated whenever it is abstracted from state of affairs so as to isolate its concept" (Deleuze and Guattari, *Difference and Repetition*, p. 159). See the excellent developments on the notion of "counter-effectuation" Paul Patton offers in "Future Politics" in Paul Patton and John Protevi, eds., *Between Deleuze and Derrida* (London: Continuum, 1999), particularly these remarks: "In counter-effectuating events, we attain and express the sense of what is happening around us. To think philosophically about the present is therefore to counter-effectuate the pure events which animate everyday events and processes. Conversely, to describe current events in terms of such philosophical concepts is to relate them to the pure events of which they appear only as one particular determination, thereby dissociating the pure event from the particular form in which it has been actualized and pointing to the possibility of other determinate actualisations" (p. 26).
14 Deleuze and Guattari, *What is Philosophy?*, p. 215 (emphasis added).
15 Romano, *Event and World*, p. 39 (emphasis added).
16 Jean-Luc Marion, *In Excess: Studies of Saturated Phenomena*, trans. Robyn Horner and Vincent Berraud (New York: Fordham University Press, 2004), p. 55.

17 Ibid., p. 37.
18 This paragraph simply summarizes some of the ideas masterfully developed by Romano on the concept of the event. See Romano, *L'Événement et le Temps* (Paris: Presses Universitaires de France ['Épiméthée'], 1999), p. 313.
19 Cited in *The Logic of Sense*, p. 148.
20 Ibid., Gilles Deleuze, *The Logic of Sense*, p. 149.
21 Deleuze, Gilles and Claire Parnet and Barbara Habberjam and Eliot Albert, trans. Janis Tomlinson, *Dialogues* (New York: Columbia University Press, 2002), p. 112.
22 Ibid.
23 Quoting Michel Cassé, Deleuze notes: "In the heart of the cloud of the virtual there is a virtual of yet a higher order ... every virtual particle surrounds itself with a virtual cosmos and each in its turn does likewise indefinitely" (ibid., p. 120, n. 4).
24 Deleuze, *The Logic of Sense*, p. 151.
25 Paul Virilio, *La Pensée Exposée. Textes et Entretiens* (Paris: Actes Sud, Collection Babel, 2012), pp. 252–3 (emphases added). In paperback format, this book collects the essays written by Virilio for his collaborations with the Fondation Cartier during the exhibitions *Terre Natale, Ailleurs Commence ici* (2008), *Marc Newson, Kelvin 40* (2004), *Ce qui arrive* (2002), *Le Désert* (2000), *1 monde réel* (1999), *Azur* (1993), *La Vitesse* (1991), and *Vraiment faux* (1988). It illustrates Virilio's visionary ideas and that his writings are still incredibly topical.
26 Jean-Pierre Dupuy, *Petite Métaphysique des Tsunamis* (Paris: Editions du Seuil, 2005), p. 25. Virilio, Paul, *La Pensée Exposée. Textes et Entretiens* (Paris: Actes Sud, Collection Babel, 2012), pp. 252–3. See also Jean-Pierre Dupuy, *Pour un Catastrophisme Éclairé. Quand l'Avenir est Certain* (Paris: Éditions du Seuil, 2001).
27 See Dupuy, *Petite Métaphysique des Tsunamis*, where he writes: "We are presently witnessing humanity's emergence as a quasi-subject: the inchoate understanding that our destiny is self-destruction; the birth of an absolute requirement to avoid this self-destruction" (p. 14). Later in this essay, Dupuy makes an appeal (to reason?): "The metaphysics that is meant to serve as the basis of prudence, adapted to the age of catastrophe, consists in *projecting itself* into the time that follows the catastrophe, and in retrospectively seeing the latter as a simultaneously *necessary and improbable* event" (p. 20).
28 Paul Virilio, *La Pensée Exposée. Textes et Entretiens* (Paris: Actes Sud, Collection Babel, 2012), p. 38 (emphases added).
29 Virilio, *The Original Accident*, p. 41.
30 Paul Virilio and Svetlana Aleksievich, *Unknown Quantity* (London: Thames & Hudson, 2003), p. 156.

31 "After Chernobyl, we didn't push our thinking to its logical conclusion: the thought that we had gone much too far, that we had gotten too close to a threshold of horror that is no longer commensurate with our human time, our moral laws, none of which work in this new space" (ibid., pp. 155–6).
32 Dupuy, *Petite Métaphysique des Tsunamis*, p. 26.
33 It might not be in philosophical texts that we can find a "vision" of what Virilio calls the "integral accident," but in certain science-fiction novels or so-called disaster films, such as *Ice Twisters, Deep Impact, The Day After, Sunshine, Tornado, Avalanche, Alien, Blade Runner, The Matrix, Planet of the Apes, Avatar, The Hunger Games*, and *Independence Day*. Some painters also have this same "vision" of the future: see, for example, "Bronx Zoo" by Alexis Rockman. If in daily life we sometimes sense the presence of disaster, it is at the cost of losing sight of the announced catastrophe.
34 Deleuze, *The Logic of Sense*, pp. 62–3 (emphasis added).
35 See Dupuy, *Petite Métaphysique des Tsunamis*, p. 15.
36 See François Jullien, *The Silent Transformations*, trans. Krzysztof Fijalkowski and Michael Richardson (London: Seagull Books, 2011), pp. 3–4.
37 We find here a manner of comprehending the real similar to Deleuze's, following the principle that singularity is not just the *predicate* of what is individual, but that it *precedes* the individual, that it is *pre-individual*. "The plant," Lleres states, "is nothing more than the *solution to a problem* caused by various elements (light, on one hand, and the earth and humidity on the other)" (Stéphane Lleres, *La Philosophie Transcendantale de Gilles Deleuze* [Paris: L'Harmattan, 2011], p. 150). In other words, the actualization of the virtual does not cancel out the "power" of the effectuation and counter-effectuation of the heterogeneous singularities that compose it.
38 Jullien, *The Silent Transformations*, p. 126.
39 Ibid., p. 142.
40 Ibid.
41 François Jullien, *Les Transformations Silencieuses* (Paris: Grasset, 2009), p. 140.
42 Jullien, *The Silent Transformations*, p. 142. This brings to mind "Parousia," for which we find in Teilhard de Chardin: "PAROUSIA, noun. CHRISTIAN THEOLOGY. Second coming of Christ on earth at the End of Days. '*The Lord Jesus will only come soon if we ardently expect him. It is an accumulation of desires that should cause the Pleroma to burst upon us … A rather childish haste, combined with the error in perspective which led the first generation of Christians to believe in the immediate return of Christ, has unfortunately left us disillusioned and suspicious. Our faith in the kingdom of God has been disconcerted by the resistance*

of the world to good'" (Pierre Teilhard de Chardin, *The Divine Milieu*, trans. Pierre Leroy [New York: Harper and Row, 1968], p. 150). Also in Camus, we find: "*The revolutionary movement at the end of the nineteenth century and the beginning of the twentieth lived, like the early Christians, in the expectation of the end of the world and the advent of the proletarian Christ*" (Albert Camus, *The Rebel: An Essay on Man in Revolt*, trans. Anthony Bower [New York: Alfred A. Knopf, 1956], p. 260).

43 Jullien, *The Silent Transformations*, pp. 142–3.

Chapter 6: The Kafka Effect: Considerations on the Limits of Interpretation in Deleuze and Guattari's Book on Kafka

1 Walter Benjamin, "Franz Kafka," in *Illuminations*, translated by Harry Sohn, edited and introduced by Hannah Arendt (New York: Schocken Books, 1969), p. 127. The following passages from Benjamin's essay will be taken from this edition; page references will appear in the text.
2 Ibid., p. 112.
3 Ibid., p. 117.
4 Ibid., p. 113.
5 P. Sollers, *Writing and the Experience of Limits* (New York: Columbia University, 1983).
6 Roland Barthes, *The Pleasure of the Text*, trans. R. Miller (New York: Hill and Wang, 1975).
7 Benjamin, p. 129.
8 Ibid., p. 131.
9 Ibid., p. 129.
10 See Jacques Derrida, "The Law of Genre," *Glyph* 7 (1980).
11 I am referring here to the concept of "*bi-langue*" that the Moroccan writer Abdelkébir Khatibi introduced in his book, *Amour Bilingue* (Paris: Fata Morgana, 1984); also available in English: *Love in Two Languages*, trans. Richard Howard (Minneapolis: University of Minnesota Press, 1990).
12 Gilles Deleuze and Claire Parnet, *Dialogues* (Paris: Flammarion, Collection Dialogues, 1977), pp. 125–6; see also the important chapter entitled "De la supériorité de la littérature anglaise-américaine," pp. 47–63.
13 Ibid., pp. 40–1.
14 These stories are to be found in Franz Kafka, *The Complete Stories*, Nahum N. Gladtzer ed., foreword by John Updike (New York: Schocken Books, 1995).

15 See Roland Barthes, *Sade, Fourier, Loyola*, trans. Richard Miller (New York: Hill and Wang, 1976).
16 Gilles Deleuze and Félix Guattari, *Mille Plateaux* (Paris: Minuit, 1980), p. 166.
17 Ibid., p. 167.
18 I am referring here to the excellent essay by Sarah Kofman, *Mélancolie de l'Art* (Paris: Éditions Galilée, 1985), pp. 26–7.
19 Gilles Deleuze and Félix Guattari, *Kafka: Toward a Minor Literature*, trans. Dana Polan (Minneapolis: University of Minnesota Press, 1986), p. 28.
20 Ibid.
21 In a letter cited in the very fine article that Irvin Wohlfarth devoted to Benjamin in the *Revue d'Esthétique*, new series, no. 1 (Paris: Ed. Privat, 1981). The article is entitled "*Sur quelques motifs juifs chez Benjamin*" ("On some Jewish 'themes' in Benjamin's work"). Wohlfarth recalls that Gershom Scholem recommended to Benjamin that he "begin every study on Kafka with the book of Job or at least with a discussion about the possibility of divine judgment": Scholem considered divine judgment to be the "only subject of Kafka's work"!
22 Deleuze and Guattari, *Kafka*, p. 45.
23 Ibid.
24 Ibid.
25 See Maurice Gandillac, in his translation of Benjamin's text on Kafka ("Kafka") in *Poésie et Révolution*, 2 (Paris: Éditions Denoël), p. 122.
26 Deleuze and Guattari, *Kafka*, p. 49.
27 Deleuze and Parnet, *Dialogues*, p. 25.
28 For further reference to these questions, see Wohlfarth's text that I mentioned above and the following articles that appear in the same issue of the *Revue d'Ésthétique*: Jürgen Habermas, "L'actualité de Walter Benjamin. La critique prise de conscience ou préservation," pp. 107–31, and Yves Kobry, "Benjamin et le langage," pp. 171–9.
29 Deleuze and Guattari, *Kafka*, p. 50.
30 Ibid.
31 Ibid., p. 51.

Chapter 7: On the Concept of "Minor Literature": From Kafka to Kateb Yacine

1 Cf. Deleuze and Guattari on the *CsO (Corps sans organes)*: "It is in no way a question of a fragmented, shattered body, or of organs without a body (OwB).

The CsO is precisely the opposite. It is not a matter of fragmented/piecemeal … organs with respect to a lost unity, nor of a return to the undifferentiated with respect to a differentiable whole … The BwO is desire; it is that which and through which we desire" (*Mille plateaux: Capitalisme et schizophrenie* [Paris: Minuit, 1980], p. 203).

2 "In 1973 Philip Roth published a beautiful short story about Franz Kafka, with the strange title 'I Always Wanted You to Admire My Fasting'; or, Looking at Kafka.'" (The quotation is from Kafka's short story "The Hunger Artist.") In this piece Roth starts out describing a photograph of Kafka taken in 1924, "as sweet and hopeful a year as he may ever have known as a man, and the year of his death." The piece goes on to imagine that Kafka "did not succumb to tuberculosis but instead emigrated to America, avoiding the war and the Holocaust and becoming a Hebrew teacher in New Jersey, where one of his young pupils was named Philip Roth." Found online at: http://www.upenn.edu/nso/prp/met/rothessay.html (last accessed March 31, 2016).

3 Deleuze and Guattari, *Kafka*, p. 19.

4 Ibid. (emphasis mine).

5 Here I have in mind, among other possible references, the beautiful, quite original text of Louis A. Renza, *"A White Heron" and the Question of Minor Literature* (Madison: University of Wisconsin Press, 1984), in which one finds the following remarks: "For Deleuze and Guattari, *then*, 'minor literature' is 'schizo' literature in its subatomic-like anti-oedipal and self-deconstructing release of literary 'intensities'" (p. 33; my emphasis); or the following, which is even more clearly stated and, in its context, appears as a symptom: "Unlike the formalist or Bloomian aesthetic conceptions of minor literature, *then*, Deleuze and Guattari's includes an ideological element. And unlike the Marxist ideological conception of minor literature, their attempts to account for its particular aesthetic operations. Yet *no less than these other conceptions*, Deleuze and Guattari's— oedipal or fissionary (*but not visionary*) delineation of minor literature *ends up* inviting the return of a repressed desire for canonicity" (p. 34; emphasis mine).

6 In the general context of Renza's analysis, the quotation marks produce the intended effect of once again canonizing a text whose primary task was to remove itself from the canon, whether literary or critical! In the previous note, the "then" and "ends up" seem to me, at the very least, to clash both with the overall project and with the details of the Deleuze and Guattari project. As I try to suggest here, their project is not to canonize Kafka—how could they do so, since they make Kafka the "somber precursor" (Deleuze) of a kind of minor literature that owes him its *theoretical* existence!—but rather to tear his

work away from the many attempts to reduce it to the literature of the major (signifying) regimes.

7   Deleuze and Guattari, *Kafka*, p. 16.
8   Ibid.
9   Ibid. I am thinking here of the work of writers such as Abdelkebir Khatibi in Morocco, Abdelwahab Meddeb in Tunisia, and, of course, writers like Nabile Farès or Kateb Yacine in Algeria, or Edouard Glissant in the Caribbean. They also found themselves, in the days following their countries' independence, in the situation that Deleuze and Guattari describe: They must write, but—whether for technical or for ideological reasons, which I will address later on with regard to Yacine—they cannot use the French language simply as a matter of course. Whatever they do, this language will remain an "official language" and the instrument par excellence of the most tragic "inner exiles." "Never," writes Yacine, "even in my days of success with the teacher, did I stop feeling deep inside myself that second rending of the umbilical cord, that internal exile that brought the schoolchild closer to his mother only to yank him away, each time a little farther, from the murmuring blood, from the reproving tremors of a banished language, secretly, of one accord, no sooner struck than broken … *Thus it was that together I lost both my mother and her language, the only inalienable—and yet alienated—treasures*" (*Le polygone étoilé* [Paris: Seuil, 1956], pp. 181–2; my emphasis).
10 Deleuze and Guattari, *Kafka*, p. 17.
11 In setting forth the elements of this problematic, I recognize the debt that Deleuze and Guattari owe to Althusser's work, particularly his work on "ideological state apparatuses." "It will be recalled that after revealing the effects of the mirror-structure of Ideology—whether the interpellation of 'individuals' as subjects; or their subjection to, the (Grand) Subject, or the mutual recognition of subjects by themselves and by one another; or, lastly the absolute guarantee that all is well," Althusser remarks: "Result: caught in this quadruple system of interpellation as subjects, of subjection to the Subject, of universal recognition and of absolute guarantee, the Subjects 'work,' they 'work by themselves' in the vast majority of cases, with the exception of the 'bad subjects' who on occasion provoke the intervention of one of the detachments of the repressive state apparatus. But the vast majority of (good) subjects work all right 'all by themselves,' i.e., by ideology (whose concrete forms are realized in the Ideological State Apparatuses). They are inserted into practices governed by the rituals of the ISAS, etc." (Louis Althusser, "Ideology and the State," in *On Ideology* [London: Verso, 1984], p. 181).

12 Deleuze and Guattari, *Kafka*, p. 17.
13 Ibid.
14 For reasons that are quite understandable in the context in which Deleuze and Guattari inscribe their analysis of the emergence of minor literature—their task is to analyze the work of an author whose work cannot yet be defined except through a demarcation from the canon and from the genres that dominate the cultural and literary scene of the moment—the collective dimension is attributed to the rarity of talents in the face of what we could term the plethora of "masters": I will attempt, later on, to show that determination by means of rarity is problematic in that it tends (unconsciously?) to confirm the validity of a model—that of *great* literature—according to the definition of which everything that is not included in the literary canon will be considered as insufficient, secondary, or even marginal. Deleuze and Guattari seem completely aware of this problem, since a little further on in their book, after defining the three characteristics of minor literature—deterritorialization of language, connection of the individual with the political immediacy, collective arrangement of enunciation—they spontaneously invoke the relation of the notion of minor literature to that of "marginal" literature. Now, as they do so, they show that the latter can be "well understood" only in comparison with the singular economy of minor literature: "There has been much discussion of the questions 'What is a marginal literature' and 'What is a popular literature, a proletarian literature?' The criteria are obviously difficult to establish if one doesn't start with a more objective concept—that of minor literature. Only the possibility of setting up a minor practice of a major language from within allows one to define popular literature, marginal literature, and so on" (Deleuze and Guattari, *Kafka*, p. 18; my emphasis). One final remark on this subject. In his fine book on the Irish author James Clarence Mangan, David Lloyd exhibits an acute awareness of these difficulties and makes a number of important points that I would like to begin to relate to the present study. Having acknowledged the work of the pioneer Louis A. Renza, Lloyd criticizes him for deferring discussion of the *political* functions of the different evaluations of minor literature that were made by the predecessors of Deleuze and Guattari, but straightaway Lloyd extends his criticism to a certain lack of vigilance on the part of Deleuze and Guattari themselves. Lloyd writes: "To produce an adequate theory of minor literature in any sense of the term, it is necessary to analyze historically the politics of culture. Deleuze and Guattari's work goes some way toward engaging this issue, though impressionistically and largely only synchronically.

What they valuably indicate, however, is the extent to which recent interest in the question of 'minor' literature recognizes the prior emergence of a combative field of literature that is expressly political insofar as the literature of the Third World, of 'minorities' or formerly marginalized communities, *calls into question the hegemony of central cultural values. A retrospective, even belated, analysis discovers* in *articulating the political structure of the canon the terms of an aesthetic culture that have already been negated by a new literature"* (David Lloyd, *Nationalism and Minor Literature: James Clarence Mangan and the Emergence of Irish Cultural Nationalism* [Berkeley: University of California Press, 1987], p. 5; my emphasis).

15 Deleuze and Guattari, *Kafka*, p. 17.
16 I am thinking here of studies such as the ones produced by researchers and critics like Pascale Casanova, *La République Mondiale des Lettres* (Seuil, 1999); Elisabeth Mudimbe-Boyi, *Essais sur les Cultures en contact (Afrique, Amériques, Europe)* (Karthala, 2006); Claudia Esposito, *The Narrative Mediterranean, Beyond France and the Maghreb* (Lexington Books, 2014); and *Writing and Translating Francophone discourse: Africa, The Caribbean, Diaspora*, Textxet, Studies in Comparative Literature, Paul F. Bandia ed. (2014).
17 Renza, 1984, p. 29.
18 Ibid., p. 30.
19 Gilles Deleuze and Felix Guattari, *Capitalism and Schizophrenia,* vol. 1, *Anti-Oedipus,* trans. Robert Hurley, Mark Seem, and Helen R. Lane (New York: Viking Press, 1977), p. 31. Quoted in Renza, *"White Heron" and the Question of Minor Literature*, p. 31.
20 Cf. *"White Heron" and the Question of Minor Literature*, pp. 32–6, particularly the following: "Their brand of minor literature clearly becomes a *privileged double* of their antioedipal revolutionary desire to overthrow all versions of a here debased reactionary or reterritorializing major literature … Deleuze and Guattari thus *privilege* only a *certain kind* of minor literature, that which like Kafka's is in the process of interrogating the oedipean tropes of major literary praxis but which the major language or canonical critical codes can misrecognize as major according to their own standards" (p. 34; my emphasis).
21 Lloyd, *Nationalism and Minor Literature*, pp. 4–5.
22 Ibid., pp. 24–5 (my emphasis).
23 Who would have ever heard of Kateb Yacine, Nabile Farès, and Rachid Boujedra without the Algerian war and the independence that followed? Yacine had written and published very beautiful texts before these events! But it is true that he still could be read only as a "minor" writer, in other words, as a *secondary*

writer. As an Algerian writer, was he not still considered as a second-class French citizen from the outlying territories?

24 I am thinking here of what Deleuze writes in *Cinema 2*: "[T]he people no longer exist, or not yet ... *the people are missing* ... No doubt this truth also applied to the West, but very few authors discovered it, *because it was hidden by the mechanisms of power and the systems of majority*. On the other hand, it was absolutely clear in the third world, where oppressed and exploited nations remained in a state of perpetual minorities, in a collective identity crisis. Third world and minorities gave rise to authors who would be in a position, in relation to their nation and their personal situation in that nation, to say: *the people are what is missing*" (pp. 216–18; my emphasis, except for first).

25 Ibid., p. 217. These are the "conditions" that explain why, historically, it is the cinema or theater, and not literature, for example, that has achieved the objectives expected from the renaissance of Algerian culture, providing the vital medium that enables a people to recognize in themselves a national "character": as an identity in the diversity of local languages and cultures, as a unity in the multiplicity of *technes* and manners, and, finally, as active solidarity amid the disparity of cities and countrysides.

26 Ibid.

27 Ibid.

28 Sheikh Mohammed el Anka was a singer of the *chaabi*, or popular style—one of the most broadly appreciated genres of music, through which the most important political, erotic, and social messages were conveyed. Rai is a form of popular dance music with strong rhythms and lyrics that often deal with the burning issues of the day, whether political, social, sexual, or affective. It is no coincidence that Rai music has been condemned by representatives of the FIS (Islamic Salvation Front) in Algeria and all forms of religious fundamentalism.

29 Bourguiba is transcribed as *bourequibat*, which in colloquial Arabic is a diminutive of "neck" and can be translated as "small neck" or "spindly neck."

30 The reference here is to the General "Q qui tue" ("Killer Q") in Yacine's *La Gandourie sans uniforme*.

31 Cf. Mouloud Feraoun, *Le fils du pauvre* (Paris: Seuil, 1954), and Rachid Boujedra, *Topographie idéale pour une agression caractérisée* (Paris: Denoël, 1975).

32 Deleuze, *Cinema 2*, p. 218.

33 Deleuze, 1989, p. 218.

34 Ibid., p. 219.

35 Ibid.

36 I have in mind here the play *L'homme aux sandales de caoutchouc* (Paris: Seuil, 1972), written in honor of Ho Chi Minh while he was still alive; this play ultimately became a hymn to the struggle of all oppressed peoples.

Chapter 8: Becoming-Animal, Becoming-Political in Rachid Boudjedra's *L'escargot entêté*

1   Deleuze, *The Logic of Sense*, p. xiii.
2   Ibid., p. xiv.
3   Ibid., pp. xiii–xiv; my emphasis).
4   Anne Sauvagnargues, "*Deleuze. De l'animal à l'art*," in François Zourabichvili, Anne Sauvagnargues, and Paola Marrati, *La Philosophie de Deleuze* (Paris: PUF, 2004), p. 219. In the same text she makes more precise observations that are useful to this analysis, saying that "nevertheless, this thinking … is not the result of a private conscience, but the ideal singularity of a differentiated virtuality. By choosing Spinozist ethics over judgment by analogy, Deleuze replaces the signifying forms of analogy with the exposition of the real forces of ethology" (ibid., p. 219).
5   I am thinking here, for example, of the way in which a Deleuzian scholar like Arnaud Villani tackles the question of the encounter in his own study of Deleuze. In the chapter analyzing "the phenomenology of the encounter" in Deleuze, after citing a long passage from Alfred Döblin's *Berlin Alexanderplatz*, Villani writes straight out: "*Everything in this text is Deleuzian*. What else can be said except that a fluid flows back and forth at the right moment between this page and the philosopher, so that, later, the latter can eventually make good use of it" (Villani, *La guêpe et l'Orchidée, Essai sur Gilles Deleuze* [Paris: Editions Belin, 1999], p. 16, emphasis added). This is a very good example of the "illusion" that consists of taking real questions in reverse: Villani "forgets" that he was able to discover this "Deleuzian" gem only because he placed it there in the first place thanks to his Deleuzian critical hindsight! This is all the more regrettable since Villani disposed of the arguments which would have helped him avoid this "mistake," namely the answer Deleuze gives to the question on his capacity to find real problems: "If it is true [that I have this capacity], it is because *I believe in the necessity to construct a concept of the problem*. I have tried to do so in *Difference and Repetition* and would want to take this question up again. But this practically forces me to ask, *in each and every case, how a problem can be posed*. In this way, it seems that philosophy can be considered

a science: in that it determines the conditions of a problem" (ibid., p. 130, emphases added).

6   Deleuze and Guattari, *A Thousand Plateaus*, p. 284.
7   Villani does this once more in his book when he, for example, endeavors to clarify (we are not sure if for himself, or for his readers?) the notion of haecceity as reinvented by Deleuze through Duns Scotus: "Haecceity. It originates in Duns Scotus. I would first like to propose an entirely personal list of haecceities (which brings to mind the Chinese Encyclopedia mentioned by Foucault): the blue beast bleeding in the thicket (Trakl), the whale's bone in Ahab's leg, Queequeg's coffin, the yellow in the view of Delft, etc." (Villani, *La guêpe et l'Orchidée*, p. 86).
8   Rachid Boudjedra, *L'escargot entêté* (Paris: Folio, 1985), p. 13.
9   Ibid., p. 12.
10 Ibid., p. 46.
11 Ibid., pp. 48–9.
12 Elsewhere, there are similar, rather unpalatable statements: "I am too faithful to the State to believe in God" (p. 31), or: "my faithfulness to the State is legendary, to such an extent that I am losing interest in God" (p. 84). Later, he adds: "In any case, personally, I am too faithful to the State to believe in all these religions, but I can't stand fornicators" (p. 118).
13 Ibid., p. 19.
14 Ibid., p. 47.
15 Deleuze and Guattari, *A Thousand Plateaus*, p. 233.
16 Ibid., p. 233. For reasons that will quickly become apparent, in this paragraph I am merely transposing almost literally what Deleuze and Guattari write about Daniel Mann's film *Willard* (cf. pp. 233–4).
17 Boudjedra, *L'escargot entêté*, p. 24.
18 Deleuze and Guattari, *A Thousand Plateaus*, p. 233.
19 Boudjedra, *L'escargot entêté*, p. 28.
20 Ibid., p. 94.
21 Deleuze and Guattari, *A Thousand Plateaus*, p. 233.
22 Boudjedra, *L'escargot entêté*, p. 97.
23 Ibid., p. 108.
24 Elsewhere, another note says: "When I'm fifty, no one will be able to blame me for a descendant. Nothing! I have no offspring. I am like the people of Uqbar, I am weary of copulation and mirrors. They multiply the number of people" (p. 108).
25 For example: "Instead of making a body without organs sufficiently rich or

full of the passage of intensities, drug addicts erect a vitrified or emptied body, or a cancerous one: the causal line, creative line, or line of flight immediately turns into a line of death and abolition. The abominable vitrification of the veins, or the purulence of the nose—the glassy body of the addict" (Deleuze and Guattari, *A Thousand Plateaus*, p. 285). Many of these "traits" can be found in the description that the narrator gives of his state of mind or his body: "The feeling, each time the day comes to a close, that I have no contours, nor margins. Veins eroded by the chaffing of words at the border of conscience..." (Boudjedra, *L'escargot entêté*, p. 98). What better "illustration" could there be of the experience of what Deleuze and Guattari call a "Body without Organs"?

26 Deleuze and Guattari, *A Thousand Plateaus*, p. 261.
27 As Boudjedra in his novel, I leave out the name of the city. But everything points to Algiers, known in its mythical history as *Alger La Blanche* ("Algiers, the White City"), of which Boudjedra seems to be thinking.
28 Boudjedra, *L'escargot entêté*, p. 79.
29 Deleuze and Guattari, *A Thousand Plateaus*, p. 233.
30 Boudjedra, *L'escargot entêté*, p. 117. "I think Onan deserved his punishment. He was killed and he deserved it. But I still have some sympathy for him. He avoided getting his brother's wife pregnant. He could have fathered twins. He refrained from doing so. He consequently did not encourage reproduction. He has nothing in common with rats, snails and pigs whose fertility is legendary. He is worthy of my respect." The narrator's loathing for reproductive sexuality in general is already established, but his attitude towards the sexuality of gastropods shows that he has definitely left the world of humans. This appears in one of his notes on the customs of snails: "What a strange animal! Walking on its tongue! As if its perverse Hermaphrodism was no longer enough. It must undulate, contract and use its tongue to go at an even slower pace than a tortoise" (ibid., p. 92).
31 Deleuze and Guattari, *A Thousand Plateaus*, p. 233.
32 Hastily, but rather symptomatically, Boudjedra translates an Arab proverb here: *Oulid El Far, yakhreuj haffar!,* which does not translate as "the son of the rat is a rodent" but more precisely, in my opinion, as "Son of a rat, posterity of a borer (of tunnels, holes etc.)." What Boudjedra's translation erases (misses?) is the displacement which transforms a rodent into a borer of tunnels and labyrinths. What is missing from his translation is the becoming: from rodent, the rat becomes a borer! Quantum leap! Deterritorialization! Line of flight!
33 Boudjedra, *L'escargot entêté*, p. 135.
34 Ibid., p. 94 (emphasis added).

35 Ibid., p. 13.
36 Ibid., pp. 16–17.
37 Ibid., p. 17.
38 Ibid., p. 77 (emphases added).
39 Ibid., p. 136.
40 Ibid., p. 17.
41 Ibid., p. 21.
42 Ibid., p. 22.
43 Boudjedra's text plays with the idea of erasure or crossing out ("***rature***" in French!). I do not think we take the interpretation of the text too far if we say that he consciously uses this expression on several occasions. The narrator spends his time crossing out the words he writes. As I will show momentarily, this behavior also relates primarily to *writing* and particularly *literary* writing.
44 Boudjedra, *L'escargot entêté*, p. 27 (emphasis added).
45 Deleuze and Guattari, 1987, p. 280.

Bibliography

Alliez, Eric, *Les Temps capitaux*, vol. 1: *Récits de la conquête du temps* (Paris: Éditions du Cerf, 1991).
Alliez, Éric, *The Signature of the World: What is Deleuze and Guattari's Philosophy?*, trans. Eliot Ross Albert and Alberto Toscano (London: Continuum, 2004).
Jean-Loup Amselle, *L'Occident décroché: enquête sur les postcolonialismes* (Paris, Stock, « Un ordre d'idées », 2008).
Ansell-Pearson, K. (ed.), *Deleuze and Philosophy: The Difference Engineer* (London: Routledge, 1997).
Antonioli, M., *Deleuze et l'histoire de la philosophie, ou De la philosophie comme science-fiction* (Paris: Kimé, 1999).
Badiou, Alain, *Deleuze: La clameur de l'être* (Paris: Hachette, 1997).
Badiou, Alain, *Manifesto for Philosophy*, trans. Norman Madarasz (Albany: State University of New York Press, 1999).
Barthélémy, J.-H., *Simondon ou l'encyclopédisme génétique* (Paris: PUF, 2005).
Barthes, Roland, *The Pleasure of the Text*, trans. R. Miller (New York: Hill and Wang, 1975).
Barthes, Roland, *Sade, Fourier, Loyola*, trans. Richard Miller (New York: Hill and Wang, 1976).
Beaulieu, A. de, *Gilles Deleuze, héritage philosophique* (Paris: PUF, 2005).
Benjamin, Walter, *Illuminations*, trans. Harry Zohn, edited and introduced by Hannah Arendt (New York: Schocken Books, 1969).
Bignal, Simone and Paul Patton (eds.), *Deleuze and the Postcolonial* (Edinburgh: Edinburgh University Press, 2010).
Bogue, R., *Deleuze on Literature* (London: Routledge, 2003).
Bouaniche, A., *Gilles Deleuze, une introduction* (Paris: Pocket, 2006).
Boudjedra, Rachid, *L'escargot entêté* (Paris: Folio, 1985).
Camus, Albert, *The Rebel: An Essay on Man in Revolt*, trans. Anthony Bower (New York: Alfred A. Knopf, 1956).
Charbonnier, Sébastien, *Deleuze Pédagogue. La fonction transcendantale de l'apprentissage et du problème* (Paris: L'Harmattan, 2009).
Clemens, Éric, *La Fiction et l'apparaître* (Paris: Albin Michel, 1993).

Colombat, André Pierre, "A Thousand Trails to Work with Deleuze," *Substance, A Review of Theory and Literary Criticism* 66 (1991).

Couchot, Edmond, *La Technologie dans l'art. Dela Photographie à la réalité Virtuelle* (Paris: Éditions Jacqueline Chambon, 1998).

Cusset, F., *French Theory: How Foucault, Derrida, Deleuze & Co. Transformed the Intellectual Life of the United States*, trans. J. Fort with J. Berganza and M. Jones (Minneapolis: University of Minnesota Press, 2008).

David-Ménard, M., *Deleuze et la psychanalyse* (Paris: PUF, 2005).

Deleuze, Gilles, "*La Photographie est déjà tirée dans les choses*," Interview with Pascal Bonitzer and Jean Narboni, in *Cahiers du Cinéma* 352 (October 1983) 38–40.

Deleuze, Gilles, *Kant's Critical Philosophy: The Doctrine of the Faculties*, trans. Hugh Tomlinson (Minneapolis: University of Minnesota Press, 1985).

Deleuze, Gilles, *Foucault, trans.* Sean Hand, with foreword by Paul Bove (Minneapolis: University of Minnesota Press, 1988a).

Deleuze, Gilles, *Spinoza, Practical Philosophy*, trans. R. Hurley (San Francisco: City Lights Books, 1988b).

Deleuze, Gilles, *Cinema 2, the Time Image*, trans. H. Tomlinson and R. Galeta (London: Athlone, 1989).

Deleuze, Gilles, *The Logic of Sense*, ed. Constantin V. Boundas, trans. Mark Lester and Charles Stivale (New York: Columbia University Press, 1990a).

Deleuze, Gilles, trans. Hugh Tomlinson and Barbara Habberjam, *Bergsonism* (New York: Zone Books, 1990b).

Deleuze, Gilles, *Expressionism in Philosophy: Spinoza*, trans. M. Joughlin (New York: Zone Books, 1990c).

Deleuze, Gilles, *Difference and Repetition*, trans. Paul Patton (New York: Columbia University Press, 1994).

Deleuze, Gilles, *Negotiations, 1972–1990*, trans. M. Joughin (New York: Columbia University Press, 1995).

Deleuze, Gilles, "The Method of Dramatization," in *Desert Islands and Other Texts: 1953–1974*, ed. David Lapoujade (New York: Semiotext(e), 2004).

Deleuze, Gilles, "Immanence et vie," *Rue Descartes* 20: *Collège International de Philosophie* (2006).

Deleuze, Gilles, *Two Regimes of Madness: Texts and Interviews, 1975–1995*, ed. David Lapoujade, trans. Ames Hodges (New York: Semiotext(e)/Foreign Agents, 2007).

Deleuze, Gilles, "l'intempestif," *Rue Descartes* 53: *Collège International de Philosophie* (2008).

Deleuze, Gilles and Félix Guattari, trans. Dana Polan, *Kafka: Toward a Minor Literature* (Minneapolis: University of Minnesota Press, 1986).

Deleuze, Gilles and Félix Guattari, trans. Brian Massumi, *A Thousand Plateaus* (Minneapolis: University of Minnesota Press, 1987).

Deleuze, Gilles and Félix Guattari, *What is Philosophy?*, trans. Hugh Tomlinson and Graham Burshell (New York: Columbia University Press, 1994).

Deleuze, Gilles and Félix Guattari, trans. Robert Hurley and Mark Seem, with introduction by Mark Seem, *Anti-Oedipus: Capitalism and Schizophrenia* (New York: Penguin Classics, 2009).

Deleuze, Gilles and Claire Parnet, trans. Barbara Habberjam, Eliot Albert and Janis Tomlinson, *Dialogues* (New York: Columbia University Press, 2002).

Deleuze, Gilles and C. Parnet, *Dialogues II*, trans. H. Tomlinson, B. Habberjam, and E. R. Albert (London: Continuum, 2006).

Didi-Huberman, Georges, trans. John Goodman, *Confronting Images: Questioning the Ends of a Certain History of Art* (University Park: The Pennsylvania State University Press, 2005).

Dumoncel, J. C., *Le Pendule du Docteur Deleuze: une introduction à L'Anti-Œdipe* (Paris: Cahiers de l'Unebévue, 1999).

Dupuy, Jean-Pierre, *Petite Métaphysique des Tsunamis* (Paris: Editions du Seuil, 2005).

Dupuy, Jean-Pierre, *Pour un Catastrophisme Éclairé. Quand l'Avenir est Certain* (Paris: Éditions du Seuil, 2001).

Dyens, Olivier, trans. E. J. Bibbee, *Metal and Flesh: The Evolution of Men Technology Takes Over* (Cambridge, MA: MIT Press, 2001).

Farès, N., *L'état perdu: Discours practique de l'émigré* (Le Paradou: Actes Sud, 1982).

Farès, N., *Un passager de l'occident* (Paris: Éditions du Seuil, 1971).

Faure, Élie, *Fonctions du Cinéma* (Paris: Éditions Gonthier, 1963).

Fiat, C., *La Ritournelle: une anti-théorie* (Paris: L. Scheer, 2002).

Flaxman, G. (ed.), *The Brain is the Screen: Deleuze and the Philosophy of Cinema* (Minneapolis: University of Minnesota Press, 2000).

Gandillac, Maurice, *Poésie et Révolution* (Paris: Éditions Denoël, 1965).

Gauthier, Guy, *Andréi Tarkovski*, Filmo 19 (Paris: Edilig, 1988).

Grande, Maurizio, "Le Temps au Miroir", in R. di Gaetano (ed.), *Deleuze. Penser le Cinéma* (Rome: Quaderni di Cinema/Studio 1, Bulzoni Editore, 1992).

Gualandi, Alberto, *Deleuze* (Paris: Les Belles Lettres, 1998).

Hardt, M. and A. Negri, *Empire* (Cambridge: Harvard University Press, 2000).

Hême de Lacotte, S., *Deleuze, philosophie et cinéma: le passage de l'image-mouvement à l'image-temps* (Paris: L'Harmattan, 2001).

Holland, E. W., *Deleuze and Guattari's Anti-Oedipus: Introduction to Schizoanalysis* (London: Routledge, 1999).

Jaglé, C., *Portrait oratoire de Gilles Deleuze aux yeux jaunes* (Paris: PUF, 2005).

Jullien, François, *Les Transformations Silencieuses* (Paris: Grasset, 2009).

Jullien, François, *The Silent Transformations*, trans. Krzysztof Fijalkowski and Michael Richardson (London: Seagull Books, 2011).

Kaiser, Birgit M., "The Singularities of Postcolonial Literature: Preindividual (Hi)stories in Mohammed Dib's 'Northern Trilogy'," in *Postcolonial Literatures and Deleuze. Colonial Pasts, Differential Futures*, Lorna Burns and Birgit M. Kaiser (eds.), pp. 123–44 (London: Palgrave Macmillan, 2012).

Kant, Immanuel, *Critique of Pure Reason*, The Cambridge Edition of the Works of Immanuel Kant, Paul Guyer and Allen W. Wood (eds.) (Cambridge: Cambridge University Press, 1998).

Kant, Immanuel, *Critique of the Power of Judgment*, The Cambridge Edition of the Works of Immanuel Kant, Paul Guyer and Eric Matthews (eds.) (Cambridge: Cambridge University Press, 2000).

Khatibi, Abdelkébir, *Amour Bilingue* (Fata Morgana, 1984). Available in English as *Love in Two Languages*, trans. Richard Howard (Minneapolis: University of Minnesota Press, Emergent Literature Series, 1990).

Leclercq, S., *Gilles Deleuze, immanence, univocité et transcendantal* (Mons: Editions Sils Maria, 2001).

Levinas, E., *Autrement qu'être ou Au-delà de l'essence* (The Hague: Nijhoff, 1974).

Lleres, Stéphane, *La Philosophie Transcendantale de Gilles Deleuze* (Paris: L'Harmattan, 2011).

Lloyd, David, *Nationalism and Minor Literature: James Clarence Mangan and the Emergence of Irish Cultural Nationalism* (Berkeley: University of California Press, 1987).

Marion, Jean-Luc, *In Excess: Studies of Saturated Phenomena*, trans. Robyn Horner and Vincent Berraud (New York: Fordham University Press, 2004).

Mbembe, A., *On the Postcolony* (Berkeley: University of California Press, 2001).

Metz, Christian, "The Perceived and the Named," *Studies in Visual Communication*, no. 6 (1980): 57.

Metz, Christian, *The Imaginary Signifier: Psychoanalysis and Cinema* (Bloomington: Indiana University Press, 1982).

Miller, Christopher L., *Theories of Africans: Francophone Literature and Anthropology in Africa* (Chicago: University of Chicago Press, 1990).

Montebello, Pierre, *Deleuze* (Paris: Librairie philosophique J. Vrin, 2008).

Nancy, Jean-Luc and Philippe Lacoue-Labarthe, *The Literary Absolute: The Theory of Literature in German Romanticism*, trans. Philip Barnard and Cheryl Leser (Albany: State University of New York Press, 1988).

Patton, P. (ed.), *Deleuze: A Critical Reader* (Oxford: Blackwell, 1996).
Patton, P., *Deleuze and the Political* (London: Routledge, 2000).
Patton, P., "The Event of Colonisation," in I. Buchanan (ed.), *Deleuze and the Contemporary World* (Edinburgh: Edinburgh University Press, 2006).
Petrosino, S. and J. Rolland, "La vérité nomade: introduction à Emmanuel Lévinas," *La Découverte* 45 (1984): 45–6.
Renza, Louis A., *"A White Heron" and the Question of Minor Literature* (Madison: University of Wisconsin Press, 1984).
Rodowick, D. N., *Gilles Deleuze's Time Machine* (Durham: Duke University Press, 1997).
Romano, Claude, *L'Événement et le Temps* (Paris: Presses Universitaires de France 'Épiméthée', 1999).
Romano, Claude, *Event and World,* trans. Shane Mackinlay (New York: Fordham University Press, 2009).
Sarrazin, Hélène, *À la rencontre d'Élie Faure: Première approche et tentative de compréhension* (Périgeux: Pierre Fanlac, 1982).
Sasso, R., and A. Villani (eds.), *Le Vocabulaire de Deleuze, Les Cahiers de Noesis* 3 (2003): 172–3.
Sasso, Robert and Arnaud Villani, *Le Vocabulaire de Gilles Deleuze, Les Cahiers de Noesis* (2003): 304–5.
Sauvagnargues, Anne, "*Deleuze. De l'animal à l'art*", in François Zourabichvili, Anne Sauvagnargues and Paola Marrati, *La Philosophie de Deleuze* (Paris: PUF, 2004), pp. 117–228.
Simondon, Gilbert, *L'Individu et sa Genèse Physico-Biologique* (Paris: Presses Universitaires de France, 1964).
Spinoza, Baruch, *Ethics: Treatise on the Emendation of the Intellect, and Selected Letters*, ed. S. Feldman, trans. S. Shirley (Indianapolis: Hackett Publishing Company, 1992).
Strauss, Erwin, *Phenomenology of Memory* (Pittsburgh: Duquesne University Press, 1970).
Teilhard de Chardin, Pierre, *The Divine Milieu*, trans. Pierre Leroy (New York: Harper and Row, 1968).
Villani, Arnaud, *La guêpe et l'Orchidée, Essai sur Gilles Deleuze* (Paris: Editions Belin, 1999).
Virilio, Paul, *The Original Accident*, trans. Julie Rose (Cambridge: Polity Press, 2007).
Virilio, P., "Les damnés de l'exode", *Le Nouvel Observateur* 2299 (2008): 16–17.
Virilio, Paul, *La Pensée Exposée. Textes et Entretiens* (Paris: Actes Sud, Collection Babel, 2012).

Virilio, Paul and Svetlana Aleksievich, *Unknown Quantity* (London: Thames & Hudson, 2003).

Zaoui, Pierre, "La grande identité Nietzsche-Spinoza, quelle identité?," Phi*losophie* 47 (1995).

Zizek, S., *Organs without Bodies: Deleuze and Consequences* (New York: Routledge, 2004).

Zourabichvili, François, Anne Sauvagnargues and Paola Marrati, *La Philosophie de Deleuze* (Paris: PUF), pp. 117–228.

Zourabichvili, François, "Deleuze et le possible (de l'involontarisme en politique)," in Eric Alliez (ed.), *Gilles Deleuze: une vie philosophique* (Le Plessis-Robinson, Institut Synthélabo ["Les Empêcheurs de Penser en rond"], 1998).

Zourabichvili, F., *Le Vocabulaire de Deleuze* (Paris: Ellipses, 2003).

Index

affect x, xiii, 6–7, 16, 35, 44, 52, 57, 59–60, 64, 111, 114, 121–2
Alliez, Éric 39, 43–4, 135, 139, 146–7, 169
art (*the subject of*) 23, 24–8, 35–6, 38, 40, 43–4, 115–16
Artaud, Antonin 52–3, 56–7, 61–2, 110
automatism (*intellectual, spiritual*) 48, 58–62, 66–7

Badiou, Alain 9, 16–18, 35, 39–40
Benjamin, Walter 83–8, 92–6
Body without Organs (BwO) 12, 17, 38, 56, 87, 90, 120
Bouaniche, Arnaud 1, 5–6, 134–5, 169
Boudjedra, Rachid 22, 118, 120–2, 126

cartography xiii, xiv
Certeau, Michel de 83
Colombat, André Pierre 56. 151
common sense (versus 'good sense') xii, 25, 27, 32–5, 41–2
concepts (*Deleuzian*) x, 4, 6–7, 11–13, 16–17, 20–1, 25–6, 29, 34–5, 39–40, 43–4, 51–2, 54, 55, 57–61, 72, 74, 88–9, 104, 112, 115–16
cinema (*specificity of*) 6, 11, 19, 29, 45–53, 57–65, 67
Clemens, Éric 25–6, 143–5, 169
Cusset, François 4, 134, 137, 140–1, 170

desire x, xiii, 30, 34, 38, 44, 56, 88, 91, 95–7, 100–1, 104, 118
difference 19, 28–9, 38, 51, 64, 70–1, 81, 100, 106–7
differentiation 28, 41
Dupuy, Jean-Pierre 76–8, 156–7, 171

event 4, 8, 11, 19–20, 36, 40, 46, 65, 70–5, 79–81

Faure, Élie 45–3
Foucault, Michel 1, 5, 7–8, 10, 17, 21, 129, 134, 136, 138, 140, 148

Gauthier, Guy 130–1, 171
Gualandi, Alberto 34, 36, 40, 135, 143, 145–6, 171
Guattari, Félix xi–xii, 1, 3, 7–9, 10, 12–14, 17–18, 21, 42–4, 56, 69, 72, 83–93, 97, 99, 100–6, 109, 112–14, 118–22, 126–7

haecceity xii, 20–1, 78, 113, 121, 127, 132, 166
Hegel, G. W. F. 18, 23, 80, 89, 92, 100, 122, 142

Jullien, François 69, 75, 79–80, 132, 154, 157–8, 172

Kafka, Franz 1, 10, 83–97
Kant, Immanuel 4, 11, 23–32, 39–40, 51–2, 71, 131
Kateb, Yacine 10, 22, 99, 107, 159

Lacan, Jacques 16–17, 39–40
Lambert, Gregg viii
limit(s) 11, 17, 36–8, 49, 51, 57, 72, 75, 83, 90–1, 97, 103, 109, 129
Lloyd, David 105–6, 162–3, 172

machine(s) (*desiring*) xiii, 8, 12–13, 19, 47, 62, 64, 67, 84–6, 88, 90–1, 93–4, 97, 99, 102–4, 120
maps, mapping xi, xiii–xiv, 13, 21, 53, 105, 125
metaphysics 15, 34, 71, 122
minor literature 6, 12, 88–9, 91–3, 99–106
Montebello, Pierre 70, 72, 133, 155, 172

Nietzsche, Friedrich 4, 7, 15, 19, 23–4, 30, 50, 92, 130, 134, 148, 151

ontology 70, 122

Patton, Paul vii, ix, 130, 134–5, 144, 155, 169–70, 173
percept x, 6, 16, 37, 44, 52, 66, 87, 111, 114, 116
philosophy x, xi–xii, 2, 5, 9, 13, 18–19, 25, 30, 35, 38–9, 42–4, 53, 59, 70–1, 74, 88, 115
postcolonial theory 2–7, 9–13, 21–2, 88
problem(matics) 2, 4, 8, 13, 14, 18, 27, 30, 32–5, 40–1, 43, 48, 61, 64, 67, 84, 101, 108–9, 114, 116
psychoanalysis 16–18, 73, 86, 104, 115

Renza, Louis A. 103, 104, 105, 160, 162
representation 3, 24, 31, 36, 40, 43, 62, 65–6, 70, 90, 96, 104

Romano, Claude 72–3, 155–6, 173

Sauvagnargues, Anne viii, 115, 165, 173
Spinoza, Baruch x, 1–2, 4, 9, 30, 50, 56–8, 115, 129, 134, 143, 148, 151, 170
stalker, stalking (in philosophy) xi, xiii–xv
stratification 80, 92
subject (theory of the) 5, 8, 10, 15–17, 19–20, 23–7, 31, 33–4, 37–44, 61, 70–3, 86–7, 92, 96, 101, 103, 106–7, 121–2

Villani, Arnaud 130, 142, 165–6, 173
Virilio, Paul 69–70, 75–80, 132, 154, 156–7, 173–4
virtual/actual 16, 19, 41, 61, 66, 68, 73–6, 80, 103, 115

Zaoui, Pierre 30, 145, 148, 150–1, 174
Žižek, Slavoj 16–17, 138, 142, 174
zone xi–xiii, 131–2

www.ingramcontent.com/pod-product-compliance
Lightning Source LLC
Chambersburg PA
CBHW051811230426
43672CB00012B/2700